Toward a Science of Accounting

Accounting Publications of Scholars Book Co.

ROBERT R. STERLING, EDITOR

Sidney S. Alexander et al., *Five Monographs on Business Income*
Frank Sewell Bray, *The Accounting Mission*
F. Sewell Bray, *The Interpretation of Accounts*
Raymond J. Chambers, *Accounting, Evaluation and Economic Behavior*
Arthur Lowes Dickinson, *Accounting Practice and Procedure*
Edgar O. Edwards, Philip W. Bell, and L. Todd Johnson, *Accounting for Economic Events*
John B. Geijsbeek, *Ancient Double-Entry Bookkeeping*
Henry Rand Hatfield, *Accounting: Its Principles and Problems*
Bishop Carleton Hunt (Editor), *George Oliver May: Twenty-Five Years of Accounting Responsibility*
Yuji Ijiri, *The Foundations of Accounting Measurement*
Kenneth MacNeal, *Truth in Accounting*
Richard Mattessich, *Accounting and Analytical Methods*
George O. May, *Financial Accounting*
Paul D. Montagna, *Certified Public Accounting: A Sociological View of a Profession in Change*
William Andrew Paton, *Accounting Theory*
William Z. Ripley, *Main Street and Wall Street*
Charles W. Schandl, *Theory of Auditing*
DR Scott, *The Cultural Significance of Accounts*
Herbert A. Simon et al., *Centralization vs. Decentralization in Organizing the Controller's Department*
Charles E. Sprague, *The Philosophy of Accounts*
George J. Staubus, *Making Accounting Decisions*
George J. Staubus, *A Theory of Accounting to Investors*
Robert R. Sterling, *Theory of the Measurement of Enterprise Income*
Robert R. Sterling, *Toward a Science of Accounting*
Robert R. Sterling (Editor), *Asset Valuation and Income Determination*
Robert R. Sterling (Editor), *Institutional Issues in Public Accounting*
Robert R. Sterling (Editor), *Research Methodology in Accounting*
Robert R. Sterling and William F. Bentz (Editors), *Accounting in Perspective*
Robert R. Sterling and Arthur L. Thomas (Editors), *Accounting for a Simplified Firm Owning Depreciable Assets*
Reed K. Storey, *The Search for Accounting Principles*
Study Group on Business Income, *Changing Concepts of Business Income*

Toward a Science of Accounting

Robert R. Sterling

Scholars Book Co.
4431 Mt. Vernon
Houston, Texas 77006

Library of Congress Cataloging in Publication Data

Sterling, Robert R   1931–
    Toward a science of accounting.

    Bibliography: p.
    Includes index.
    1. Accounting. I. Title.
HF5635.S835 1980   657   80-14502
ISBN 0-914348-31-0

Printed in the United States of America

Contents

Preface

> The dogmas of the quiet past are inadequate to the stormy present. The occasion is piled high with difficulty and we must rise with the occasion. As our case is new, so we must think anew and act anew.
>
> ABRAHAM LINCOLN, *Second Annual Message to Congress*, Dec. 1, 1862

Accounting was born without notice and reared in neglect. It was of primary interest only to anonymous, faceless accountants. To some accounting was of secondary or tertiary interest but to most it was a subject to be ignored. That was the past and it was quiet. In the 1960s this began to change. Shareholders began to complain of losses caused by misleading financial statements. Courts began to find accounting culpable. The sleepy SEC awoke and cried loudly. The still Congress was stirred by investment credits and deeply agitated by more debits than credits. Today the arcane terms of accounting are a part of the daily vocabulary of attorneys and journalists. Every financial statement is a potential spectacular court case. Our every action, or inaction, is a potential headline. This is our present and it is stormy.

Our quiet past produced dogmas that are inadequate for the stormy present. The most inhibiting dogma is that accounting is an art, that it is necessarily unscientific. The development of accounting practice, and the attendant development of accounting thought, contains some forces which explain how that dogma arose, was reinforced, and passed on by subsequent generations. (I examined those forces in "Accounting in the 1980s.") But we now face different forces. Our case is new so we must think anew and act anew.

This essay is an attempt to think anew, to throw off the yoke of the inherited dogma and reexamine the fundamentals. To add a footnote on replacement costs, to propose price-level adjustments of historic costs may be improvements, but they are appendages to a model clearly constrained by the inherited dogma. What we needed was

ix

a new engine; what we got were new tailfins. To replace the APB with the FASB may be an improvement, but is is a continuation of the process of legislating accounting conventions which flows directly from the inherited dogma that accounting must be based upon conventions, that it cannot be an empirical science. What was needed was a new scientific foundation; what we got was a new institutional penthouse.

This essay is an unabashed attempt to demolish the dogma. In its place I try to lay a few stones for a scientific foundation. Part One is the attempted demolition, an examination of the dogma and its consequences. Part Two is the attempted construction, an application of scientific criteria to the fundamental problems of accounting. My purpose is to get others to think anew, to complete the foundation and build the structure.

Our stormy present also requires that we act anew—that we reform accounting practice. The prerequisite of acting anew is thinking anew, but in accounting there is no automatic connection between thinking and acting. The problem, as Zeff ("Comments," p. 177) puts it, is that "the academic literature has had remarkably little impact . . . upon the policies of the American Institute or the SEC." The reason is that the establishment of accounting practices has become a political process. It is a matter of legislation, not a matter of science, under the control of the FASB, SEC, AcSEC, and other legislatures. The function of legislatures is to record the compromises they can effect among their various constituencies. Thus, reform of practice requires that the legislators think anew *and* that the various constituencies think anew.

I have no illusions that this essay will persuade the legislators and their constituencies to think anew. The problem is that it is very difficult to think anew. Thoreau's (*Journal*, p. 24) observation is particularly apropos for accounting: "When any real progress is made, we must unlearn and learn anew what we thought we knew before." But unlearning is extraordinarily difficult. Therefore, my hope lies in the new generation who are not required to unlearn. I cannot improve on the words of Darwin (*Origin of Species*, pp. 422–23) who expressed both the problem and the hope: "Although I am fully convinced of the truth of the views given in this volume . . ., I by no means expect to convince experienced naturalists whose minds are stocked with a multitude of facts all viewed, during a long course of years, from a point of view directly opposite to mine. . . . Any one whose disposition leads him to attach more weight to unexplained difficulties than to the explanation of a certain number of facts will certainly reject the theory. A few naturalists, endowed with much flexibility of mind, . . . may be influenced by this volume; but I look with confidence to the future—to young and rising naturalists, who will be able to view both sides of the question with impartiality."

To rely upon the new generations requires a very long time. It also requires that we connect accounting research with accounting education. The teaching of accounting does not provide for reliance upon new generations because our undergraduate curricula consist almost entirely of present practices. Only in graduate seminars do we consider research. The undergraduates go into practice and implement what we taught them; the graduate students go into academia and advance the research; the gap between research and practice grows wider and wider. Young and rising accounting practitioners cannot view both sides of the question with impartiality because we teachers do not present both sides of the question. Instead, we pass along and thereby reinforce the inherited dogma. Thus, the long-run reform of accounting practice requires the reform of accounting curricula. My suggestion is that we teach both—we consider alternatives to present practices concurrently with the description of present practices. (See Staubus, "Responsibility," Sterling, "Accounting Research, Education," and Bowman and Lookabill, "Accounting Research Revisited," for further discussion.)

In presenting the alternatives in the classroom, as well as considering the alternatives discussed in this essay, the reader may find it helpful to classify them by empirical domains. This taxonomy has helped me to see similarities and differences that I did not see before. The question to be asked is: What are the empirical inputs and outputs? The broadest classification is between complete and incomplete systems. Some accounting systems specify empirical inputs but the outputs are not empirically testable—they are incomplete in this sense. (See Sterling "Theory Construction" for a schematic and further discussion.) Other systems are complete in that they specify empirical inputs and provide for empirical testing of the outputs. This exposes a fundamental difference between traditional accounting—whose outputs are admittedly not subject to empirical tests—and the proposal of this essay. It also reveals a similarity between the proposal of this essay and, for example, Thomas's proposal to report allocation-free figures. On the same basis, it reveals similarities between this proposal and the unallocated entry-value proposal of Johnson, Bell, and others, the physical-capacity domain of Revsine, Weygandt, and others, the undiscounted cash flows of Lee, Ijiri, and others. It also permits one to discern important differences. For example, there are vast differences between replacement-cost proponents—between allocated and unallocated entry values, between monetary and physical capacity—despite the fact that they use the same name for their proposals.

Other research groups can also be classified by empirical domain. For example, behaviorists use financial statements as inputs and the decisions of individuals as outputs; capital market efficiency researchers use financial statements as inputs and the prices in the securities market as outputs. The similarity of inputs is apparent; the similarity of outputs is revealed by recognizing that capital market agents are individuals whose collective decisions set the prices. An as yet unnamed group specifies changes in supplied information as inputs and the resultant changes in welfare—the social welfare effects—as outputs. Previous accounting theorists utilized the actions of practicing accountants as inputs, but their outputs were not specified.

In addition to this being a convenient taxonomy, in addition to its enabling us to see similarities and differences, examination of the empirical domain is important in its own right. As Boulding (*Economics*, p. 155) says: " . . . just as no stream can rise above its source, no science can rise above its data collection." The development of accounting thought has previously been restricted by an essentially unexamined constraint on its empirical domain. Proponents of reform have not explicitly recognized that their proposed systems are, at base, proposals for changes in or extensions of the empirical domain. I think that future development would be enormously enhanced by an explicit, careful examination of the various empirical domains.

It is customary to say that all this hard labor was undertaken for the good of society or, at least, the good of the accounting profession. Perhaps I should make some altruistic comment of that sort but honesty requires that I confess that I do it for fun. I enjoy wrestling with these ideas. Of course, I think my ideas are right, else I would not present them, and I hope that they will find their way into elementary courses and eventually into practice because I think they would be beneficial to the profession and to society. But these ideas need to be tested against your reason as well as against nature. I invite you to test the ideas, correct my errors, extend any ideas that survive the tests, and join in the fun.

RRS
Hoover Visitor, University of New South Wales
Bastille Day, 1979

Acknowledgments

Drafts of various parts of this essay were prepared for presentation at the following: The Arthur Young Colloquium at Florida A&M University, the University of Washington, Bowling Green University, Texas Tech University, the University of Pennsylvania, Washington University at St. Louis, the Southwest Regional Meeting of the American Accounting Association, the Price Waterhouse Distinguished Lecture at Stanford University, again at Texas Tech University, the Price Waterhouse Distinguished Lecture at Georgia State University, the Hoover Lectures at the University of New South Wales, the University of Sydney, and the Australian National University. I am grateful to Sybil Mobley, John Grant Rhode, Edwin Bomeli, Doyle Williams, David Solomons, Robert Virgil, Kenneth Most, William Beaver, Bruce Collier, Gary Luoma, Ronald Ma, Athol Carrington, Murray Wells, and Allan Barton for making the presentations possible. Valuable comment and criticism were received from various members of these audiences. I especially remember the insightful criticism of Kermit Larson, William Schrader, and a group of students from Macquarie University.

The Price Waterhouse Distinguished Lecture was published by Stanford, along with critiques by Nicholas Dopuch and Kenneth P. Johnson. The lecture was also published by the *Financial Analysts Journal*. It is used here with the kind permission of the publishers.

James Anderson, Thomas Dyckman, and Arthur L. Thomas read parts of the manuscript and made many helpful comments. A draft of the complete manuscript was insightfully critiqued by Ronald Ma.

Kay Preston, Bob Bunch, Pat Hefren, Catherine Harrison, David Harvey, and Jean Haug have served ably as research assistants over the years. Kay and Bob were especially valuable as critics of the content and of the exposition.

Students in various classes provided assistance in a number of ways, not the least of which was convincing me that the ideas contained herein are comprehensible and plausible, perhaps even correct. I especially remember Tim Lucas for anticipating every conclusion, as well as the questions and comments of Carey, Chini, Doris, Janet, Jeff, Jim, Mel, Peggy, Rich, Tom, and many others.

Pat Armentor did that myriad of things that editors are expected to do, and more. Bonnye Karger performed all those miracles that secretaries are expected to perform, and more.

To all the above my warm thanks and the usual absolution.

Symbols

Several symbols are defined in context and are not used again. Others are defined here for reference.

d_{it} Discounted value of asset i at time t

p_{it} Price (undifferentiated between entry and exit) of asset i at time t

n_{it} Entry value of asset i at time t

x_{it} Exit value of asset i at time t

In capitals the symbols refer to values of the firm.

D_{ft} Discounted value of firm f at time t

P_{ft} Price (undifferentiated) of firm f at time t

N_{ft} Sum of the entry values of the assets of firm f at time t

X_{ft} Sum of the exit values of the assets of firm f at time t

In the symbols listed above, the first subscript is varied to indicate o = owned, u = unowned, and r = rented. A presubscript is used to indicate who assigned the value, for example, $_cD$ = discounted value assigned by creditor as opposed to $_oD$ = discounted value assigned by owner. Bars are used to indicate average value per share outstanding, for example, $\bar{x}_{ft}$ = per share average of sum of exit values of assets of firm f at time t, that is, X_{ft}/λ where λ is total shares outstanding. Superscripts $+$ and $-$ are used to differentiate increments from decrements.

A Alternatives set

A_{ft} Sum of unspecified values of the assets of firm f at time t

a_{it} Stocks of i at time t

a_n The nth alternative

B_{ft} Change in all balance sheet accounts of firm f at time t

b_{mt} Inflows and outflows of account m at time t

C Consequences set

$\bar{C}_{fT}$ Vector of composition exchanges of firm f for time period T

c_n The nth consequence

F_t Available funds at time t

I_{fT} Sum of investment and disinvestment exchanges of firm f for time period T

i_{mt} Investment and disinvestment exchanges for account m at time t

L_{ft} Liabilities of firm f at time t

P Preferences set

s_{it} Required sacrifice for asset i at time t

Y_{fT} Net income of firm f for period T

y_{mt} Income of account m at time t

γ A risk indicator

μ A measurement operation

λ_{ft} Total shares outstanding of firm f at time t

¢   Specific means of combination

Part One

From the Elusive Art

1

Introduction to Part One

> Science must begin with myths—and with the criticism of myths.
>
> POPPER, "Personal Report," p. 177

This essay is an attempt to take a first step in transforming accounting from an elusive art[1] into a science. The transformation process must, as Popper says, begin with the criticism of myths. Part One is critical of some of accounting's most cherished beliefs—beliefs which I think are myths. I hope that from this criticism a science will emerge, that the criticism will destroy some myths, and that science will fill the void.

1.1 The Problem

> No inquiry can even get under way until and unless *some difficulty is felt* in a practical or theoretical situation. It is the difficulty, or problem, which guides our search.
>
> COHEN and NAGEL, *Logic and Scientific Method*, p. 199

The felt difficulty that motivated this essay is that we accountants seem incapable of solving accounting problems. When we confront a problem, we almost invariably disagree about its proper solution. The solution itself becomes an issue about which various accountants advance various arguments for or against various proposed solutions. We accountants do not resolve these issues; we abandon them. I am not implying that we ignore issues: quite the contrary, we debate them long and loud. Instead of resolving the problem, however, we

---

1. As Howard Ross called it in the title of his book.

continue the debate until another more current and more controversial issue arises, and then we forget the former issue. Consider the LIFO–FIFO debate that occupied so much of our attention and journal space a few years ago. Presently, LIFO versus FIFO is a dead issue. Note that I said "dead issue." I did not say "resolved issue." Although the issue was never resolved, very little attention or journal space is devoted to it at present because other pressing issues came along to divert our attention. In fact, a number of issues—tax allocation, accelerated versus straight line, pooling versus purchasing, full versus direct costing, and so forth—were abandoned in favor of newer issues. For example, we quit debating full versus direct costing not because the issue was resolved but rather because the merger movement caused us to divert our attention to the more pressing issue of purchasing versus pooling.

Further evidence of our inability to resolve issues is that we periodically resurrect dead issues. The treatment of interest as a cost and the classification of bad debts were controversial issues in the 1920s and 1950s. Conclusive evidence that these issues were not resolved at that time is provided by the fact that they are once again, in the 1970s, being debated in the literature. Such issues are periodically brought up for debate, neglected for a while, and then resurrected and debated again. Accountants anticipated the ecology movement by some years; instead of disposing of issues, we recycle them.

The problem then is that instead of resolving issues in accounting, we move from one unresolved issue to another, and our inventory of such issues grows. Additions to the stock of unresolved issues come from the natural course of events; however, we have been virtually unable to subtract from that stock.[2] The stock of resolved issues grows imperceptibly if at all.

The purpose of Part One of this essay is to examine the reasons for our inability to resolve issues in accounting. Despite the pressing need to solve our current, specific accounting problems, no attempt is made to do so in Part One. Instead, the main focus is on the broader question: why are we unable to resolve issues in accounting? I hope that an answer to this general question will yield insights into how to resolve the specific issues.

2. In 1967 Catlett ("Achieving Progress," p. 67) wrote: "If you carefully analyze the actual progress that was made during the period from 1940 to 1960, you will find that very little was accomplished. . . . Not only were many of the old problems left unsolved, but new ones, such as those relating to leases, pensions, mergers and tax allocation, were also unsolved." The subsequent years have not resulted in solving these problems; instead we have added more unsolved problems to the list.

1.2 The Cause of the Problem

> Upon the whole, I am inclined to think that the far
> greater part, if not all, of those difficulties which have
> hitherto . . . blocked up the way to knowledge, are
> entirely owing to ourselves—that we have first raised
> a dust and then complain that we cannot see.
>
> BERKELEY, *Treatise,* p. 8

My essay advances the argument that our inability to resolve issues
is entirely owing to ourselves—we raise a dust that prevents us from
seeing. The explanation of our inability to resolve issues can be found
by examining the way we conceive of the issues. We conceive of
them in such a way that they are *in principle* unresolvable. We cannot
answer our questions because we phrase the questions in a way that
prohibits our obtaining answers. We define our problems so that the
very definition *precludes the possibility* of a solution.

1.3 The Solution

> The significance of a thought lies in the actions to
> which it leads.
>
> RUSSELL, *Philosophical Essays,* p. 80

If the cause of our problem has been correctly identified, the solution
is apparent: we must reformulate our questions; we must redefine
our problems. If our present formulation of questions prohibits
obtaining answers, we must reformulate those questions in order to
obtain answers to them; if our present definition of problems precludes
the possibility of solutions, we must redefine the problems in order
to solve them.

Such reformulations and redefinitions are common in the history
of science.

> It is just this sort of change in the formulation of questions and answers
> that accounts, far more than novel empirical discoveries, for the
> transition from Aristotelian to Galilean and from Galilean to Newtonian
> dynamics. (KUHN, *Scientific Revolutions,* p. 139)

Thus, in science a question that has remained unanswered for a long
period of time is often never answered in its original formulation;
the answer comes only after the question has been reformulated.

I believe that a general reformulation of questions and a redefinition
of problems are necessary to obtain answers and solutions in accounting. Reformulation of accounting questions will not provide automatic,
easy answers any more than the Newtonian reformulation provided

automatic, easy answers in physics. The solution to redefined accounting problems may be extraordinarily difficult, as was often the case
in physics. However, I believe our choice is between the difficult
and the impossible. In our present state, answers and solutions are
impossible to obtain. Reformulation and redefinition will make them
merely difficult to obtain.

1.4 An Example of a Redefined Problem

> Do people gather grapes from thorns, or figs from
> thistles? So every healthy tree bears good fruit, but
> a rotten tree bears defective fruit.
>
> MATTHEW 7: 16–17

A reader familiar with the accounting literature can get a preview
of my intent by reflecting on the history of the concept of objectivity.
As originally defined that concept bore no fruit—we were trying to
reap grapes from thorns and thistles.

The literature of the past reveals that objectivity was one of the
most slippery concepts in accounting. Conclusive evidence of its
slipperiness is shown by the fact that it was used to support both
sides of diametrically opposed positions. When considering alternative
reporting procedures x and y, those who favored x would invariably
claim that x was more objective than y, while those who favored
y would invariably claim that y was more objective than x.

Such a situation caused some of us to think the term was completely
vacuous. On one occasion I argued that the term was a quagmire
that should be avoided (Sterling, "ASOBAT Review," p. 100). On
another occasion I stated that the term had only emotive content
and recommended it be completely expunged from the vocabulary
of accounting (Sterling, "Operational Analysis," p. 136). However,
I was troubled by my recommendations. I thought that objectivity
ought to have a place in accounting as it has in science. Toward
that end I presented some suggestions that objectivity be defined
as observer agreement (*Enterprise Income,* pp. 42–44), but those
suggestions were not sharply focused.

My point is that considerable confusion attended the notion of
objectivity. I use my past writing to illustrate the confusion that existed
and the unsuccessful attempts to correct the situation. I was unsuccessful because the problem as it has been formulated was in principle
unresolvable—a reformulation of the problem was required before
we could approach resolution.

It was Ijiri and Jaedicke ("Reliability and Objectivity") who proposed a reformulation of the problem, a redefinition of "objectivity." They proposed a method of *measuring* the divergence of observer agreement. The results were twofold: (1) "objectivity" was given a definite meaning so that we could improve our communications and our thinking; (2) one could use the proposed measure to adjudicate disputes regarding the relative objectivity of various proposals.

The significance of the redefinition can hardly be overstated. Prior to the redefinition our discussions of objectivity were little more than vague assertions. The redefinition put us on a higher plane—we could make tests instead of assertions. McDonald ("Test Application") made the first test. I followed with another test (Sterling and Radosevich, "Valuation Experiment," p. 94) and was surprised because the result of that test was antithetical to some of my previous conjectures. Had it not been for the Ijiri and Jaedicke redefinition, I would probably still be making those erroneous conjectures.

Parker ("Testing Comparability") has subsequently performed a field experiment. In that experiment he corrected the conclusion drawn in Sterling and Radosevich while replicating some of our previous results. Had it not been for the Ijiri and Jaedicke redefinition, neither the correction nor the replication would have been possible.

Of course, not all of the problems of objectivity have been solved. McKeown ("Empirical Test"), Staubus (*Accounting Decisions*), and others have suggested alternative statistical tests. While there are still arguments about objectivity, they are on a higher plane. The current arguments are about refinements—the redefinition remains intact.

In summary, objectivity has a long, ignoble history. We were confused about the basic meaning of the term, and this confusion hindered our communications and our thinking. In addition, we never resolved any issues about the relative objectivity of alternative reporting procedures in its previous formulation. The reformulation of the problem permitted us to clarify our communications and our thinking and to resolve some problems regarding the relative objectivity of various proposals. It was the reformulation of the problem that permitted us to begin to make progress. We began to replace assertions with tests. Some of the test results had high informational content because they were a surprise to us. We also began to see suggestions for refining the reformulated problem.

2

The Art of Accounting

> It is desirable that the accountant conceive . . . of his statements as creative works of art.
>
> AMERICAN INSTITUTE OF CERTIFIED PUBLIC ACCOUNTANTS, "Accounting Terminology," p. 10

The accountant is instructed to conceive of his financial statements as creative works of art. Of course, no accountant literally conceives of his product as a creative work of art. He knows that his product is different from that of a Rembrandt or a Picasso. Figures of speech are not meant to be taken literally. We know that "a heart as hard as flint" is false, but we also know that such similes convey messages that affect actions.

> "A mere matter of words," we say contemptuously, forgetting that words have power to mold men's thinking, to canalize their feeling, to direct their willing and acting. Conduct and character are largely determined by the nature of the words we currently use to discuss ourselves and the world around us. (HUXLEY, *Words and Meanings*, p. 9)

It is the belief that our words affect our conduct that motivates the consideration of defining accounting as an art and the consequences of that definition.

2.1 The Subject and the Approach

> We have to recognize that here [replacing the theory of impetus with inertia] was a problem of a fundamental nature, and it could not be solved by close observation within the framework of the older system of ideas—it required a transposition in the mind.
>
> BUTTERFIELD, *Origins*, p. 17

Sometimes problems cannot be solved by close observation or hard thinking within the framework of a given system of ideas because that framework is a misconception of the nature of the subject. The solution requires a transposition in the mind. I believe that we have misconceived the nature of the subject. We misconceive our subject at the very beginning in regard to the broadest of issues—the definition of accounting. In the official pronouncements of our societies,[1] in journal articles,[2] in symposia proceedings,[3] as well as in textbooks,[4] we find accounting defined as an "art" as opposed to a "science." As Devine ("Discussion," p. 18) says, the "assertion that accounting is an art and not a science . . . is common in accounting literature." The authors who make the assertion typically claim that accounting is necessarily an art, that it cannot be a science.[5]

This definition of accounting stems from two misconceptions. First, the authors have a misconception of the nature of science. They seem to believe that in order for a discipline to be scientific, it must consist of immutable laws and absolute truths. The fact is that laws in even the most exact sciences are mutable. Witness the recent overturn of the Newtonian laws of physics by Einstein. To a scientist, laws are empirical generalizations which *must* be subject to falsification. If

---

1. "Accounting is the art of recording, classifying, and summarizing in a significant manner and in terms of money, transactions and events which are, in part at least, of a financial character, and interpreting the results thereof. . . .

"If accounting were called a science, attention would be directed (and perhaps limited) to the ordered classifications used as the accountant's framework, and to the known body of facts which in a given case are fitted into this framework" (American Institute of Certified Public Accountants, "Accounting Terminology," p. 9).

2. "Accounting is the art of measuring and communicating financial information" (Bierman, "Measurement," p. 501). Although Bierman defines accounting as an art in the beginning sentence, the remainder of his article is concerned with scientific measurement. See also the quotations by Lawler ("Accounting Philosophers") and Stone ("Public Confidence") infra.

3. "Accounting is an art and not a science. Its principles are not natural laws but rules developed by man to meet the needs of the business community" (Blough, "Accounting Principles," p. 12).

4. "It would be incorrect to suggest that the rules which establish whether a given accounting procedure is acceptable or unacceptable are in the nature of principles like those found in physics or chemistry. Accounting principles are more properly associated with such terms as *concepts, conventions,* and *standards.* It is important to remember that accounting principles are man made, in contrast to natural law.

. . .

"Principles cannot be established in accounting, as they are in the realm of natural sciences, by experimentation; nor have they been determined, as in the law, by authoritative pronouncement" (Finney and Miller, *Principles of Accounting,* pp. 165–166).

5. In response to my Price Waterhouse lecture, one critic (Dopuch, "Discussion") argued that defining accounting as an art is not prevalent, while the other critic (Johnson, "Discussion") provided additional evidence of the prevalence of the definition by arguing that "trying to transform accounting into a science is impossible" but that "this is not to say that accounting cannot be made into a more precise art."

they were immutable, scientists would call them "definitions," not "laws."[6]

In direct contrast to scientists, accountants conceive of laws as immutable and seem to believe that there are no uncertainties in science. For example, Lawler ("Accounting Philosophers," p. 88) writes: "If, in truth, a practitioner of the accounting art is a truth-seeker, he is confronted by a host of uncertainties. There are no natural laws of accounting which he can employ, only conventions validated by experience, estimates born of human judgments, guidelines developed by his professional societies." We can all agree that there are a "host of uncertainties" in accounting. The existence of such uncertainties seems to cause accountants to define accounting as an art. If one conceives of science as consisting of absolute truths, one must conclude that accounting is not a science since there is so much uncertainty in accounting. However, that conclusion is based upon a misconception of the nature of science. There is also uncertainty in science; else there would be no reason for scientists to continue their research. Thus, when accountants define accounting as an art because of its uncertainty, they are basing their definition upon a misconception of science.

We can also agree with Lawler that there are "no natural laws of accounting." But we might pursue that accurate description a little further. The quotation clearly indicates that the absence of laws is a necessary condition—that we must rely on conventions. This is the basis of the second misconception which causes us to define accounting as an art.

Specifically, the second misconception is that there is something about accounting that makes it inherently unscientific. That accounting is more like an art than a science may be an accurate description of accounting at present, but it is not a necessary condition of accounting. Compare the primitive medicine man to the modern medical scientist. Both study illness—they have the same subject matter. However, they differ greatly in their approach to that subject matter. One performs artistic rituals designed to exorcise demons.

---

6. Caws (*Philosophy*, pp. 85–86), for example, draws the distinction: "The same statement can at different times and under different circumstances be a principle, a definition, or a law. If its truth is *asserted* and not considered liable to empirical challenge, it is a definition; if not—that is, if it is taken to be empirically significant—then it is a principle if it contains theoretical terms, otherwise a law. A principle turns into a law if what before could not be observed becomes observable by virtue of some advance in experimental technique." See Popper (*Logic*, et passim especially pp. 40–42) for a discussion of the falsifiability requirement in science.

The other performs the rather arduous scientific task of looking for empirical generalizations (i.e., laws) and trying to construct logical connections among the laws (i.e., theorizing). Thus, the difference between them is not the nature of the subject but rather their approach to that subject matter. The medicine man *defines* illness as the product of the inexplicable caprice of demons. Once he has defined it that way, he is trapped. His problems will remain unresolved because he has defined them in such a way as to make them in principle unresolvable. The first step toward science is to change the definition. The modern medical scientist faces a host of uncertainties—for example, the cause of and cure for cancer—but he does not fall into the trap of conceiving of his subject matter in such a way as to preclude the possibility of obtaining answers.

The analogy applies to accounting. Nothing about our subject matter requires accounting to be an art instead of a science. It is an art because we define it that way. It is possible to define it in some other way. There is nothing inherently unscientific about accounting: it is our approach to accounting that has been unscientific. It is possible for us to adopt a scientific approach.

2.2 Objectives and Objectivity

> Perfection of means and confusion of goals seem, in my opinion, to characterize our age.
>
> EINSTEIN, *Later Years*, p. 113

Many accountants have criticized our literature for its excessive attention to the "how" and its almost complete absence of attention to the "why." (See, e.g., Spacek, "Accounting Court," p. 4.) We have been busily engaged in perfecting our means, our techniques, with precious little attention and much confusion about the goals or objectives of accounting. I believe that part of the confusion of goals or objectives arises from defining accounting as an art instead of a science.

Although I have never found the notion of accounting associated with science in accounting texts, I often find such associations in science and philosophy texts. "In the language of scientific explanation and philosophical criticism the word 'account' seems to crop up with surprising frequency" (Caws, "Accounting Research," p. 72). In fact, many scientists include "account for" or "account of" as an integral part of the definition of science. For example, Torgerson (*Theory*, p. 1, italics added) writes: "The principal objective of a science, other than the description of empirical phenomena, is to establish, through laws and theories, general principles by means of which the empirical phenomena can be explained, *accounted* for, and predicted." In my view, this ought to be the objective of accounting as well as the objective of science; that is, accounting ought to be redefined as a science and then it ought to adopt the principal objective of science. Our financial statements ought to provide descriptions and explanations of empirical phenomena. We should also seek laws and theories which will allow us to predict (in the scientific sense) those phenomena.[7] In short, as "accounting" seems to imply, the principal objective ought to be to account for empirical phenomena.

A prepublication reader protested: "Your use of 'account' seems no better than a pun. Torgersen presumably was not thinking of accounting, but of the lay sense of 'account for.' " Agreed, but that is precisely the point I am trying to make: the way in which we define the term is a matter of choice. One lay sense of "account" given by *Webster's Unabridged Dictionary* is: "A statement or exposition of underlying or explanatory reasons, causes, grounds, or motives [as used in] no satisfactory account has been given of these phenomena." I venture that this is an older definition, that it predates the technical definitions we accountants have given the term. If this is true, it means that we accountants have *previously* redefined the term, thus providing conclusive proof that it is possible to redefine it. Once we recognize the possibility of redefinition, perhaps we could redefine it in accord with the scientific meaning of the term.

The objective of science is not in conflict with the usefulness objective of accounting. Science is the pursuit of knowledge. The knowledge provided by science is useful knowledge. One must understand empirical phenomena in order to use them effectively. The prediction of empirical phenomena provides the basis for the useful control of those phenomena. Indeed, scientific laws and theories are a prerequisite to usefulness. One cannot determine what facts are useful in the absence of scientific laws and theories. One of the primary functions of scientific theory is to provide a guide for the selection of useful facts. Without a theory to guide us, all facts would appear to be equally relevant, and the bewildering number of facts would prohibit understanding. Thus, to accomplish the usefulness

7. "Predict" in the scientific sense means to anticipate unobserved phenomena without regard to the temporal locations of those phenomena. Thus, in science "predict" often refers to present phenomena. "Forecast" refers exclusively to anticipated phenomena that lie in the future. Whether or not we want to predict in the sense of issuing and certifying to forecasts will be discussed in Chapter 7.

objective of accounting, we must first provide scientific laws and theories.

Compare the objective of art to that of science. The principal objective of the fine arts is to create beauty, to create objects that please the observer. This is an aesthetic, not a useful or utilitarian, objective. In order to accomplish the aesthetic objective, the artist perceives his specific objective to be to present his personal "interpretation" of an object, not to present an accurate representation of that object.[8] Thus, the image that shows up on the canvas is due more to the imagination of the artist than to the object he is painting. Artists (at least post-Renaissance artists) strive to be different—to present different depictions of the same object. For example, if Picasso had painted a picture of Madame Matisse, he might have depicted her with only one eye since there are in fact Picasso paintings showing one-eyed women. On the other hand, Matisse depicted her with two eyes—and a green nose. It is unlikely that Picasso would have chosen green as the color of her nose. Both Picasso and Matisse would have been looking at the same object, but the representations on the canvas would have been quite different. In art different representations of the same object are not only acceptable, they are desirable. They are intended to depend upon the imagination of the artists, not upon the object.

By contrast, scientists strive to avoid such differences. If two scientists were to count the number of Madame Matisse's eyes or to determine the color of her nose, differences between them would be cause for alarm. A basic tenet of science is agreement among independent observers. As Hempel (*Fundamentals,* p. 43) puts it: "Science strives for objectivity in the sense that its statements are to be capable of public test with results that do not vary essentially with the tester." Thus, in science the representations are intended to depend upon the object, not upon the imaginations of the scientists.

Defining accounting as an art is, unfortunately, a fairly accurate description of the current condition. There is that infamous memo in the Penn Central Case (Daughen and Binzen, *Penn Central,* p. 224) which praises an accountant because his "imaginative accounting is adding millions of dollars annually to our reported income." Certainly in that case the representation depended more on the

---

8. Matisse clearly drew the distinction between scientific or accurate representation and artistic imagination: "I replied to someone who said I didn't see women as I represent them: 'If I met such women in life, I should run away in horror.' First of all, I do not create a woman, I make a picture" (Escholier, *Matisse,* p. 124).

imagination of the accountant than on the operations of Penn Central. I fear that there may be a good many such instances. In the present unscientific state of accounting, I fear that the representation may depend more on the imagination of the accountant than on the firm being accounted for. In this sense accounting may, in fact, be more like an art than a science.

Undoubtedly, this is not the way that things *ought* to be. If two accountants were to count Madame Matisse's eyes, a difference in the result should be cause for alarm as it should be cause for alarm when we obtain different measures of income and assets. A basic tenet of accounting ought to be agreement among independent observers because the measure ought to depend upon the condition of the firm, not upon the imagination of the accountant. We have a choice. We can adopt the principal objective of science—to explain, account for, and predict empirical phenomena—or we can continue to lament the artistic nature of accounting. We can strive for observer agreement or we can continue to permit, and perhaps to unintentionally encourage, artistic interpretations. The adoption of a principal objective or the striving for observer agreement is not imposed on us by external forces: it is a matter of choice.

2.3 Independence

> The game must go on: that is Nature's command. But it is up to man to determine the ground rules and the teams.
>
> HARDIN, *Nature,* p. 318

The extant ground rules and the makeup of the teams present a major impediment to progress in accounting. On the one hand our fees are paid by management, and on the other hand we are required to be independent of management. The problem is too complex for me to attempt to resolve it here.[9] Despite my inability to resolve the problem I can point to one contributory factor. I am convinced that defining accounting as art exacerbates the problem.

The dangers of such a definition can be illustrated by considering Oliver Cromwell's instructions to his portrait painter:

> Mr. Lely, . . . I desire you would use all your skill to paint my picture

---

9. My belated recognition of the existence of the problem and some preliminary suggestions toward a solution are given in Sterling, "Accounting Power." After that belated recognition, I invited others to consider the problem and make proposals in Sterling, *Institutional Issues.*

> truly like me, and not flatter me at all; but remark all these roughnesses, pimples, warts, and everything, otherwise I never will pay a farthing for it. (FIRTH, *Oliver Cromwell*, p. 453)

The very fact that Cromwell could give such instructions is significant. It implies that he could have given instructions to do the opposite.

This quotation is famous because it expresses a rare trait. It is much more common to want to be flattered, to be shown in the most favorable light. Since managements are human, I cannot imagine that they would instruct their accountants to "paint me as I am, warts and all." I suspect that they would give opposite instructions:

> Flatter me just a little—about 10 percent increase in earnings—by selecting the most cosmetic conventions, and conceal my warts with aesthetically phrased footnotes.

Since most managements are not as blunt as Cromwell, I omitted the threat to never pay a farthing if the instructions were not followed. Nonetheless, I suspect that the threat is often there, albeit tacit. Moreover, I am sure that the auditor (or controller) is keen enough to recognize such a tacit threat. This puts him in a untenable position. Despite his desire—indeed his obligation—to tell it like it is, he has no defense. There are a large number of alternative conventions with no clear criteria for selection. The result is the danger of artistic accounting to the extent of selecting the most cosmetic of the available conventions.

Contrast other verifiers, for example, a construction inspector. He is required to use judgment, but he has no alternative laws of physics to select from. In inspecting electrical circuits, for example, one cannot measure the resistance by choosing between Ohm's law—$R = V(1/I)$—and Sterling's law—$R = V(2/I)$. The example seems absurd, but compare it to the "measurement" of first-year depreciation by choosing between straight line—$D = C(1/L)$—and double declining balance—$D = C(2/L)$. Instead of being required to use his judgment in *selecting* alternative *conventions*, the construction inspector used his judgment in *applying* scientifically established *laws*. As a consequence, the construction inspector is in a much stronger position than the accountant. The existence of scientifically established laws does not make one more independent, but it does permit one to be in a better position to exercise independence.

An additional advantage of scientifically established laws is that the demarcation between deliberate misrepresentation and errors in judgment is much sharper. The existence of alternative conventions in accounting has permitted both critics and courts to confuse fraud with error. As long as we allow the possibility of the representation to depend on one's imagination in the selection of conventions, I expect that this confusion will continue.

In summary, by defining accounting as an art, we have left ourselves wide open to receiving instructions and threats—to having our independence weakened—and, when we have erred, to accusations of deliberate misrepresentation. If we defined accounting as a science, we would be considerably less vulnerable. Of course, the act of redefining will not result in scientifically established laws. Redefinition is, however, a prerequisite. We are not likely to ever seek scientifically established laws as long as we define accounting as an art.

2.4 Tastes Versus Tests

> *De gustibus non disputandum.*
> LATIN PROVERB

As the proverb says, tastes are not disputable. Even the language used to express tastes indicates this status. The comment, "I like Matisse's work," does not provide evidence that his work is good; instead it merely expresses an indisputable taste—it is an incorrigible statement not subject to scientific test.

As Johnson ("Discussion," p. 19) has pointed out in response to an outline of this essay, "Our output—financial statements—depends, at many steps, on judgments and decisions made by people. . . . Produced under those flexible conditions, the output is much more apt to resemble art than science." Again the description is accurate.[10] But that makes the contents of financial statements a matter of indisputable taste. This in turn calls into question the auditing function. We recognize that is is impossible to audit art since it depends on indisputable tastes, yet we require audits of financial statements while defining them as artistic conceptions. The contradiction is manifest. Recognition of the contradiction requires that we either: (1) give

---

10. Stone ("Public Confidence," p. 53) makes an almost identical point: "But I must point out that accounting principles are intellectual concepts. They are not subject to the kinds of proof that are applied to laws of physical science. So legitimate differences of opinion within the profession itself are virtually inevitable." Matters of opinion are similar to matters of taste in that both are not subject to test. My comments in the text apply to matters of opinion with equal force. Namely, I agree with Stone that the answers to most accounting questions are now matters of opinion, but I want to go further and argue that reformulation of the questions will convert them to matters of test.

up the auditing function since we cannot audit art, or (2) redefine the contents of financial statements so that they are not matters of indisputable tastes.

I prefer the second alternative: let us redefine the financial statements so that they are matters of test rather than matters of taste. Selecting this alternative requires that the financial statements be designed so that they reflect empirical phenomena. If a figure on a financial statement is *intended* to represent empirical phenomena, that figure can be subjected to scientific tests—it is not a matter of taste. On the other hand, if the figure is arrived at by convention, if the figure refers to some unobservable fiction (such as an "unexpired cost"), it cannot be tested and will forever remain a matter of taste.

The current question of how to audit unexpired costs is not answerable. We must reformulate the question before we can obtain an answer. Specifically, we must ask how to audit empirical phenomena. The answer will not be easy to obtain. Indeed, it may be quite difficult. But auditing unexpired costs is impossible. Our choice then is between the impossible and the difficult. I choose the difficult.

Some Terms of Art in Need of Redefinition

> Term of Art: A word or phrase having a specific significance in a particular art, craft or department of knowledge.
>
> *Webster's Unabridged Dictionary*
>
> It is thanks to words and to words alone that, as the poet says:
>> Tasks in hours of insight willed
>> May be in hours of gloom fulfilled.
>
> And let us remember incidentally that by no means all of our tasks are willed in hours of insight. Some are willed in hours of imbecility, some in hours of calculating self-interest, some under the stress of violent emotion, some in mere stupidity and intellectual confusion.
>
> HUXLEY, *Words and Meanings,* p. 14

We accountants have adopted certain terms of art that have a specific significance to us. Linguists have long known that the structure of languages determines to a large extent the structure of our thought processes. Some languages facilitate thinking and others hamper thinking. It is my view that many of our terms of art hamper our thinking and, hence, hamper progress in accounting. Many of our terms of art have imbedded tasks that seem to have been adopted in hours of intellectual confusion instead of in hours of insight. Consequently, those terms are in sore need of redefinition.

3.1 Conventions Versus Laws

> A fundamental principle of modern science is that a *logical gulf* exists between nature and convention.
>
> KARL R. POPPER quoted by SZASZ, *Mental Illness,* p. 170

19

Accounting principles are defined as conventions rather than laws. I think the definition is an accurate description. I think that our current "principles" are in fact conventions. However, I also think that it is an error to call a convention a "principle." It confuses the nature and function of two disparate things. Both laws (which are similar to principles—see Caws's distinction in Section 2.1) and conventions are necessary to science, but it is important to clearly distinguish between them.

All sciences have need for conventions, but they are relatively unimportant matters. For example, 0° (Celsius) is defined, by convention, to be the temperature of freezing water. It could have just as easily been defined as some other number, such as 32° (Fahrenheit), and that fact makes it a relatively unimportant matter. Conventions are general rules that are agreed upon either formally by the vote of an assembly or informally by custom and usage. There may be marginal reasons for selecting one convention over another (such as computational ease), but the selection of a convention is essentially an arbitrary choice.

At the present time we define accounting as being based upon conventions in general: "Earnings, therefore, are based on conventions" (Trueblood Committee, *Financial Statements,* p. 22). In addition, our texts describe various allocation procedures as "cost conventions." For example, LIFO is described as one convention and FIFO as another. The type of depreciation used is also said to be a matter of selecting a particular convention. The texts present rather vague arguments about the relative merits of the alternative conventions, and then they conclude that the choice in a specific case "depends upon the circumstances."

Defining the problem as one of selecting a convention has caused much mischief. Consider the convention of driving on the right side of the road in the U.S. That it is truly a convention is evidenced by the fact that they drive on the left in England. Since it is a convention, the choice is arbitrary. A similar convention exists in accounting: we put the credits on the right. Since putting the credits on the left would be equally acceptable, it is easily recognized to be a convention. The choice is arbitrary. Once the choice has been made—the agreement reached—we cannot allow individuals to choose. If we allowed each individual to choose which side of the road to drive on, the result would be chaos. If we let each individual choose which side to put the credits on, the result would be chaos. We have let each individual choose between LIFO and FIFO, accelerated and straight-line depreciation, and so forth, and the result has been chaos.

We academic accountants have assured ourselves that the market is not fooled by the use of different conventions—that competing sources of information permit capital market agents to adjust for different conventions. This finding provides comfort to some accountants, but the source of their comfort is a puzzle to me. Consider an analogy. Suppose that some meteorologists report temperature in Fahrenheit and others report it in Celsius. Suppose further that there are competing sources of information that adjust from Fahrenheit to Celsius (or vice versa) so that the figures are comparable. I think that all of us would be justifiably critical of the meteorologists. First, the differences in conventions introduce the possibility of unnecessary error. Some of the figures may not be adjusted or some may not be adjusted correctly.[1] This error would be unnecessary because of the possibility of standardizing the convention at the outset. If the convention were standardized, no adjustment would be required. Second, the situation would require unnecessary costs. Adjustments cost something; and since the conventions could be standardized at the outset, this cost is unnecessary. For these reasons (and others) all of us who use temperature information would probably demand that the conventions be standardized—we would not be satisfied to have competing sources of information make the adjustments. Nonaccountants are critical of accounting for the same reasons, and I think that their criticism is justified for the same reasons.[2]

1. Although the adjustment from Fahrenheit to Celsius is simple and straightforward, errors have occured. One example of such an error caused an early Apollo unmanned test vehicle to go off course, and the vehicle had to be destroyed. In calculating the effects of atmospheric pressure, a technician made a mistake in converting some of the measurements from Fahrenheit to Celsius. Since the adjustment from, say, LIFO to FIFO is much more complex, it would seem much more susceptible to error.

2. The discussion in the text assumes that the market can make such adjustments. I must confess that I have some doubts about that. My doubts spring from four sources. First, individual research clearly reveals that such adjustments are impossible in the absence of an immense amount of disclosure. I regularly run such an experiment in my seminar for first-year graduate students. The purpose of the experiment is to encourage the students to think about the issue instead of merely parroting the ancient text-book assertions that disclosure negates the problem or the more recent assertions that competing sources of information negate the problem. Since sameness or difference is the most elemental discrimination of any measurement system—even the nominal scale permits discrimination of sameness or difference—the experiment is designed to test the ability of students to determine whether or not two sets of financial statements refer to the same firm or to different firms. In spite of their superior knowledge of accounting, over the years the students have done no better than chance.

Second, market studies on adjustments of accounting reports present some inherent experimental design difficulties. Since we do not know the true or correct price, we cannot compare the observed price to the true price. In the absence of a true or correct price, we would like to have two or more identical firms utilizing different

This problem has been with us for a long time. As early as 1967, *Forbes* named it "The Growing Credibility Gap." The problem was never resolved. Instead, as usual, it was abandoned when other issues demanded our attention. The issue went unresolved because we defined it in such a way that it was unresolvable. The definition caused problems for both the practitioners and the researchers.

3.1.1 Practitioners.

The definition of the problem put practitioners in an untenable position. The problem was defined as the selection of conventions by individual practitioners. Conventions are not subject to selection by individuals; they are agreed to by a group. Selecting a convention is an arbitrary choice that should be made by a group and then standardized. The burden of choosing should not be placed on individuals since standardization is essential. The problem was compounded when the selection, an arbitrary choice, was defined

---

accounting conventions. If adjustments are made, we could expect to find identical prices for identical firms. But we do not have identical firms to study. Instead, we have different firms utilizing different accounting conventions. We do not know how to separate the differences in the firms from the differences in the accounting conventions; therefore, we cannot run a cross-sectional experiment. For these reasons, market experimenters have performed longitudinal studies. They select firms that change accounting conventions and observe the price reactions to those changes. This approach also presents a formidable experimental design problem since other factors affect the market price. Thus, the findings are contaminated by other factors, and we cannot be sure that their effects have been correctly separated.

Third, I am troubled by the inability to reconcile the findings of the market studies with the findings of individual research. Such a reconciliation is essential because capital market agents are, in fact, individuals. The "market" is a collection of individuals. I think that the findings of both the individual researchers and the market researchers will remain suspect until such a reconciliation is accomplished.

Fourth, there are some anomalies in the market studies. To cite just one example, consider Sunder's findings ("Accounting Changes") that the market seems to adjust from FIFO to LIFO but does not seem to adjust from LIFO to FIFO. This finding appears to be a gross anomaly that cries out for explanation. How can we continue to flatly assert that the market adjusts for differences in conventions when a market study designed to detect such adjustments concludes that the market adjusts one way but not the other? I find a one-way adjustment to be enigmatic.

My previous expression of such doubts has brought forth an avalanche of criticism. Usually the criticism is in the form of a proof that I have rejected capital market efficiency. The present confession of such doubts is likely to bring forth further proofs of such rejection. If that is the result, I will be sorry because such proofs are a waste of scarce, valuable resources. It would be more productive if the critics were to demonstrate my errors by responding to the points directly instead of proving that I do not "believe" in capital market efficiency.

The anticipated criticism is one reason I place these doubts in a footnote. Another reason is that they are not germane to the credibility gap. Even if adjustments are made perfectly, the fact that such adjustments are required provides grounds for justifiable criticism.

as depending upon circumstances. It is a contradiction to make an arbitrary choice depend upon criteria. If there are criteria, the choice is not arbitrary. The problem was further compounded, and the dilemma revealed, when the circumstances upon which the choice was supposed to depend were never specified.[3] I think the reason they were not specified is that they are unspecifiable. We defined the question in a way that precludes the possibility of an answer. Practice cannot be blamed for the chaotic situation, the credibility gap. Practice is the application of a theory; it cannot be better than the theory being applied. The fault lies in the theory, not in the practice.

3.1.2 Researchers. The definition of the problem put the researcher in an untenable position. Originally the problem was attacked by logical research—theorists argued about which convention was best. This method of attack was most prevalent in the late 1930s and early 1940s, especially in regard to inventory and depreciation conventions. Despite an inordinate amount of time and effort devoted to the problem, it was not resolved. Since the problem was defined as the selection of conventions and since conventions are arbitrary, the failure to resolve the issue should not come as a surprise. The researchers were trying to resolve an issue which was, by reason of the way it was defined, unresolvable.[4]

3. Chasteen ("Empirical Study," p. 508) attempted to discover the circumstances which correspond to different inventory methods applied in practice. He concluded, "Generally, no significant differences in economic circumstances were consistently found among firms which use different methods of inventory pricing." Cadenhead ("Differences") arrived at a similar conclusion.

I have previously expressed doubt about the existence of such circumstances: "The disputes are empirically unresolvable since there are no observations which could be used to confirm or disconfirm either convention. It is sometimes said that the 'appropriate' inventory or depreciation method 'depends upon the circumstances' but I am unable to discover any particular circumstances which imply any particular method. My inability to discover the circumstances does not prove that they do not exist but the fact that no one has yet made them explicit, even though the problem is a pressing one, casts some doubt upon their existence" (Sterling, "Explication," p. 160n).

4. One incidental but particularly noxious bit of mischief that resulted, in part, from this failure of logical (some call it "a priori") research was that this method of research became suspect. I am in full agreement with those who charge that the arguments about LIFO versus FIFO, for example, were sterile. However, I am in equal disagreement with those who use such failures as a basis for concluding that "a priori" is a dirty word, that logical research has no place in accounting.

The failure of logical research was due to the way the problem was defined, not to an inherent inability of logic to contribute to the solution of our problems. This misunderstanding has caused some internecine strife that is almost sure to be detrimental to our long-run research efforts. In an empirical science both logic and empirics are necessary and neither is sufficient; they are of equal importance. For further discussion

This failure of logical research, among other causes, resulted in an increased emphasis on empirical research. Many accountants looked for answers in behavioral research. Although the behavioral findings provided important insights, they did not provide an answer to the question of which convention ought to be selected. In addition to behavioral research, propitious developments in the theory of finance permitted accounting researchers to examine the actions of the stock market. Although this research also provided important insights, it also failed to answer the question of what we should report or which convention should be selected.

Thus, both logical and empirical research failed to resolve the issue.[5] Reaction to this failure has been to criticize the "pure research" or "academic research" and to demand more "applied research" or "impactive research." I predict that these research efforts, if undertaken, will also fail for the same reason: the issue is in principle unresolvable. Another reaction to the failure has been to become disenchanted with the efficacy of research in general. The blame is, once again, misplaced. Research cannot be expected to provide answers to questions that are defined in such a way as to preclude an answer. In effect, we have asked for research on unresearchable issues. The fault lies in the definition of the problem, not in the efficacy of research.[6]

---

about accounting, see Sterling "Introduction" and "Theory Construction." For a better, more general discussion see Einstein's foreword in Galileo's *Dialogue*.

5. Both logical and empirical researchers have tried to go through the horns of the dilemma via additional disclosure. They have suggested that we allow free choice of reporting and let the user adjust the figures to make them comparable. The logical researchers have argued that disclosure permits adjustment, and the empirical researchers have argued that adjustments are made in the market. As stated above, I think that reliance upon disclosure and adjustment fails to get to the root of the problem. Additional reasons for this position appear in Sterling, *Enterprise Income*, pp. 86–89.

6. It is probably more accurate to say that the fault lies in our unwillingness to accept and implement the results of research. My early training in economics led me to believe that accounting had been implicitly defined as a process of allocating joint costs. It has been an accepted maxim of economics since John Stuart Mill (*Political Economy*) that joint cost allocations are arbitrary. I drew a number of conclusions from that, the least radical of which was that it is better to standardize arbitrary allocations than to research them to make them depend on unspecified circumstances.

Thomas (SAR #3), in the highest and best tradition of logical research, has systematically considered all of the allocation proposals in detail. After an exceptionally careful analysis and after overcoming his reluctance to announce his results (for fear they would be too disruptive), he concluded that all allocations are arbitrary and suggested that we quit allocating. The outcome was that we awarded him our highest research prize (the Gold Medal) and then, in effect, rejected his conclusion. The reasons given for rejection are many, but without too much distortion they may be summarized

3.1.3 The Solution. That we have defined the allocation procedures as conventions suggests an intermediate solution. Conventions must be decreed, not selected by practitioners or researched by academics. The legislature decreed that we all drive on the right. If such things as LIFO and FIFO are conventions, and I am convinced that they are, we need to let our legislature decree that we all use LIFO (or FIFO). Let Marshall go up to Mount Stamford and fast for 40 days and 40 nights and return with a series of "Thou Shalts" on stone tablets. If Marshall has any difficulty deciding which convention to choose, I will loan him my binary solid-state decision maker—he can flip my coin.

After Marshall has selected the conventions, we can quit debating the long unresolved issues of uniformity versus flexibility and which conventions ought to be used in what circumstances. After the selected conventions have been implemented consistently, we can quit debating the ability of disclosure or the market to adjust for different conventions. It is only an intermediate solution, but it has the advantage of freeing us from engaging in debates that are in principle unresolvable. Perhaps we can then use our energy to begin research on a long-run solution. In my view, the long-run solution is to carefully distinguish laws from conventions and then to replace conventions with laws as such laws are discovered. I think that it is possible to discover testable accounting laws. I cannot be certain that such laws will be discovered. However, I can be certain that such laws will not be discovered (because they will not even be sought) as long as we define accounting as necessarily consisting of conventions instead of laws. We have a choice. We can redefine accounting in a way that encourages laws to be sought, or we can continue to define it as being based on conventions.

If we continue to define it as being based on conventions, we will continue to require legislation. Conventions (if not informally adopted by custom and usage) must be formally adopted by vote of an assembly. Whether that assembly is in the private sector (such as the APB or FASB) or the public sector (such as the SEC or CASB)

---

as: Thomas reached the *wrong type* of conclusion. We *must* allocate, and we need help on *how* to allocate, not told to quit allocating.

Thus, we came full circle. We defined the problem so that it is unresolvable. We did not recognize it to be unresolvable, so we asked for research on the issue. When the research told us that the problem was unresolvable and suggested an alternative approach, we, in effect, rejected the research and insisted on continuing to define the problem as an allocation and demanding research on how to allocate.

is not germane since both issue regulations or legislation. That is, the alternative to scientific laws is legislated conventions. The alternative to scientific accounting is legalistic accounting.[7] The choice is ours. I choose scientific accounting.

3.2 Forecasts Versus Measurements

> To confess ignorance in the face of the future is the tragic duty of all scientific philosophy.
> REICHENBACH, *An Analysis*, p. 404

Accountants have long held the belief that our reporting problems would be solved if we knew the future. We are preoccupied with the future because we have defined the *present* magnitude of assets and income as an allocation of a *past* magnitude which depends upon a *future* magnitude. Oft heard examples are depreciation and income. We say that the "true depreciation" cannot be known until the asset is sold because only then will we know the true life and true salvage value. We say the "true income" cannot be known until the firm has been liquidated[8] because only then will we know the final cash balance. These beliefs have been held for a long time. Paton and Littleton (*Corporate Accounting*), for example, articulated them clearly in 1940, and they were recently reconfirmed by the Trueblood Committee (*Financial Statements*, p. 22) when it presented the traditional definition of the problem and the standard three-step argument:

(1) If we had "perfect knowledge" of the future, then income and asset magnitudes would be "readily determinable."
(2) We do not have perfect knowledge of the future.
(3) Therefore, income and asset magnitudes are "of necessity . . . based on allocations and similar estimates."

This is conceptual error, not an inherent limitation of accounting. Although we must admit that the future is unknown, we are not required to define the present as being dependent upon that unknown future. If we phrase our questions about the present so that it is

---

7. For further discussion of the alternatives of science versus legislation see Sterling, "Accounting at the Crossroads," "Accounting in the 1980s," and "Board to Adjudicate Disputes."

8. We confound ourselves further when we assume that the firm will not be liquidated (going concern assumption) while defining income so that it can be determined only after the firm has been liquidated. (See Sterling, "Going Concern," p. 482ff.)

dependent upon the future, then we have precluded an answer.[9] Since the future is unknown and since the present depends on the future, by definition we have committed ourselves to an inability to know the present. And this is true at all instants in time: since each today depends upon the unknown tomorrow, all todays are unknown.

The definition also prohibits us from knowing the past until some "final" event occurs. We define the problem so that yesterday also depends upon tomorrow and therefore commit ourselves to an inability to know yesterday until a "final" event occurs. For example, the final event for the determination of true income is defined to be the liquidation of the firm. Hence, not only have we precluded the possibility of knowing the income of this year, we have also precluded the possibility of knowing the incomes of all past years.

It is instructive to consider the nature of the "final" event. Liquidation of the firm means the conversion of all of the noncash assets to cash. The reason given for the necessity of waiting for this conversion is that we say we cannot measure noncash assets (because their measure depends on the future) but we can measure cash (because, evidently, its measure does not depend on the future). This is a definitional distinction. A counterexample will make the definitional aspect apparent. Recall the outline of the problems taken from the Trueblood Committee presented supra. The ideal measure of assets is defined to be the discounted value of future cash flows, and the ideal measure of income is defined as the difference between the discounted values at two dates. But, so the argument goes, this ideal measure cannot be made because it depends on the unknown future. The question is, how does the application of this ideal measure permit the "true income" at liquidation? The cash obtained from liquidation is likely to be reinvested in other noncash assets. So why not apply the ideal measure to the cash? Why not discount the future cash flows from the intended investment and assign that measure to cash? I am not seriously suggesting this procedure.[10] Instead, I am trying to point

---

9. We accountants suffer from the same foolish optimism as the Nigerian maid.
> There was a young lady from Niger
> Who smiled as she rode on a tiger;
> They returned from the ride
> With the lady inside,
> And the smile on the face of the tiger.

The future is our tiger. We repeatedly begin optimistic journeys on the back of that tiger, and it always devours us. The solution is to choose a more tractable mode of transport.

10. If the example sounds too far-fetched, compare it to the argument that foreign currency cannot be truly valued because its conversion to domestic currency depends

out that the value of cash could be *defined* so that it also depended on an unknown future. That is, we could define the problem of measuring cash so that the problem is also in principle unresolvable. If we did, then we could all lament the fact that true income cannot be known even at liquidation.

The point is that there is no natural characteristic of cash that makes it independent of the future, and there is no natural characteristic of noncash assets that make them dependent on the future. It is possible, albeit strange, to conceptually make the value of cash depend on the future instead of the present. Likewise it is possible to conceptually make the value of noncash assets depend on the present instead of the future.[11]

The above discussion was concerned with discounted values, a method which has been rejected by accountants because it requires forecasting and we want to avoid forecasts. Grady (*Inventory*, p. 73) "emphasized that the income statement is historical and not prophetic." Perhaps Grady should have emphasized that we desire our statements to be historical, but that despite our desires, they are in fact prophetic because earlier (p. 41, quoting Bulletin 43) he defines net income to be a series of "allocations . . . based on assumptions as to future events."

Thus, we want to avoid forecasts, so we reject discounted values

---

upon unknown future foreign exchange rates. From this type of reasoning, we reach the odd conclusion that foreign currency is a nonmonetary asset when price level adjustments are to be made. Defining currency as nonmonetary strongly suggests that something is wrong. At the very least, it suggests that we should clean up our language so that money is monetary.

11. It is strange for us to think about making cash depend upon the future and making noncash assets depend upon the present because we have been *conditioned* to think in a certain way. Our generation was conditioned by the previous generation (and our generation is in the process of conditioning the coming generation) to *define* noncash asset magnitudes as *necessarily* dependent upon the future. Therefore, it looks strange when someone makes the suggestion, which would be obvious in other contexts, that a present magnitude depends upon the present, not the future.

Reichenbach (*Scientific Philosophy*, p. 141) states the point generally: "The power of reason must be sought not in rules that reason dictates to our imagination, but in the ability to free ourselves from any kind of rules to which we have been conditioned through experience and tradition. It would never have been possible to overcome the compulsion of established habits . . . before the scientist had shown ways of handling structures different from those for which an age-old tradition had trained our minds."

Thomas (SAR #9, pp. 113–14) makes the same point in an accounting context: "Naturally, such an income calculation looks strange if it is incorrectly perceived as a way of calculating allocated income. But the fault here lies in the perception. . . . [Unconventional] reports seem strange to . . . critics because these critics are conditioned to deem them strange."

because they require forecasts, but then we conceive the alternative to forecasting to be the allocation of past costs, allocations which require forecasts. Let us consider one kind of allocation—the familiar and long unresolved problem of depreciation.

Suppose we were to allocate my weight in the same way that we allocate the cost of an asset. We know that at acquisition (birth) Sterling weighed 10 pounds. I forecast that his salvage weight at time of disposal (death) will be 210 pounds and that his useful life will be 50 years. On the basis of a straight-line allocation, I would report his weight at age 25 as 110 pounds. If another accountant were to forecast that Sterling's useful life will be 100 years, he would report Sterling's weight at age 25 to be 60 pounds. If a third accountant were to forecast Sterling's future salvage weight to be 250 pounds, he would report at age 25 a weight of 130 pounds or 70 pounds, depending upon the life forecast.[12] There should be some way to resolve the disagreement—to determine which of these four figures is correct—or to put it another way there should be some way to audit the figures. Unfortunately, the disagreement is in principle unresolvable because we have *defined* the problem so that Sterling's present weight depends upon a forecast of his future life and future weight. Since we cannot resolve disagreements about the unknown future, we cannot resolve disagreement about the present.

Because we cannot resolve the disagreements, the four widely divergent figures are equally acceptable. Since they are equally acceptable, accountants may freely choose which one to report, and different accountants may report different figures for identical phenomena. Worse, an auditor would certify that all four different figures present fairly the weight of identical phenomena. The result is nourishment for the continuing growth of the credibility gap.

The problem does not end with different futures for identical phenomena. It plagues us throughout the life of an asset. It commits us to a continual correction of past magnitudes or else to an admission that all past magnitudes are wrong. Suppose that we have been reporting Sterling's weight (on the past balance sheets) and his weight change

---

12. If the divergence in forecasts of life seems too great, compare it to empirical tests that have been conducted on asset lives. When I did a questionnaire study some years ago, I was surprised to learn that the differences in book values caused by differences in life estimates were so great that they overshadowed differences caused by selecting different conventions (Sterling, "Uniformity Hypothesis"). Parker ("Testing Comparability") has done a field test using actual lives of the same asset. His findings show an even wider divergence in life forecasts. Parker's results are particularly germane to many current disputes as well as to this essay.

(on the past income statements) on the basis of a 50-year life forecast. Suppose that present events cause us to change the forecast of his useful life from 50 to 100 years. What do we do? Do we correct all of the past balance sheets and income statements, or do we admit that all of the past statements are wrong? If we decide to correct all of the past statements, what good does it do? That is, how much does it benefit a reader to discover today that all the past financial statements are wrong? Although we can change our past statements, the reader cannot change the past decisions he made on the basis of those statements. Also, if we adopt the policy of correcting past statements, we must correct all of the past statements again next year when next year's events cause us to again change our forecasts of the future life and salvage value.

Given these considerations, we will likely decide that correcting past statements is not a desirable policy. But what is the alternative? Changing the forecast of my useful life from 50 to 100 years means that there is a change of 50 pounds in my recorded weight, a write-down from 110 to 60 pounds. Do we report that 50-pound weight loss on that year's income statement? It seems odd, to say the least, to report a 50-pound loss in a year when my weight did not change—the only thing that changed was the forecast of my future life. Given these considerations, we will likely reject this alternative. But we have already rejected the other alternative. We have only two alternatives, and we have rejected both: a classic example of the horns of a dilemma.

Some people tried to go through the horns of the dilemma by dirtying the surplus. This approach resulted in abuses as well as logical conundrums. But, as noted above, the alternative was to "distort" the present statement. Debate on this issue was at its height around 1947. That it was not fully resolved is evidenced by the fact that we still permit some prior period adjustments and that we are still debating the definition of "current operating performance" under the new name of "extraordinary items." Another current controversial issue is "big bath accounting." It is a similar problem with a different name. When a firm takes a "big bath," the firm's management changes past, overly optimistic forecasts of its future to a present, more pessimistic forecast of its future for the purpose of changing past profits to losses so that they can change future losses to profits.

As long as we define present magnitudes as allocations based upon forecasted future magnitudes, such problems will remain unresolved. We have phrased the question in a way that precludes an answer. Nothing inherent in our subject matter impels us to forecast instead of measure. We have *defined* it that way. We could define it as a measurement. Changing the definition will not automatically solve our problems, but it will shift our attention from unresolvable forecasting problems to resolvable, albeit difficult, measurement problems.

3.3 Allocations Versus Measurements

> It sometimes happens that two different commodities have what may be termed a joint cost of production.
> . . .
>
> A principle is wanting to apportion the expenses of production between the two.
>
> MILL, *Political Economy*, pp. 569–70

The allocation problem is fundamentally different from the forecasting problem. As mentioned in section 3.2, accountants have long believed that our reporting problems would be solved if we knew the future. The exact opposite is the case. Even if we knew the future, we would still face an unresolvable allocation problem.

To demonstrate this point, let us make the heroic assumption that we know the future with certainty. Specifically, let us assume that we know that at acquisition (birth) Sterling's weight was 10 pounds, that at time of disposal (death) his weight will be 210 pounds and that his useful life will be exactly 50 years. These hard, objective facts are shown as x_1 and x_2 in Exhibit 3.3-1. But what do these hard, objective facts contribute to the answer to the question of what weight to report at age 25? The answer is that they contribute nothing at all. An infinite number of curves will connect points x_1 and x_2; thus, an infinite number of allocated weights could be reported at age 25. The problem is to select one of those curves—to select the weight to be reported.

The problem has no solution. It is easy to generate *plausible arguments* for or against *any* curve that connects the two points. But there is no way to *demonstrate* the superiority of any curve. That is what Thomas (SAR #3 and SAR #9) means when he says that all allocation methods are totally arbitrary.[13] The root of the problem

13. Thomas has been widely misunderstood on these points. He is not saying that we cannot generate arguments about various allocation methods. Of course we can generate arguments as is evidenced by the fact that we have been arguing about them for over 100 years. He is not saying that the problem is forecasting the future. Of course the future is uncertain, but the allocation problem remains under conditions of certainty. He is not saying that the allocation problem exists only in accounting or in regard to depreciation. It extends to physics as the weight example demonstrates, as well as pervading all of accounting by extending to inventory methods, manufacturing cost accumulation methods, amortizations, assignment of costs to various products

Exhibit 3.3-1

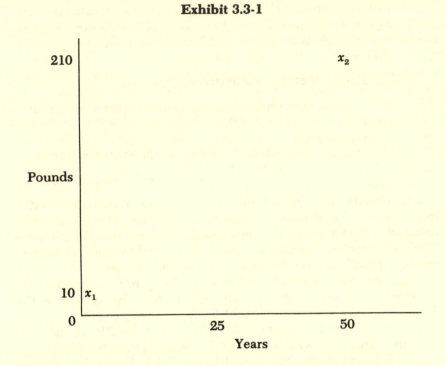

is that we decided to allocate instead of deciding to measure. When we made that decision, we created two vastly different kinds of things: (1) real weight and (2) allocated weight. The former refers to real-world phenomena, and as such it causes us relatively few problems. That is, the numerals of 10 and 210 pounds refer to "real weight" and, therefore, can be verified or falsified by relatively straightforward (scientific) procedures.[14] By contrast, "allocated weight" is a fiction. It does not refer to real-world phenomena; therefore, it is impossible

---

or processes or departments, and so forth. He is not saying that sterilized allocations solve the problem. He is saying that sterilized allocations avoid the mischief of nonsterilized allocations.

14. I say "relatively" because the verification of weight, especially past weight, is not quite as easy as it seems at first glance. Another reason for saying "relatively" is that the history of science reveals that there were many problems with weight that required the attention of some of the greatest intellects of the past to solve, for example, the concept of mass. Today, we consider determining my weight to be the trivial operation of reading a bathroom scale; but at one time the diversity of weight measures was a problem of vast proportion, and it took a good deal of effort to reduce it to a simple pointer reading.

to verify or falsify any element of the infinite set of numbers that could be reported. The problem is in principle unresolvable.

In this case the solution is obvious: redefine the problem. Get rid of the fictional "allocated weight," and retain only the "real weight." Then we can treat the various curves that connect x_1 and x_2 as scientific hypotheses. Each curve can be tested by measuring my weight at various ages to determine whether it accurately predicts weight. If we find regularities which stand up to repeated testing, we have discovered a law that can be used to predict weight. If we do not find such regularities, we will have to measure the weight each time we need to know it.

We probably will not find regularities, so we will be forced to go to the trouble and expense of measuring. This is unfortunate. However, if we must know the weight, measuring is infinitely superior to allocating. Resolution of the allocation problem is impossible. The measurement problem is merely difficult. The benefits of allocating are zero; if allocation costs anything, the costs will exceed the benefits. The benefits of measuring are greater than zero; it is at least possible for the benefits to exceed the costs.

4

Prerequisites for a Science

> Most of our beliefs, we have already indicated, rest on the tacit acceptance of current attitudes.
> COHEN and NAGEL, *Logic and Scientific Method,* p. 192

> The real problem is not the conversion of financial accounts but the conversion of financial attitudes.
> SIR RONALD LEACH, quoted in "Inflation Accounting,"
> Accounting," p. 115

One of the major impediments in accounting is the tacit acceptance of current attitudes. Since the propensity for tacit acceptance of current attitudes has been in existence for a long time, there is little difference between ancient attitudes and current attitudes. One of the more pervasive and pernicious attitudes is that accounting is inherently unscientific. An even more pernicious attitude is one of helplessness—that accounting is inherently unscientific and there is nothing we can do about it. When the two attitudes are coupled, it is obvious that no progress can be made toward a science. The real problem then, as Sir Ronald Leach said, is not the conversion of financial accounts but the conversion of financial attitudes.

4.1 Adopting a Scientific Language

> Non-human beings seldom produce the signs which influence their behavior, while human individuals in their language and post-language symbols characteristically do this to a surprising degree.
> MORRIS, *Signs, Language,* p.198

I have argued in the previous chapters that we err when we define our problems. Such definitions have a significant effect on our attitudes, on our approach to problems. Linguists long ago discovered that different languages had pronounced effects on different cultures. The structure of the language imposes a structure on the world. For example, some cultures view the world as a continuous process, while others view it as a series of discrete states. This difference is associated with the fact that one culture employs a process language and the other a state language. In comparing English to the Hopi language, Whorf (*Language, Thought,* p. 85) writes: "We [English speakers] have to think and boggle over the question for some time, or have it explained to us, before we can see the difference in the relationships . . . whereas the Hopi discriminates these relationships with effortless ease, for the forms of his speech have accustomed him to doing so." I believe that our language has the same effect on accountants. We define accounting as an art and use a nonscientific language to describe it. As a result, we have to think and boggle about the very possibility of scientific relationships. We often boggle when presented with suggestions that we seek laws instead of resigning ourselves to using conventions or that we seek measurements instead of resigning ourselves to allocations. It *sounds strange* to hear someone talk about laws and measurements in regard to accounting. "Law" and "measurement" are scientific terms, and we are not accustomed to hearing or using them.

The danger in continuing to use a nonscientific language is that we will not even understand the questions of science, much less seek answers to those questions. If we begin to use the language of science, we may begin to ask the right kinds of questions. Asking the right kinds of questions is a long way from obtaining answers, but it is a prerequisite.

Another advantage of adopting the language of science is that the scientific community has had considerable experience in making their communications more precise. The major contributor toward precise communications is the adoption of technical terms by each scientific subspecialty. We accountants seem to have a negative attitude toward technical terms. On the one hand, this attitude is well founded since we need to communicate with nonaccountants via our financial reports. On the other hand, the absence of technical terms inhibits communication among accountants. The language that we currently use in trying to communicate with each other is most imprecise. It would be wholly beneficial if we adopted technical terms to communicate with each other and then translated those terms into plain English when we communicate with nonaccountants.

A prime source of ambiguity in accounting communications is the use of a single term with many different meanings. For example, "cost of goods sold" refers to a numeral that is derived from a host of different calculations—LIFO, FIFO, average, moving average, retail, and lower of cost or market to name a few. Thus, the single term "cost of goods sold" has many different meanings. "Depreciation" also has many meanings. "Income" has an astronomical number of meanings, since it depends upon the various combinations of "cost of goods sold," "depreciation," and other revenue and expense terms.

An elementary principle of communication theory is that having many meanings for one term leads to confusion. The difficulty is compounded because each person thinks he knows what the other means when, in fact, each has a different meaning in mind. The problem is not recognized and, therefore, no attempt is made to solve it. The confusion is perpetuated. In response to a similar problem in physics, Bridgman proposed that each term be "operationally defined." Although it is now recognized that Bridgman went too far when he demanded a different term for each different operation, he made a significant contribution to the language of physics—one which we accountants would do well to emulate. At least, different terms for different operations would forcefully and continually remind us of the intolerably large number of operations in existence. At best, different terms for different operations would result in more precise communications with others as well as more precise self-communication, that is, in more precise thinking.

To illustrate the confusion more fully, consider the simple example of the different uses of "historic cost." For a long time I was totally confused by my colleagues who argued in the context of valuation disputes that "historic costs" were completely objective, while in other contexts these same colleagues lamented the subjectivity of "historic costs." I could not understand how my respected colleagues could hold such an obviously contradictory position. While pursuing the research for a tangentially related project, I accidentally discovered that it was not a contradiction but rather the case of two different meanings for the same term. On the one hand, the term "historic costs" was used as a synonym for past purchase prices; while on the other hand, it was used to refer to allocated past purchase prices, that is, those numerals that we report on financial statements. Thus, there was no contradiction because historic costs qua purchase prices are quite objective, while historic costs qua allocated purchase prices are quite subjective. Although in retrospect the distinction seems trivial, I was confused by the imprecision for a number of years. After I made the distinction, I discovered that a number of other people were also confused. Indeed, some of my colleagues who were making the arguments were not aware that they were changing meanings while making the arguments. Had we had different terms for the two different meanings, that confusion in both communication and thinking would not have occurred.

Another simple example of the same type of confusion arises from the common textbook assertion that "all assets are valued at cost." I originally thought that the assertion was a harmless fiction. I considered it to be a fiction because in my way of thinking there were two different types of exchanges—purchases and sales—which resulted in two different types of valuation procedures for assets—dependent and independent. On the one hand, in a purchase exchange we value the acquired asset dependently by imputing the independently valued sacrifice. That is what we mean by "cost." On the other hand, in a sale exchange we value the acquired asset independently without regard to the value previously assigned to the sacrifice. This is what we mean by "realization." For example, when we acquire inventory and sacrifice cash we classify the exchange as a "purchase," and we independently value the cash and then impute that value to the inventory. On the other hand, when we acquire cash and sacrifice inventory, we classify the exchange as a "sale," and we independently value the cash without regard to the value previously assigned to the inventory. For this reason, I thought that "all assets are valued at cost" was a harmless fiction because I assumed that no one would be misled by the common textbook assertion. However, during the debate over the valuation of marketable securities by the Accounting Principles Board, I was surprised to find that the fiction misled a number of people. One group participating in that debate used "all assets are valued at cost" as a premise. Given that premise they argued that marketable securities should be valued at cost in order to be consistent with *all* other assets. This argument turned out to be one of the more prevalent and convincing ones presented during that debate. In my view, no consistency issue was involved. Instead, I thought the argument should turn on which *category* of assets marketable securities should be assigned. That is, should they be assigned to the category that is valued independently (e.g., cash and receivables) or to the category that is valued dependently (e.g., inventory and plant)?

It seemed to me then, as it does now, that our language was hampering our thinking. Had we followed the precedent set by scientific languages, we could have discriminated such differences with effortless ease. As it was, our language caused us to think and boggle over the question for a very long time; and then, although it was explained to us, we could not see the differences. If we had a scientific language, we would have discriminated these differences in our thinking, and our communications would have been more precise.

In summary, I think it would be wholly beneficial if we were to discard our nonscientific language and adopt the language of science including technical terms. The language of science in general would allow us to ask the right kinds of questions. The technical terms would allow us to be more precise in our communications and in our thinking.

4.2 Defining Scientific Hypotheses

> If a statement or set of statements is not testable at least in principle, . . . then it cannot be significantly proposed or entertained as a scientific hypothesis or theory, for no conceivable empirical finding can then accord or conflict with it.
>
> HEMPEL, *Natural Science*, p. 30

The first requirement for a proposition to be considered a scientific hypothesis is that it be empirically testable—it must specify a measurable attribute. It is not required that the attribute be immediately measurable. On the contrary, measurement of the specified attribute may depend upon as yet undeveloped instruments. However, the attribute must be in principle measurable. It is not required that the attribute be easy to measure. On the contrary, the measurement difficulties may seem overwhelming. Difficulty of measurement is not a sufficient reason for refusing to classify a proposition as a scientific hypothesis; however, defining a proposition that is in principle unmeasurable is sufficient reason for excluding it from the domain of science.

The history of science contains many cases of hypotheses being proposed before the necessary measuring techniques were developed. In writing about the history of the first law of thermodynamics, for example, Epstein (*Thermodynamics*, p. 32) says: "An experimental test of this hypothesis required measurements extremely delicate and difficult for the primitive technique of those times. A long time passed, therefore, before they were even attempted. At length (in 1821), the Académie des Sciences announced a prize for the investigation of this problem, and this induced Dulong and Despretz to start work on it." There are three things to learn from such historical cases. First, such hypotheses (later laws) specify something that is in principle measurable, not something easily or immediately measurable. Second, the sequence flows from the conception to the development of the measurement, not from measurement to the conception. As many historians of science have noted, measurable attributes are conceived, and *then* the techniques for measuring them are sought; they are not thrust upon us by nature. Third, the Academy of Science encouraged the development of the measurements; it did not reject the conception because it was difficult to measure. More importantly, the academy did not define, say, heat transference as an allocation not subject to measurement.

The distinction between "in principle measurable" and "unmeasurable" can be used to illustrate the difference between conventions or allocations and laws. Consider the formula for the distance travelled by a free-falling body. Suppose two methods are proposed:

Accelerated method $\qquad d = \frac{1}{2} gt^2$

Straight-line method $\qquad d = \frac{1}{2} gt$

where d is distance travelled, g is a constant, and t is elapsed time. Suppose that the problem were defined as the selection of conventions and/or as an allocation. Under such a definition, we could measure the initial resting place, but we would have to forecast the final resting place and the total time of fall. After these forecasts we could solve for g. For example, for the straight-line method

$$g = (p_2 - p_1) 2 / T$$

where p_1 is the measured initial resting place, p_2 is the forecasted final resting place, and T is the forecasted total time of fall. We could then insert the conventional value of g in the straight-line equation, measure the elapsed time t, and calculate d. A similar procedure would be required for the accelerated method.

The immediate problem is that the two methods yield different values for d. The Bible tells us that

Diverse weights and measures are an abomination to the Lord.
(PROVERBS 20:10[1])

The long-run problem is to devise a method of eliminating diverse measures. To put it another way, the long-run goal is to devise a way of resolving issues in accounting. We can contrast two approaches:

---

1. Often when I debate accounting issues, my opponent invokes the criterion of "reporting economic reality" to support his argument. Then if I disagree with him, I am placed in the awkward position of explaining why I am opposed to reporting economic reality. In retaliation, I am here invoking the criterion of obeying God's will. If you disagree, not only must you explain why you are opposed to obeying God's will, you also run the risk of incurring God's wrath.

Accounting Approach: Define the problem as a conventional allocation of the total distance.

Scientific Approach: Define the problem as an attempt to establish a testable scientific law.

The accounting approach does not permit a solution because it defines d in such a way that it cannot be measured.[2] If our physicist ancestors had selected the accounting approach, we would still be arguing over accelerated versus straight-line free fall, just as we still are arguing over accelerated versus straight-line depreciation.

The scientific approach, by contrast, requires that d be measurable. A scientific law is an empirical generalization that must be subject to empirical test. The value of d may be very difficult to measure, but it must be defined in such a way that it is at least possible to measure it. We will consider the difficulties of measurement in the next section. For the present, I only want to emphasize that to resolve the problem, d must be defined as a quantity that can be measured.

4.3 Accepting the Challenge of Measurement

> Contrary to widely held belief, measurement is not a simple "look-and-see" procedure.
> HENRY MARGENAU, Personal Communication

When presented with the term "measurement," we accountants seem to boggle because we are accustomed to thinking about allocations. We often confuse the terms. We use "measuring depreciation" as a synonym for "allocating original cost." In our nonaccounting pursuits, we have no difficulty with the distinction. In regard to the weight example presented in Section 3.3, no accountant would find it difficult to distinguish between allocating my weight and measuring my weight. However, the general reaction to the simplistic weight example is to reply that measuring weight is too easy to require analysis, while it is impossible to measure income or assets.

Perhaps an historical perspective would be helpful. In Biblical times there was a problem of the existence of diverse weights, as is evidenced by the admonition in the proverb quoted in Section 4.2. If our ancestors had resigned themselves to the impossibility of measuring weight,

---

2. As noted in Section 3.1, an intermediate solution to the problem of diverse measurements is to have an authority, such as the FASB, select one of the conventions and standardize it.

we would probably still be arguing about how to allocate it. Luckily, they viewed the problem as a challenge; so we now consider measuring weights to be so easy that it is not comparable to the problems of measuring income or assets.

The history of science is replete with examples of quantities that at one time were exceptionally difficult to measure. The scientific attitude, however, is that these difficulties "present a constant *challenge* to the skill and imagination of the experimentalist and observer" (Kuhn, *Scientific Revolutions*, p. 26, italics supplied). Had our ancestors resigned themselves to their limitations instead of viewing them as a challenge, the special telescopes necessary to confirm Copernicus's prediction of the annual parallax would not have been built (because they would not have been attempted); Atwood would not have built his machine to test Newton's second law; Foucault would not have designed his apparatus to test the speed of light; and so forth.

More specifically, let us return to the development of the law of free-falling bodies and sketch its history. Aristotle observed bodies falling in air and made some generalizations about them. Disputes arose over those generalizations. Measurement methods were exceptionally primitive by today's standards and so, from the critics' viewpoint, the measurement of *d* seemed completely impossible.

Galileo took the difficulty of measuring as a challenge. The problems he faced were formidable. He had neither the logical aids (e.g., the calculus) nor the measuring devices (e.g., a finely calibrated clock) that seem, in retrospect, to have been indispensable. Instead of resigning himself to these inherent limitations, he proceeded. It was a slow, arduous task, not the romantic (and apocryphal) story of the sudden revelation at the Leaning Tower of Pisa. Since he could not think of a way to measure *d* directly but did have some notions about how to measure acceleration, he logically reversed the law to make it imply constant acceleration. Next, he had to overcome the obstacle that bodies fell too rapidly to be timed by his crude water clock. He accomplished this task by slowing down the effects of gravity by rolling balls down an inclined plane instead of dropping them. From these results, he again reverted to logic and reasoned what would happen if the angle of incline were increased until the plane became vertical; that is, what would happen if the balls were dropped. Since the air pump had not yet been invented, he could not eliminate air resistance; but he could decrease its effects. From the measurements made with the decreased effects of air resistance, he reverted to logic once again and reasoned what would be the case in a vacuum.

It was Newton, after the invention of the air pump, who performed the famous experiment of simultaneously dropping a feather and a gold coin in a vacuum. This experiment was taken as a crucial test of the law of free-falling bodies. Thus, Galileo "failed" in the sense that he was never able to devise measurement methods that would allow him to perform the crucial test. His measurement methods were so crude that he described distances in such terms as "four fingers" and his clock could not even distinguish seconds. In comparison to the present era of micrometers and nanoseconds, Galileo's "failure" is apparent. In a much more important sense, his success was immense.

It seems clear that the measurement problems faced by Galileo were much more formidable than those faced by accounting. The difference is not in the difficulty of the respective measurement problems but in the respective attitudes. Instead of resigning himself to the inability to measure, Galileo accepted the challenge. We accountants seem to have the attitude that the measurement problems are too difficult to solve, and therefore we must allocate. This has become self-fulfilling prophecy.

4.4 Learning from Scientific Simplifications

> Simple statements, if knowledge is our object, are to be prized more highly than less simple ones *because they tell us more; because their empirical content is greater; and because they are better testable.*
>
> POPPER, *Logic*, p. 142

Practitioners must attest to (or disclaim) the financial statements of very large and complex firms. They must tackle the problems as they exist; they cannot simplify. Since they face complex problems, it is rather natural for them to become impatient with research on simplified cases. Many academics also become impatient with research on simplified cases. They also think that we must study the real world in all of its complexity. They fear that studying simplified cases is more apt to mislead than to inform. There is a real danger in studying simplified cases, but my reading of the history of science leads me to believe that our only hope is to simplify. I think our choice is either to simplify and run the risk of being misled or resign ourselves to being mystified by the complexities.

The point can be illustrated by returning to the law of free-falling bodies. Aristotle was searching for a way to make generalizations about bodies falling in the normal atmosphere, in the real world. He failed. The problem was just too complex for it to be comprehended even by someone with the acumen of Aristotle. The problem is still too complex—no one has yet been able to formulate a law that will describe the fall of diverse kinds of bodies, such as feathers and cannonballs, in diverse kinds of air resistance, such as updrafts and crosswinds. A major part of Galileo's contribution was his recognition that the problem had to be simplified before it could be solved. He thought that the Aristotelians had hopelessly entangled themselves in the complexities of the real world (Rogers, *Physics*, p. 9ff). For this reason, he postulated the unrealistic, oversimplified case of zero air resistance, a perfect vacuum.

With the present attitude in accounting, Galileo's simplification would be met with incredulity and scorn. Since nature abhors a vacuum, we accounting academics would think that a law concerned with bodies falling in a vacuum was ridiculous on the face of it. Since vacuums were thought to be impossible (and since the air pump had not been invented), Galileo's law would be rejected out of hand because it is concerned with conjectures about the impossible. Accounting practitioners would scorn it not because of its impossibility but because of its uselessness. Even if the law holds in a vacuum, they would argue, it is at best a useless curiosity because air resistance exists and we must contend with it. We cannot retreat to our ivory tower and postulate ideal states; we must operate in the complex real world, they would say.

We have come to recognize that Galileo's law was an immense contribution. It was exceptionally fruitful in science. To cite just one example, it led to Stokes's law for fluid friction which, in turn, led to the measurement of the electric charge of a single electron which, in turn, led to a host of other scientific discoveries. It also led to many practical applications in such fields as ballistics and, later, airplane and rocket design. In addition, it is practical in and of itself. We have discovered that it approximates the fall of dense bodies in the real world. That is, we know the effects of air resistance on dense bodies are negligible or, as we accountants would say, "immaterial." For less dense bodies, such as feathers, we know that the law is not applicable because the effects of air resistance are not negligible—they are "material." Scientists would say that deciding when the effects are or are not negligible requires the use of one's "intelligence." The accounting synonym for "intelligence" is "professional judgment." But many accountants would reject the law precisely because it requires professional judgment. Evidently they believe that a law must be perfectly applicable to all realistic, complex cases in order to avoid utilizing professional judgments on the materiality of the deviation.

Thus, the current attitude of accountants prohibits research on and application of such simplifications. Given the requirements that practice must deal with complex problems, and given the almost universal tendency of practical men to disdain theory, the practitioners' attitude toward simplifications comes as no surprise. I have more difficulty understanding my fellow academics' attitude.

Consider behavioral research in accounting. Since we do not know how to research the complex cases, behavioral researchers must simplify. I agree with Goodman (*Fact, Fiction*, p. xii) that such simplification "far from being an intellectual sin, is a prerequisite for investigation." Some of my fellow academics consider it to be an intellectual sin. They seem to reject the findings solely because the researchers simplified the problem. I think that behavioral research can provide important insights to accountants, and I regret the decrease in the quantity of such research. I never expected behavioral research to provide answers to *all* of our problems, but I did expect it to provide insights; and I, for one, received insights from the findings. We are now deprived of all but a dribble of those findings, and consequently we are deprived of the attendant insights. I think that one reason for the lack of behavioral research is the belief that researching simplified cases is inappropriate.

I think that there is a particular segment of accounting academics who misunderstand the purpose of simplification. As a consequence of the misunderstanding, they require so much realism-complexity that no scientific law could meet the test. If the ideal gas (Boyle's) law were required to be so realistic-complex, it would be rejected, precisely because it refers to a simple ideal gas and not to a real complex gas. If Galileo's law were subjected to the realistic-complex criterion that has been required of behavioral research, the law would have been demolished. Consider the criteria of "external validity" and "subject surrogation." Obviously, Galileo's law is not externally valid. It is valid only under the very simple conditions of a perfect vacuum. When we remove it from those simple conditions and put it in the complex real world, we must use our intelligence to decide when the approximation is close enough for the effects of air resistance to be considered negligible and when it is not. Many accounting critics do not seem to recognize that they must use their intelligence for such purposes. Instead, they set the standard that a law must be so general that it can be applied to realistic-complex cases. No law can meet that standard, and therefore no law can withstand the criticism that follows from that kind of standard. The "subject surrogation" criticism is similar. A ball rolling down an inclined plane is only a surrogate for a falling body. Since Galileo could not examine the principal directly, his choice was to admit defeat or examine a surrogate. It seems that some present-day accounting critics would prefer us to admit defeat rather than to examine the surrogate. Galileo chose to examine the surrogate and then to perform an ingenious "thought experiment"—he imagined what would happen if the plane were rotated until it became vertical. Some present-day critics forbid thought experiments. They require research on the principal because they mistakenly believe that it is improper to employ logic to reason from surrogate to principal. Some denigrate logical or a priori research in general and embrace an exclusive empirical methodology. This attitude would have committed us to ignorance in physics because "the mere empirical study of all falling bodies would never have given us the law of gravitation" (Boulding, *Economics*, p. 100). I fear this attitude will commit us to ignorance in accounting.

I do not mean to imply that external validity and subject surrogation are not legitimate questions. On the contrary, they raise some thorny issues which researchers must worry about. My concern is that we may fail to discover an important law by applying the realistic-complex standard. We may inhibit future research by applying that standard to discredit past research on simplifications. For example, some have mounted broadside attacks on behavioral research because it was not performed in the "real marketplace" by observing "real economic agents" who risk "real money" making "real decisions" with "real accounting data" with "real competing sources of information" and so forth, ad infinitum. It is an error to require research on "real" things. The plain fact is that laboratory research is *not* real world research: it is a simplification. More important, the history of science reveals that many great contributions have come from research on simplifications. To cite just one more example, at one time the attitude toward genetics was similar to the attitude toward accounting—that it was beyond the realm of the scientific method. The breakthrough in genetics came from a simplification: "Only by these hypothetical and methodological simplifications is it likely that one could have achieved Mendel's results" (Morris and Irwin, *Modern World*, p. 946).

The scientific attitude is to try to learn from research on simplifications. Some accountants' attitudes have been to reject the findings because the research was performed on a simplification. It is a long way from research on simplifications to the solutions of complex problems, but adopting the attitude of learning from simplifications provides some hope for eventually solving those problems, while the alternative almost guarantees that they will remain unresolved.

4.5 Employing Scientific Criticism

On a sunny day in September, 1972, a stern-faced, plainly dressed man could be seen standing still on a street corner in the busy Chicago Loop. As pedestrians hurried by on their way to lunch or business, he would solemnly lift his right arm, and pointing to the person nearest him, intone loudly the single word "GUILTY!"

Then, without any change of expression, he would resume his stiff stance for a few moments before repeating the gesture. Then, again, the inexorable raising of his arm, the pointing, and the solemn pronouncing of the one word "GUILTY!"

MENNINGER, *Sin*, p. 1

A prepublication reader of this essay remarked that the Chicagoan described by Menninger was right—each person he pointed at was undoubtedly guilty of something. I agree. Moreover, given the impossible religious standards employed by this Chicagoan, I would venture that he would have been right had he pointed his finger at Moses or Jesus or Buddha, had they chanced by. It is quite easy to adopt impossible standards—standards that no one could meet. One can then point the finger at everyone because everyone is guilty of failing to meet those standards. In such a case we ought to question the appropriateness of the standards instead of continuing to point the finger.

Criticism is an integral part of the scientific process. The standards are high but not impossible. A scientist's work must be corroborated by others before it is accepted. Conversely, the work will be rejected if it cannot be corroborated or if errors are discovered. In order to correct errors we must discover them by carefully scrutinizing each other's work. Thus, criticism is essential. Although it appears to be destructive, it is in fact constructive in the sense that it helps to separate truth from error.

Academic accountants often criticize the work of their colleagues. Most of this criticism is in the scientific mode—the critics read sympathetically and look for insights while at the same time being vigilant for the inevitable errors. Unfortunately, there are other accounting critics who, in my view, err by employing impossible standards. They level a kind of criticism that no research can withstand. If we discover that no research, not even the great scientific discoveries of the past, can satisfy the standards, it is clear that the standards are impossible. If no research can withstand a particular kind of criticism, we can easily see that the criticism inhibits progress instead of facilitating it. Such criticism does not help to separate truth from error, because the inevitable conclusion is that *all* research fails to meet the standards. In that sense, such criticism is nothing more than pointing the finger.

To provide evidence that the problem exists, I will present quotations which illustrate the impossible standards.[3] My purpose is not to point out errors in these particulars but rather to try to get us out of our present impasse by attempting to demonstrate that the kind of criticism exemplified leads to nihilism rather than helping to separate truth from error.

4.5.1 Imposing a Different Paradigm. A reseacher performs his research within the framework of a particular paradigm. Others may employ different paradigms. The problem is that the different paradigms are disjoint. They pose different questions, examine different empirical domains, use different languages, or confusingly use the same language with different meanings for the terms, and, in general, employ different world views. As Kuhn (*Scientific Revolutions*, p. 149) puts it, "the proponents of competing paradigms practice their trades in different worlds."

Since the paradigms are disjoint or incommensurable, the standards of one paradigm cannot be used to criticize the research performed under a competing paradigm. The reason is that *all* research will fail to meet the tests of a competing paradigm. Obviously, it is not productive to impose standards when one knows a priori that the object under review cannot possibly meet those standards. Since "their standards are not . . . the same" (Kuhn, *Scientific Revolutions*, p. 147), it is clear that paradigm *A* cannot possibly meet the standards of paradigm *B*, and vice versa.

There is no universally accepted paradigm in accounting at the present time. Instead, there are a number of competing paradigms, one of which is "capital market efficiency," henceforth "CME." Some

3. The purpose of the following discussion is to try to demonstrate that impossible standards are currently being employed by some accounting critics. Some prepublication readers were of the view that such impossible standards did not exist. Evidence in the form of specific citations is needed to convince those readers of the existence of such impossible standards. Other prepublication readers, however, felt that my comments might evoke an angry reply yielding more heat than light. My purpose is to expose an error, not to expose those who have committed the error. I have no desire to engage in a fruitless quarrel. For this reason, I decided to omit the specific citations and reference the quotations as coming from anonymous "Critics." For those readers who need the evidence, who want to examine the original sources, I will supply the citations upon request.

of the proponents of the CME paradigm have failed to recognize that paradigms are disjoint. Evidence of this failure is provided by their rejection of competing paradigms solely because those paradigms failed to meet CME tests.

The Critics (p. 162) have such a strong commitment to CME that they evidently consider it to be prima facie proof of error to show that someone has "effectively rejected capital market efficiency." By making the existence of error depend upon whether one has accepted or rejected CME, rather than upon the subject matter being questioned, they present CME as an article of faith not open to investigation.[4]

Scientific findings depend upon scientific tests, upon corroboration or falsification by other researchers. They do not depend upon whether or not the researcher accepts a given paradigm or upon evidence that the researcher questioned certain elements of a paradigm. They do not depend upon whether or not the reported findings conform to or conflict with a competing paradigm.

Consider again the criticism of behavioral research in accounting. Much of this criticism appears to stem from the fact that it *is* behavioral research rather than CME research. The Critics (pp. 164–65) object to the fact that the behavioral "methods reviewed . . . often have been proposed as methods that can yield insights on the external accounting issues . . . namely, the desirability and effects of alternative accounting techniques." Thus, in regard to external accounting issues, the Critics not only reject the possibility of receiving answers, they also reject the possibility of receiving insights from behavioral studies.

This rejection of behavioral research findings follows directly from the CME paradigm. That paradigm specifies the empirical domain of accounting to be the aggregate capital market. That is, the Critics seem to be convinced that the answers to external accounting issues

---

4. The similarity to heresy trials is striking. Galileo, for example, was charged with heresy because he proposed a heliocentric paradigm. The case was tried not on the basis of the evidence about the movement of the planets but rather on the basis of whether or not Galileo had rejected the geocentric paradigm, a paradigm the inquisitors held to be so true that it could not be investigated.

For example, none of the inquisitors ever bothered to look through the telescope to test Galileo's claim that there were moons revolving around Jupiter. This test was directly pertinent to the geocentric belief that the Earth was the only center in the universe about which bodies revolved. However, the test was not pertinent to the trial. The only question pertinent to the trial was whether Galileo had violated the precept that had prohibited him from advocating the heliocentric paradigm. If he had, it was considered to be prima facie proof that he was guilty of heresy. See Geymonat, *Galileo*, for a general discussion. See Langford (*Galileo, Science*, p. 41) for a case in which an Aristotelean critic refused to look through the telescope; that is, refused to look at pertinent, direct evidence.

could be found *only* on the price tapes. Since the behavioral researchers studied individuals instead of the price tapes, it follows that their research could not provide insights into external accounting issues. The reasoning is simple:

> Axiom: Insights into external accounting issues can be found only by studying the aggregate capital market.
>
> Fact: Behavioral researchers do not study the aggregate capital market.
>
> Conclusion: Behavioral research results cannot provide insights into external accounting issues.

The conclusion is valid, but it is the axiom that is being questioned. The question is whether or not at the present time we have sufficient grounds for believing that external accounting issues can be resolved by examining the price tapes instead of examining other empirical domains such as individual behavior.

The Critics' commitment to the CME paradigm is so strong that they apparently fail to recognize that the axiom is in question. Instead of defending the axiom, they repeat it and present examples of others who are guilty of *not* studying the price tapes. Dyckman ("Investment Decision") is their prime example. The Critics (p. 165) selected the following quotation and presented it as prima facie evidence of his guilt.

> The results, it is true, apply to a particular group of students and for this reason cannot be statistically extrapolated to the investing population. Nevertheless, if the subjects used in this study are thus mystified, and if these subjects possess an advantage over the typical investor, *then it seems that investors in general would also exhibit similar confusion relative to financial statements.* . . .
>
> Thus to the extent that the investment decisions of individuals are influenced by the mere accounting procedures used to prepare financial reports rather than the underlying economic facts, *the accounting system fails to facilitate the rational operation of the economic system.* (DYCKMAN, "Investment Decision," p. 294, italics supplied by Critics)

I do not understand Dyckman's error. I am confused by the criticism in regard to several things, three of which will be considered.

First, I have no difficulty in replicating Dyckman's thought experiment. If I were a subject in his lab and if I had been confused and mystified by simplified financial statements in the experiment, I would also be confused and mystified when I left the lab, walked back to my office, read some complex financial statements and called my broker. I am also willing to extend the implication to other individual investors, particularly in light of a rather large amount of additional supporting evidence. If the confusion holds for a sample of individual investors, then it is also likely to hold for the population of individual investors.

Instead of replying to the point that Dyckman and others raised, the Critics (p. 106) dismissed them as irrelevant because: "Since the lab/field studies concentrated on individual behavior rather than competitive market phenomena, their relevance to the [external accounting] issues at hand seems nonexistent." Thus, the basis for rejecting Dyckman's findings is that he examined individual behavior rather than competitive market phenomena.

Second, I do not understand why the Critics reject Dyckman's statement about confusion of investors. A group of confused individuals can play in a fair game. The fact that they are confused does not imply anything at all about the fairness or lack of fairness of the game. Confusion does not imply anything at all about whether or not the prices are a random walk. I once supervised a pilot test of 100 subjects with equal beginning wealth and the ability to set prices by inputting bids and asks at a remote computer terminal. The different firms were in fact the same firm with different asset and income figures derived from applying different accounting conventions. All but one of the subjects had access only to past and current condensed financial statements. The other subject had access to the complete past and current financial statements. In addition, he was explicitly told that the statements referred to the same firm. The 99 subjects were confused (thought the firms were different) because of the condensation; the one subject was not confused. Despite this "inside" information, the one subject did not, on the average, earn a significantly different rate of return. I interpreted this result as a confirmation that the participants were playing a fair game—as consistent with the strong form of efficient market hypothesis in the fair game sense. I also inferred that it was a fair game because all the subjects set the price but the 99 confused subjects had 99 times as much influence on the price. The one subject was a price-taker because he had only 1 percent of the aggregate demand. The confusion of the 99 subjects had nothing to do with the fairness of the game.

This is slim evidence, but it at least raises a question. It seems possible, on both logical and empirical grounds, for Dyckman's findings and implications to be correct without conflicting with the finding that the market is a fair game.

Third, I do not understand why the Critics think that Dyckman's second quoted paragraph is in error. The portion they italicized simply says that "the accounting system fails to facilitate"; it does not say anything about fair pricing or random walks. One of the major points of the CME paradigm is the effects of competing sources of information. It could be that the economic system operates rationally on the basis of information from competing sources and that accounting merely fails to facilitate this rational operation. Thus, it is quite possible for Dyckman's conclusion to be consistent with the CME paradigm.

To this outsider (neither a behavioral nor a CME researcher), it appears possible to interpret Dyckman's work as at least not in conflict with, perhaps even supportive of, the CME paradigm. This lack of conflict did not seem to be of interest to the Critics; instead they seemed to be intent on rejecting Dyckman's work for the main, perhaps the sole, reason that he did not examine the price tapes.

In short, Dyckman and others have examined individual investors as they made decisions; CME researchers have examined the aggregate market as it sets prices. It seems to me to be quite appropriate for Dyckman to look at individuals in a lab and for others to look at the aggregate market on a price tape. Dyckman never claimed that his findings implied anything about what one would find on the price tapes, about the random walk or the fairness of the game. Indeed, Dyckman was a model of scientific caution in that he carefully set limits on his findings and warned the readers of the dangers of extrapolation. He repeatedly cautioned the readers that his experiment was conducted with a sample of individuals and specifically addressed the problem of a simplified, controlled experiment. The Critics evidently decided a priori that such studies could not yield insights or implications for external accounting issues. Thus, Dyckman's only error was that he examined individuals instead of price tapes. Instead of responding to Dyckman's drawn implications directly, the Critics dismissed them because he did not examine the empirical domain that they had defined for accounting. Instead of looking for insights into Dyckman's work and wondering about the connection to their work, the Critics charged him with violating the CME paradigm.

The same type of criticism was leveled at a number of other studies. The main basis of the criticism was the same: the Critics showed that all non-CME studies did not access the CME empirical domain. Since the Critics consider the CME empirical domain to be the only place where answers can be found, this is sufficient reason to reject the studies. The Critics (p. 113) provide the following summary: "The available studies that did not use the prices of firms' ownership shares in examining the effects of alternative techniques do not, in our judgment, provide much reliable evidence on the effects of alternative accounting techniques."

This conclusion should not come as a surprise. It follows directly from the imposition of the CME paradigm. If a chemist rejected the research of a psychologist because the psychologist did not examine the atomic composition of chemical elements, we would easily recognize it to be inappropriate. In my view, when the complexities and verbiage are stripped away so that we can see the structure of the criticism, the same type of inappropriate criticism is occurring in accounting—the Critics are imposing a CME paradigm and then rejecting all non-CME studies *because* they are non-CME studies.

This type of criticism errs in two ways: First, it fails to recognize the nature of competing paradigms. Second, and more important, it has the effect of restricting the different kinds of accounting research. Such restriction is likely to inhibit scientific progress.

Breakthroughs in scientific research often come from unexpected places; therefore, it ill behooves accountants to rule out any area of research. Instead, if we are to follow the scientific norm, we will do our individual research on the basis of our individual beliefs about the likely source of answers, while at least tolerating, preferably encouraging, others to do likewise. This strategy increases our chances of achieving breakthroughs. It is at least possible (and may be highly probable) that breakthroughs will come from sources other than CME research. Therefore, it is entirely inappropriate for the CME proponents to attempt to restrict research in accounting to CME questions and CME data.

My view was epitomized by Alexander Pope (*Essay on Man*, p. 23) in reference to a similar, ancient debate:

> Know then thyself, presume not God to scan;
> The proper study of mankind is Man.

If the behaviorists want to study man, then the proper study of man is man. If others want to study the price tapes, it is equally proper for them to study those. It is *improper* for either side to try to intimidate the other from doing research by imposing its own paradigm.

4.5.2 Hyperbolic Criticism. The Critics engage in a kind of criticism that no scientific research could withstand. For lack of a better name, I call this "hyperbolic criticism." In order to illustrate the problem, I will apply their criticism to some well-known scientific efforts.

The Critics (pp. 103 and 167) look with a jaundiced eye upon behavioral findings because "they are not based upon a strong theoretical foundation that provides the necessary linkage between" them and other important questions. This criticism would apply to Galileo since his work also lacked a strong theoretical foundation. It was Newton who later provided the theoretical foundation. Newton's contribution was to synthesize the previous findings, including Galileo's. It is difficult to imagine Newton's being able to make his contribution in the absence of Galileo's previous work. Thus, if we were to apply the above criticism to Galileo, we would stop his research because it lacks Newton's strong theoretical foundations. Newton's providing the strong theoretical foundations would, in turn, be impossible because of the absence of Galileo's findings. The literal application of such a criticism would have stopped progress in physics. I fear that it might also stop progress in accounting.

The Critics (p. 167) confound themselves with such statements as: "One cannot argue that, say, X is a simplification of Y if one does not know what Y is and, therefore, how Y must be altered in order to get X from Y." The statement is either trivial or absurd. If the Critics mean that one cannot "argue" in the sense of "prove," then it is trivially true that one cannot prove that X is a simplification of Y without knowing about Y. If the Critics mean that one cannot "argue" in the scientific sense of jumping the "logical gap," then it is an absurdity which is belied by the whole history of science.[5] Prior to Galileo, the arguments about falling bodies were couched in terms of a very complex theory of impetus. In this complex world there was a prime mover and "things that were in motion had to be accompanied by a mover all the time" so that a "projectile was carried forward by an actual impetus which it had acquired." When a body was falling, it was explained as "accidental gravity . . . due to effects of impetus being continually added to the constant fall due to ordinary weight" (Butterfield, *Origins*, p. 19 and p. 23). Galileo could not prove that gravity was a simplification of impetus. However, he could (and did) "argue" that gravity was a simplification.[6] Had he been prohibited from making such arguments, the law of free-

---

5. Jumping the "logical gap" is Polanyi's (*Personal Knowledge*, p. 123) term. Hempel (*Natural Science*, p. 15), following an ancient precedent, uses "happy guesses" as a synonym. Popper calls them "conjectures" as indicated by the title of his book: *Conjectures and Refutations*. Others use still other terms in trying to explain the phenomenon of achieving the right answer from what is at the time inadequate evidence.

6. Galileo was particularly fond of *reductio ad absurdum* arguments in which he tried to show that if one did *not* accept his simplification, then one would get absurd consequences. That is, he employed a priori research. One particularly interesting proof about the absurdity of speed being directly proportional to distance travelled has subsequently been shown to be unsound. That is, he also erred.

falling bodies might not have been developed.

The Critics (p. 167) continue: "If a researcher has no conceptual framework or perspective (however tentative) bearing on what he is investigating and if he has no ideas (however tentative) on the linkage(s) between his specific project and his ultimate object(s) of analysis, then he ought not to be doing his 'research' until those issues have been attacked." Previous scientists did not follow this advice to refrain from doing research until they had attacked the "prior" issues. Galileo's work would not stand up to this criticism. A better counterexample is provided by the exploratory research of Semmelweis. (See, e.g. Slaughter, *Immortal Magyar* for a history of Semmelweis's research.) The problem that Semmelweis faced was that of a large number of women dying of "childbed fever." Semmelweis had *no* conceptual framework or perspective. He had *no* ideas about linkages; instead he made wild guesses. The absence of a conceptual framework or ideas about linkages can be ascertained from his own statements, as well as from the great variety of hypotheses that he tested. For example, he entertained the notion that the ringing of the bell by a priest's attendant terrified the patients and increased the mortality rate. He tested the notion by silencing the bell. Another notion was that the mortality rate was connected to the position of delivery. He tested that by changing the position of delivery.

In retrospect such notions seem too obviously wrong to have even been entertained, much less tested. However, we have the benefit of looking at such tests with the clear hindsight provided by the germ theory of medicine. Semmelweis faced his problem before germ theory was developed; and, as a consequence, he did not have the conceptual framework and linkages which the Critics would require that he attack before doing his research. In fact, Semmelweis discovered the cause of and cure for childbed fever without attacking those prior issues. This result provides some evidence that the criticism is in error, not the research. The danger of such erroneous criticism is that we may inhibit a Semmelweis-type researcher in accounting.

It was the accidental death of a colleague that allowed Semmelweis to guess the linkage between "cadaveric matter" on the hands of the physicians and the mortality rate. Once the cause was discovered, the cure was, at the time, unbelievably simple: require the physicians to wash their hands with a chlorinated lime solution after an autopsy. The prior view was that the cause of the disease was some complex entity known as an "atmospheric-cosmic-telluric epidemic." The Critics (p. 167) would say that: "One cannot argue that [cadaveric matter] is a simplification of [atmospheric-cosmic-telluric] if one does not know what [atmospheric-cosmic-telluric] is and, therefore, how [atmospheric-cosmic-telluric] must be altered in order to get [cadaveric matter] from [atmospheric-cosmic-telluric]." Semmelweis was not cognizant that he could not argue that cadaveric matter was a simplification, and his ignorance allowed him to guess the linkage.

Once he had the idea, Semmelweis began to notice additional infections and additional means of transmission. He isolated infected patients in an attempt to prevent airborne transmissions of the disease. By observed increases in infections when they were not isolated and reductions in infections when they were isolated, Semmelweis was, in effect, conducting a controlled experiment. Semmelweis's controlled experiments would not stand up to the criticism of the Critics (p. 167): "[Semmelweis] can hardly claim that he is dealing with a simplified model because he has no perspective on what it is that he is simplifying. Indeed, if he is in this position it is not clear that he can even design an experiment." Semmelweis was not aware that it was unclear that he could even design an experiment, and his ignorance allowed him to design several.

Since mortality is a complex function of a large number of variables and since Semmelweis was able to guess and control for only cadaveric or ichorous matter, he was able to reduce the post partum mortality rate but not eliminate it—he had a large "error term." Subsequently, it was discovered that there are competing bacteria in our biomedical systems and that an equilibrium is required for health. For example, staphylococcus was once classified as benevolent, but when broad spectrum antibiotics were introduced which killed off its competitors and destroyed the equilibrium, staphylococcus became malevolent. Since it is a competitive system, the Critics (p. 106) would reject Semmelweis's work for the following reasons: "[Mortality] is a function of the interactions among rivalrous [bacteria]. The attainment of [biomedical] equilibrium in such a [system] is induced by the workings of the system as a whole, or *aggregate* [bacterial] behavior, and not by the actions of particular [bacteria]. Since [Semmelweis's] studies concentrated on [the] individual behavior [of cadaveric matter] rather than on competitive [bacterial] phenomena, their relevance to [mortality] seems nonexistent." The relevance of Semmelweis's studies hardly seems nonexistent. In fact, he discovered a factor relevant to mortality.

In another place the Critics (p. 168) permit "partial equilibrium analyses"—they relax their requirement that the "system as a whole" be studied—but, "the usefulness of such exercises depends upon the extent to which one can attain a linkage between the behavior of the part(s) under investigation and the behavior of the system as a whole." Semmelweis had not attained the linkage between requiring the physicians to wash their hands with chlorinated lime and the bacterial system as a whole. Yet he discovered a useful procedure.

The analogy would fit better if we were to require that Semmelweis specify the linkage between washing hands with a chlorinated lime solution and the atmospheric-cosmic-telluric epidemic instead of the linkage to the bacterial system. The Critics (p. 113) refer to their previous summary as evidence of their tolerance of partial equilibrium analyses. The summary specifies "the connection between whatever framework is used in a nonprice study and capital market agents' behavior." Thus, the Critics predetermined that the specific findings must be linked to the capital market agents' behavior. In terms of the analogy, this statement means that we would assess the usefulness of washing hands with chlorinated lime on the basis of attaining linkages to a predetermined atmospheric-cosmic-telluric epidemic. Such a linkage was never discovered. In fact, predetermining what hand washing must be connected to would have inhibited the development of the germ theory (which hand washing could be linked to).

A scientific attitude is one of agnosticism. I think accountants would do well to adopt the same attitude. Despite the "considerable appeal" of predetermining that everything must be linked to capital market efficiency, we should allow for the possibility of somebody developing something in accounting that would serve as our germ theory.

According to the Critics, Semmelweis's methodological error was that the relevance of the factor he controlled for was not identified by a theory. Therefore, the Critics (p. 105) would reject his controlled experiment for the following reasons: "If these kinds of factors [cadaveric or ichorous matter] really do have systematic effects on the observed results then they should have been identified as important factors by some body of theory. In the absence of such a theory, we do not know what variables must be controlled in the invented decision [about mortality] settings." Semmelweis did not know that his factors had to be identified by the as yet undeveloped germ theory. Yet he identified factors in the absence of that theory.

The Critics (p. 106) are also suspicious of controlled experiments in general. They complain that the behavioral "studies fail to simulate competition among sources of information. Indeed, the information available to subjects is usually deliberately limited to accounting information." When it was pointed out that the very purpose of a controlled experiment is to "deliberately limit" the subjects to accounting information so that the effects of accounting information could be isolated and thereby determined, the Critics presented a proof that it could not be done.

Within the complicated context of the way we currently talk about CME research, such proofs appear plausible. However, they are manifestly absurd in other contexts. The following proof is a slightly altered quotation taken from the Critics (p. 169). The original proof is in the footnote.[7] The alteration consists of substituting Galileo's subject matter for accounting subject matter. The only essential substitutions are "gravity" for "accounting information" and "competing effects of air resistance" for "competing sources of information."

> Galileo's argument is based upon a critical implicit assumption: that the effects of gravity can, in general, be assessed (or at least defined) independently of the competing effects of air resistance. That assumption is, in general, not satisfied. Consider, for example, the following scenario. Suppose that we want to assess the effects of gravity, G, on the distance of a body's fall, d, where the distance is a function, $f(\cdot,\cdot)$ of G and the competing effects of air resistance R. That is, $d = f(G,R)$. With no loss of generality, we assume that $f(\cdot,\cdot)$ is differentiable with respect to G. Galileo would have us attack this problem by altering G and observing the associated alterations in d, holding R fixed. That is, he would have us observe $\partial d/\partial G = \partial f(G,R)/\partial G$. But, in general, $\partial f(G,R)/\partial G$ is a function of both G and R; i.e., $\partial f(G,R)/\partial G = g(G,R)$. Consequently, one cannot, in general, assess (or even define) the effects of gravity, G, independently of the competing effects of air resistance, R.

We have just witnessed a proof that Galileo could not even define, let alone assess, the effects of gravity independently of the competing

7. [The] argument is based upon a critical implicit assumption: that the effects of accounting information can, in general, be assessed (or at least defined) independently of competing sources of information. That assumption is, in general, not satisfied. Consider, for example, the following scenario. Suppose that we want to assess the effects of accounting information, A, on some agent's decision, d, where his decision is a fuction, $f(\cdot,\cdot)$, of A and competing sources of information, C. That is, $d = f(A,C)$. With no loss of generality, we assume that $f(\cdot,\cdot)$ is differentiable with respect to A. SH would have us attack this problem by altering A and observing the associated alterations in d, holding C fixed. That is, they would have us observe $\partial d/\partial A = \partial f(A,C)/\partial A$. But, in general, $\partial f(A,C)/\partial A$ is a function of both A and C; i.e., $\partial f(A,C)/\partial A = g(A,C)$. Consequently, one cannot, in general, assess (or even define) the effects of accounting information, A, independently of competing sources of information, C.

CRITICS, p. 169

effects of air resistance. From this we must, I suppose, conclude that Galileo perpetrated a gigantic hoax and that no subsequent physicist has exposed that hoax. Alternatively, we might conclude that there is an error in the proof.

The Critics erred in two ways. First, they overlooked the oft-observed phenomenon in the history of science sometimes called "investigator ingenuity." No one can deny the validity of their mathematics:

$$\partial d/\partial A = \partial f(A,C)/\partial A = g(A,C)$$

Despite the validity of that equation, Galileo did in fact both define and assess the effects of gravity independently of the effects of air resistance. Moreover, he performed this experiment before the invention of the air pump, so he could not have experimented with the air resistance at zero. To call this "investigator ingenuity" merely names the process; it does not explain it. Although we cannot explain it, it has often happened in science and therefore the Critics erred when they "proved" that it could not be done.

Second, there was technical oversight. In the quotation, the Critics wrote that C was *fixed* at some *unspecified* magnitude. In the previous quotation they correctly noted that the behaviorists "deliberately limited" their subjects to accounting information and "fail[ed] to simulate competition among sources of information." Thus, the Critics erred in the formulation of the problem. They should have said that C was *fixed at zero*. Had they correctly formulated the problem, their proof would have read:

The partial of f is a function of A and C.

$$\partial d/\partial A = \partial f(A,C)/\partial A = g(A,C)$$

However, if C is *fixed* (at zero in the typical lab study), g becomes a function of A only.[8]

$$\partial f(A,0)/\partial A = g(A,0) = h(A)$$

Then one can assess the effects of accounting information, A, independently of the competing sources of information, C.

$$f(A,0) = \int g(A,0)\,dA = \int h(A)\,dA$$

Thus, the correct formulation of the problem would have permitted the Critics to correctly conclude that one can both assess and define

---

8. It is important to note that it is only the fixing of C which makes $\partial f/\partial A$ independent of C in the experiment, not the fixing at zero. Presumably a lab study could be designed with C fixed at some level other than zero. In that case, $\partial f/\partial A$ would still be independent of C in the experiment, but $\partial f/\partial A$ would be a different function of A than if C had been fixed at zero.

the effects of accounting information independently of the effects of competing sources of information.

The fact that the Critics erred is not important. We all err. However, the effects of such criticism are of utmost importance. Had Galileo been faced with a proof that he could not develop the law of free-falling bodies, he might not have attempted it. Had Semmelweis been required to connect hand washing with chlorinated lime to an undiscovered germ theory, he might not have pursued his research. Accounting may be affected similarly: no results because of no attempts; no attempts because of the impossibility of withstanding the hyperbolic criticism.

There are other points in the example as well as other examples. I will not pursue them further here. My purpose was only to demonstrate that it is possible to reject great scientific breakthroughs by employing hyperbolic criticism. Obviously, if great breakthroughs cannot withstand that kind of criticism, there is no chance for current accounting research to withstand it. Therefore, the error is in employing hyperbolic criticism, not in the research being criticized.

Scientific criticism is a sympathetic search for insights and errors. If we search for insights in the works of others, there is some (perhaps small) chance that we will find them and benefit from them. If we search for errors, we may help others avoid pitfalls in their research. On the contrary, if we apply a hyperbolic criticism that no scientific research could withstand, we are more apt to inhibit research than to contribute to progress.

Part Two

Toward an Embryonic Science

5

Introduction to Part Two

A journey of a thousand miles must begin with a single step.

LAO TZŬ

This essay is an attempt to transform accounting from an elusive art to an embryonic science. The transformation must begin, as Lao Tzŭ says, with a single step. Part Two is an attempt to take a single step by proposing the transformation of a single accounting convention to a single scientific hypothesis. As with most first steps, it is rather feeble. But we cannot travel until we begin and this path looks promising.

5.1 An Apology

Theories are nets: only he who casts will catch.

NOVALIS

I apologize for the highly specialized and rather feeble hypothesis that I am going to propose. I am reluctant to propose the hypothesis because I fear that readers will focus on it and ignore the more important point of moving toward a science of accounting. I also fear that a negative reaction to my feeble hypothesis may result in an associated negative reaction to the move toward a science. I accept these risks because the alternative is also unattractive: if I do not present something specific and concrete, the message of Part One may be too general to be understood.

My specific proposal should not be taken as an indication that other proposals are not worthy of consideration or that other research efforts are not worthy of undertaking or are unscientific. On the contrary, although I do not believe that all roads lead to insights (there are some blind alleys), I do believe that many roads lead to insights. Obviously, I think my proposal is best, else I would not propose it. But there is the likelihood that I am wrong. As I have said before, I encourage each researcher to select his research questions and research methods because he *believes* that he can obtain an answer and that the answer is likely to be important (Sterling, "Introduction," p. 2). I do not want to restrict or constrain research in any way. Instead, I want to echo the remark attributed to P. W. Bridgman that, "The scientist has no other method than doing his damnedest."

5.2 A Challenge

> Reflect on the moral history of mankind which can be summarized: They *hang* prophets. Or ignore them, which hurts worse.
>
> MENNINGER, *Sin,* p. 1

I wish to distinguish "negative reaction" from "refutation" or "falsification." As I said above, I fear a negative reaction to the hypothesis because of the possibility that such a reaction may hinder the move toward a science. I do not, however, fear falsification of the hypothesis or a refutation of my arguments. On the contrary, I have deliberately tried to make them vulnerable to such scientific pursuits.

All scientific propositions, both empirical and logical, contain an implicit challenge: that is what "corroboration," "public test," "observer agreement," "falsifiable," and such terms mean. Since the implicit challenge is understood, scientists seldom offer explicit challenges; but since accounting is not yet a science, I explicitly challenge readers to prove me wrong. I offer the challenge for several reasons: First, such proofs provide the self-correcting aspect of science. Second, since I do not hesitate to criticize you, you should not hesitate to criticize me. Third, I relish a good argument. Finally, it hurts less to be hanged by errors than to be ignored.

5.3 A Preview

> It [pragmatism] will serve to show that almost every proposition of ontological metaphysics is either meaningless gibberish, —one word being defined by other words, and they by still others, without any real conception ever being reached,—or else is downright absurd; so that all such rubbish being swept away, what will remain of philosophy will be a series of

> problems capable of investigation by the observational
> methods of the true sciences,—the truth about which
> can be reached without those interminable misunder-
> standings and disputes.
>
> PEIRCE, "Pragmatism," p. 171

In my attempt to move toward a science, I will employ two related criteria: (1) empirical testability and (2) relevance. Although each of these criteria will be developed in the following chapters, the reader can get a preview of what I am driving toward by considering the two criteria in the context of the quotation by Peirce.

One of the major problems of ontological metaphysics was the existence of the "interminable misunderstandings and disputes." Those disputes could not be adjudicated because the problem was defined in such a fashion that it was not "capable of investigation by the observational methods of the true sciences." Consider the familiar question, "How many angels can dance on the head of a pin?" Since "angels" are not observable, are not measurable, this question led to those interminable misunderstandings and disputes. Had "angels" referred to empirical phenomena, we could have adjudicated the dispute by the simple process of counting.

Although adjudication of disputes is important, usefulness or relevance is even more important. Obviously, meaningless gibberish is not useful or relevant. Many propositions of ontological metaphysics were of this nature—even if we could have adjudicated the disputes, the answer would have been useless. The reason that it would have been useless is related to the reason that disputes could not be adjudicated—the questions did not refer to empirical phenomena. Instead, they were words which were defined by other words which, in turn, were defined by other words, *none* of which ever referred to empirical phenomena. Consider again the example of angels dancing on the head of a pin. The word "angel" was defined by other words which in turn were defined by other words. Since these words never referred to empirical phenomena, the answer to the question would have been useless. Thus, even if we were able to adjudicate the dispute (by, say, an ex cathedra edict), we would still have to question the usefulness of the answer.

Such considerations reveal the interrelated character of the criteria. If a concept does not refer to empirical phenomena, does not refer to a measurable attribute, or does not lead to another concept which refers to empirical phenomena, the concept will be found to be useless. It will have no practical value.

The converse is not necessarily true. Although it is possible, perhaps even likely, for concepts that refer to empirical phenomena to be useful or relevant, it is not guaranteed. As Brodbeck (*Readings,* p. 7) says: "Counting is sterile only when it is not guided by the attempt to arrive at a scientific law relating what is being counted to something else." This idea is indicated in ordinary language when we talk about a measurement's being useful *for* something or relevant *to* something. In science, the object of the preposition "for" or "to" is a law or a theory. Unless a measurement is related to something else by a law or a theory, it is an isolated fact—isolated in the sense that it is not useful for anything or relevant to anything.

In short, concepts that refer to empirical phenomena will allow us to adjudicate disputes. Reference to empirical phenomena is also a necessary, but not a sufficient, condition for usefulness or relevance. The additional condition for usefulness or relevance is that the concept be specified by a law or theory.

These related criteria will be applied to accounting and discussed in greater detail in the following chapters. First, I will propose that we define a concept that is empirically testable in the specific context of depreciation. The immediate benefit to be derived from this proposal is that it will allow us to adjudicate our disputes—it will allow us to avoid those interminable misunderstandings and disputes. Second, I will turn to the criterion of relevance. I will present some examples of the relevance of the proposed definition and raise some questions about the relevance of competing definitions.

6

Depreciation:
From a Convention to a Law

> Depreciation is probably the most discussed and most disputatious topic in all accounting.
>
> DAVIDSON, "Depreciation, Income Taxes," p. 191

Depreciation has long been an unresolved issue. Since so much effort over such a long period of time has been devoted to attempts to resolve the depreciation issue and since all these attempts have failed, it must be one of the most difficult issues in accounting. I have been told that no one or no approach can possibly resolve the issue. For this reason, I selected depreciation for consideration. It presents quite a challenge.

6.1 Defining a Convention

> If depreciation is a matter of fall in an asset's value over time, then the primary step in measuring it must be to establish the successive value figures. When these figures have been found, the depreciation costs emerge as a by-product. . . . If the accountant declines to treat his asset figures as a part of a valuation process, then he divorces his values and costs from the reality that he is striving to measure, and reduces them to empty abstractions.
>
> BAXTER, *Depreciation,* p. 27

Baxter states the issue clearly and succinctly: we have a choice between measuring and reporting reality or reporting empty abstractions. I agree with Baxter's formulation of the problem. However, I disagree with his statement that the accountant is striving to measure reality. I think that the root of the problem is that the accountant does *not* strive to measure reality. Instead, accounting in general and

67

depreciation in particular have been defined as a process of allocation, not a process of measurement.

The American Institute of Certified Public Accountants ("Accounting Terminology," p. 24) provided the following official definition:

> The term [depreciation] is broadly descriptive of a type of process, not of an individual process, and only the characteristics which are common to all processes of the type can properly be reflected in a definition thereof. These common characteristics are that a cost or other basic value is allocated to accounting periods by a rational and systematic method and that this method does not attempt to determine the sum allocated to an accounting period solely by relation to occurrences within that period which affect either the length of life or the monetary value of property. Definitions are unacceptable which imply that *depreciation for the year* is a measurement, expressed in monetary terms, of the physical deterioration within the year, or of the decline in monetary value within the year, or, indeed, of anything that actually occurs within the year.

This is a most curious definition. It almost seems that we deliberately set out to define an impossible task. The definition specifically states that depreciation is *not* a *measure* of *anything* that actually occurs within the year. Since it is *not* a *measure* of *anything*, no conceivable empirical finding can accord or conflict with it. Instead, the definition has the effect of divorcing the depreciation figure from reality and reducing it to an empty abstraction. It also implicitly defines a present magnitude as depending on a future magnitude. That is, the present amount of depreciation or book value is defined as a function of the future life and future salvage value. Thus, we are committed to definitional ignorance of the present magnitude.

This *official* definition explicitly repudiates the attempt to measure reality. A prerequisite for the resolution of the depreciation problem is to change the definition—to change the objective from one of reporting conventional allocations (which reduce to empty abstractions) to the objective of measuring some kind of reality. Once we have done that, we can adjudicate disputes about the amount of depreciation by the relatively simple process of performing empirical tests.

The difficulty extends beyond the definition of historic-cost depreciation. The notion that accounting is a process of allocation is, evidently, an ingrained habit of thought. Reformers also define depreciation as an allocation. One such definition has been provided by replacement-cost proponents. Although replacement-cost theorists have made great contributions to accounting thought, they fell into the same trap when they defined depreciation. The only difference between historic-cost depreciation and replacement-cost depreciation is that the former allocates a past purchase price, while the latter allocates a current purchase price. Assume, for example, that an automobile was purchased for $5,000 last year and that the same automobile new would cost $6,000 this year. A forecasted life of three years and a zero salvage value would result in historic-cost depreciation of $1,667 (= $5,000/3) and replacement-cost depreciation of $2,000 (= $6,000/3). Replacement-cost depreciation also is not a measure of anything, and therefore no conceivable empirical finding can either accord or conflict with it.[1] It too is an allocation—an arbitrary allocation. It also requires a forecast of the life and salvage value. As such, it defines a present magnitude to depend upon a future magnitude and commits us to definitional ignorance.

Another definition is that depreciation is the change in the discounted value of the asset. This definition requires us to forecast the future net cash flows to be derived from the asset and then to calculate a discounted value. Of the three, this definition is the most explicit in defining a present magnitude to depend upon a future magnitude. Thus, it also commits us to definitional ignorance. The procedure also results in a figure that has no empirical referent. Of course, cash flows are observable, but the discounted value of those flows is not observable. To demonstrate, consider how one would resolve a dispute about which of two different discounted values is correct. It could not be resolved by empirical test, even if one waited to observe the cash flows, since the difference may be due to different discount rates instead of different forecasts. Hence, no conceivable empirical test can accord or conflict with it. It is also an allocation—an arbitrary allocation. That is, although the initial figure is determined by forecasting and discounting, the subsequent figures are calculated as a function of time.

In summary, all three definitions—historic cost, replacement cost, and discounted value—present us with all those problems discussed in Part One. They define conventions instead of laws; they define allocations instead of measurements; they define empty abstractions instead of representations of reality; they define meaningless gibberish

---

1. An exception is provided by Johnson and Bell ("Current Replacement Costs"). They have redefined "replacement cost" as the immediate purchase price of an identical used asset. Depreciation is the difference between such purchase prices at two dates. It is a measurement subject to empirical test; therefore, the above discussion does not apply. For more discussion of this definition, see Section 9.2.

we cannot find an identical used asset!

instead of problems capable of investigation by scientific methods. As such, they present problems that are in principle unresolvable.

6.2 Defining a Measurable Attribute

> The principal functions in accounting are usually recognized as being those of recording, reporting and interpreting. But underlying all of these is the necessity for measuring. The problem facing the accountant is that of measuring something. He therefore needs concepts which are capable of measurement. In charging "depreciation," accountants purport to measure something. What is it?
>
> GOLDBERG, "Concepts," p. 484

If we are to resolve the depreciation problem, if we are to move toward a science, we must answer Goldberg's question. We must cease defining depreciation as a conventional allocation—the antithesis of measurement—and ask what it is that we purport to measure. We must specify a measurable attribute.

In tracing the origins of modern science, Whitehead (*Science,* p. 114) has written: "It grounded itself upon what every plain man could see with his own eyes, or with a microscope of moderate power. It measured the obvious things to be measured, and it generalised the obvious things to be generalised." Since accounting is, at best, an embryonic science, perhaps we ought to take a lesson from this history and consider the measurement of one of the obvious quantities, namely, market prices. Of course, there are other measurable attributes; so we must consider the question of which measurable attribute(s) ought to be measured and reported. I will consider that question in the following chapters. For the moment, I will focus only on the question of the measurability of market prices.

I define an "exit value" as the amount of money that could be received from an immediate sale of an asset. It is a price, an immediate sale price. Market exchanges are observable phenomena. One can observe that asset a was exchanged for d dollars at time t in market m. Then, one can infer that identical assets could be exchanged for identical amounts under identical conditions. One can also infer that similar assets could be exchanged for similar amounts under identical conditions or that identical assets could be sold for similar amounts under similar conditions. Thus, the measurement sought is the amount of money that would be received if the asset were sold.

Many accountants object to the described measurement operation. They claim that exit values can be measured only by selling the asset—that it is impossible or illegitimate to make the proposed inferences.[2] Others claim that exit values can be verified only by selling the asset. I freely admit that exit values present difficult measurement and verification problems, but requiring assets to be sold before their exit values can be measured or verified is a conceptual error, not a measurement difficulty. Compare, for example, the measurement of potential energy in science. Scientists may measure the energy expended by one object and then infer that an identical object has an identical amount of potential energy. They do not require that the potential energy actually be expended in order to measure it. If it were required, we could not say that we have x Btu's of potential heat energy in our coal reserves. The analogous accounting requirement would be to burn the coal before we could measure the potential heat energy, and then it would no longer be potential. Thus we would only be able to measure the "realized" heat energy. We would, by definition, commit ourselves to ignorance of the amount of all potential energy. Scientists have managed to avoid the definitional ignorance, meet the measurement challenge, and in fact measure and verify potential energy. I am confident that we accountants could also overcome the measurement and verification difficulties if we first cleared away the conceptual errors.

Scientists often make inferences such as the one I suggest for measuring exit values. For example, Rogers (*Physics,* p. 8), a physicist, writes: "We trust the 'Uniformity of Nature': we trust that what happens on Friday and Saturday will also happen on Sunday; or that a simple rule which holds for several different spiral springs will hold for other springs." Thus, scientists do not require that all spiral springs be subjected to direct measurement. Instead they infer that the force from some springs will be the same as that for other springs. Compare the following two statements:

(1) When a few spiral springs were compressed under c conditions, they exerted f force; therefore, if other similar uncompressed springs were compressed under c conditions, they would exert f force.

(2) When a few automobiles were sold at time t in market m, they fetched d dollars; therefore, if other similar automobiles were sold at time t in market m, they would fetch d dollars.

---

2. Dopuch and Sunder ("Financial Accounting: A Review") state: "The 'true' replacement costs of assets are not observed until those assets are actually replaced (nor are 'true' exit prices observed unless the assets are sold)."

The statements are structurally identical. The same type of inference is required for both statements. I hardly see how we accountants can continue to deny the possibility or legitimacy of the inference in (2) without also denying (1) which would, by extension, require us to deny the possibility or legitimacy of all of physics, indeed, all of science. To put it another way, scientists have in fact made such inferences for a very long time. There is a plethora of evidence that it is possible to make such inferences. What evidence do we accountants have that it is impossible or illegitimate?

Opponents will continue to object on grounds that there is something unique about prices and markets. We accountants think that we face problems which are fundamentally different from those faced by scientists. In truth, scientists face identical kinds of problems. Rogers (*Physics*, p. 8n) footnotes the previous quotation as follows: "The obvious condition, 'all other circumstances remain the same,' is often difficult to maintain, and we blame many an exception to the Uniformity of Nature on some failure in that respect. Magnetic experiments in towns that have streetcars may give different results on Sundays, when fewer cars are running." All scientific endeavors have need of—and also problems with—the condition that "all other circumstances remain the same." Differences in the number of streetcars in operation caused problems for physicists in measuring magnetic force. Different circumstances will also cause accountants problems in measuring exit values. At the present time we do not know what circumstances will cause problems and what circumstances need to be held constant. But the problems we face are those that are common to all measurement endeavors. They are not problems that are fundamentally different nor fundamentally more difficult.

Consider allocating as the alternative to measuring. Had physicists allocated instead of measured, they would have never discovered that the number of streetcars in operation is a circumstance pertinent to measuring magnetic force. The discovery was made because they were measuring and because they encountered a problem. The "problem" of a variation in the measurement of magnetic force eventually turned into a "discovery" about the causes of such variations. Such problems have often been converted to discoveries. At one time, gas pressure variations were a problem. Later the pressure variations were found to be related to variations in temperature and volume, that is, the discovery of Boyle's law. Had Boyle allocated instead of measured, this exceptionally useful discovery would never have been made. If we accountants continue to allocate, we preclude the possibility of making such discoveries. We will never know which circumstances need to be kept constant.[3]

Opponents have also objected that exit values will be different in different markets and at different times. On one level, this objection is met in the previous discussion. For some purposes, markets and times are circumstances that need to be held constant while the measurement is being made. On another level, this objection reveals a basic misunderstanding of the purpose of measurement. The very purpose of measurement is to discover the extant magnitude at a given place or given time and/or the variation in magnitude from place to place or time to time. Some accountants think that such variations invalidate the measurement.

Exit values will vary from market to market just as barometer readings vary from altitude to altitude. The fact that the exit value is d_1 dollars in market m_1 and d_2 in m_2 does not invalidate exit value measures any more than the fact that the barometer reads b_1 at altitude a_1 and b_2 at a_2 invalidates barometric measures. Indeed the purpose of the measurement may be to discover that variation. Exit values will also vary over time. The fact that an automobile will fetch d_1 dollars at time t_1 while it will fetch d_2 at t_2 does not invalidate exit value measures any more than the fact that it was 80° yesterday and it is 85° today invalidates temperature measures. Indeed, the purpose of the measurement may be to discover that variation. Thus, stating the time and the market provides a means for discovering the amount of exit value variation associated with the variation in time and place.

The opponents will continue to object on grounds of (a misunderstanding of) "the fallacy of composition." I cannot answer. I do not know what would happen if everybody tried to sell all of their automobiles at once. (Would the exit value go to zero, or would some

3. As this essay was going to press, I had the privilege of an extended conversation with Robert Woodrow Wilson, the 1978 Nobel Laureate in Physics. The measurements that he made with his radio telescope did not yield the expected quantities. Making those measurements was extraordinarily difficult because of the need to separate the radio waves emitted by the earth and other extraneous objects that he did not want to measure. Obtaining results different from expected also caused an extraordinarily arduous search for the source of the variations. Among other things, he entertained the notion that pigeons roosting in his telescope caused the variations. He sought a number of other possible explanations for the variations. His final discovery of the difference between the expected and the actual was support for the "Big Bang Theory" and resulted in his being awarded the Nobel Prize. The point is that the "problem" turned into a "discovery." Despite the difficulty of measurement he continued to search for the source of the variations. Had he allocated instead of measured, he would not have faced the problem nor made the discovery.

of you join me in putting in a ridiculously low bid?) I also do not know what would happen if we tried to burn all of our potential heat energy at once. (Would there be enough oxygen to support the fire necessary to convert all of the energy, or would we care since the heat would kill us all anyway?) The condition that all other circumstances remain the same includes the circumstance that only a few automobiles are offered for sale or that only a small amount of potential energy is converted. If those circumstances are different, the measurements will be different. This situation is not peculiar to measuring exit values. It pervades all of science.

Other accountants object on the basis of intentions. They say that it is "obviously irrelevant" to measure an attribute if one does not intend to do what is "implied"[4] by the measurement. In regard to the specific case, exit values are said to be "obviously irrelevant" because the firm does not intend to sell its depreciable assets.

This objection is based on a misconception of the purpose of measurement. The purpose is to provide information about the state of the world. That information may be necessary to a decision, a decision that may alter our intentions. For example, it is quite legitimate (and, more importantly, quite useful) to measure the potential heat energy in a coal reserve even if the present intention is not to convert that coal to heat. The present intention may be instead to convert it to nylon. If we allow present intentions to prohibit the measurement—to prohibit discovering that the reserve contains x Btu's—we also prohibit a rational decision. We must compare the benefits of converting coal to nylon to the benefits of converting it to heat. We must know that coal will produce y amount of nylon *and* x Btu's of heat. Without both of those bits of information we cannot compare, we cannot rationally decide. Thus, to prohibit a measurement on the basis of some previously formulated intentions is to prohibit a rational decision.

More generally, all measurements are comparisons. They provide

---

4. This is a particularly unfortunate locution because *nothing* is "implied" by measurement. I am sure that the opponents who employ this locution understand that, but I sometimes think that they get tangled up in their own words. They react negatively to measuring exit values solely because we do not intend to sell the assets. If they really think that there is a connection between measurements and intentions, I hope that we keep it secret from the Atomic Energy Commission. On several occasions the AEC has gone to some pains to try to measure the number of people that would be killed if an atomic bomb were dropped in various metropolitan areas. I would hope that we would not employ the opponents' "logic" and tell the Atomic Energy Commission that since they have made the measurements, they must intend to drop the bombs.

information about what is possible regardless of intentions. Even such simple things as length measurements are comparisons. Knowing the length of my desk *means* that I can compare it to the length of various other objects. I can say, "If I were to move the desk, then it would fit (or not fit) in room x." I can make that statement in regard to King Tut's Tomb, the Oval Office, or my study. The statement may merely be a mental exercise, or it may be a prelude to a rational decision. The point is that the purpose of measurement is to permit such comparisons. The purpose of measurement is to inform by comparing the object at hand to a general unit, which in turn permits a comparison to all other objects which have also been compared to that unit, that is, a comparison to all other objects that have been measured. Such comparisons permit us to make rational decisions.

There is an entire class of scientific terms (called "dispositional terms") ending in "ble" which are quite useful (relevant) but which do not imply anything about intentions. Flexible, soluble, and flammable are examples of such terms. It may be useful for me to know that a sugar cube is soluble in coffee even though I do not intend to dissolve it because I do not use sugar in my coffee. In choosing building materials, it is often useful to know that a wooden two-by-four is flexible under a certain amount of stress even though we do not intend to flex it. I suggest that we add the term "salable" to this class of scientific concepts and try to measure the number of dollars that assets would fetch if they were sold without regard to intentions.

There are other objections to the measurability of exit values. It would be tedious to reply to all of them. I hope, however, that I have said enough for you to tentatively entertain the possibility of measuring exit values so that I can proceed to define depreciation as a measurable attribute.

> Sterling's Definition: Depreciation is the decline in the exit value of productive assets.

6.3 The Proffered Hypothesis

> [This] according to Galileo [is] not a pure convention but a hypothesis which is either "true" or "false."
> EINSTEIN, "Foreword," p. xv

Now that we have defined a measurable attribute, we can formulate hypotheses. The hypotheses must be stated in such a manner that they can be empirically tested. They must be especially vulnerable to falsification. I offer the following highly specialized hypothesis.

> Sterling's Hypothesis: The exit value of an automobile at this year's end is approximately 60 percent of its exit value at last year's end.

The hypothesis is equivalent to the double-declining balance method with a five-year life, assuming the starting value to be the purchase price. However, that is accidental. I did not select the hypothesis because I think that it results in "better matching." I selected it because I think it fits the facts—because I think that it will predict the year-end exit value. I will present the case for the relevance of exit values in the following chapters. For the moment let us focus only on the structure of the hypothesis.

Sterling's hypothesis has all of the characteristics of any scientific hypothesis, the prime one being that it is a testable empirical generalization. The possibility of empirical test means that if an issue arose, it would be possible to resolve it. Suppose that an opponent offered the following hypothesis.

> Opponent's Hypothesis: The depreciation (decline in exit value) of an automobile is approximated by the straightline method.

The two competing hypotheses are not conventions to be selected by the individual practitioner or legislated by the FASB. Instead, the dispute can be adjudicated by empirical test. Researchers can begin the arduous task of observing the exchange of used automobiles for dollars.[5] They can fit a curve to these observations and then decide which of the two competing hypotheses best approximates the decline in exit values of automobiles.

Once the researchers have confirmed one of the hypotheses, it can be termed a law. That is what a scientific law is—a confirmed hypothesis. I have done some testing of the hypothesis using "Blue Books" of second-hand automobile dealers. My tests are undoubtedly inadequate, but it seems that the decline in the "average wholesale" prices conforms fairly closely to 40 percent per year. The major difficulty is in adjusting for different equipment (such as air condi-

---

5. Beidleman (*Valuation*) has made a promising beginning on this effort in regard to several different kinds of machinery; McKeown ("Empirical Test") has examined the availability of prices for a medium-sized road construction company. Mining inventories were investigated by Foster ("Mining Inventories"); primary production and steel inventories were examined by Wolnizer ("Primary Production Inventories" and "Current Prices").

tioning) which affects the price. But the exact percentage of decline
is not important. The objective is to obtain *some* empirical generalization which can be used to predict *some* empirical phenomena as
opposed to conventionally allocating. Once we have a law, we can
cease lamenting the conventional nature of accounting and begin to
use the law in practice. The practitioner will have to apply his
professional judgment to the individual cases. The law will not be
applicable to all assets or even to all productive assets and, in some
special cases, it may not even be applicable to automobiles. For
example, it is not likely to be a good approximation of the exit value
of a perfectly maintained Rolls Royce reserved for the use of the
president. Nor is it likely to be a good approximation of the exit
value of abused automobiles, such as jeeps in combat. In short, even
after the law has been well confirmed, it cannot be unthinkingly
applied to all cases. Its application will require intelligence.

Many practitioners fear that such laws will commit them to a series
of specific rules which would reduce them from a "professional"
to a "technician." I believe that the exact opposite would occur. The
current status of auditing depreciable assets is less professional than
the intelligent application of the law. Currently, we say that since
they are "management's statements," it is management's duty to select
the depreciation method to be used, as well as to supply the forecasts
of the life and salvage value.[6] Thus, management selects the particular
formula and then provides the magnitudes of the terms of that formula.
Under these conditions, what is left for the auditor to do but to check
the accuracy of the arithmetic? The computer is a much more efficient
device for checking arithmetic, but no one endows the computer with
professional status. I think that the application of such laws by the
auditor would increase the use of his professional judgment and
enhance his professional stature, not reduce it.

Once the law has been well confirmed, it can be applied in the
same way that the laws of physics are applied in engineering. Indeed,
in engineering they use a form of scientific accounting which should
be instructive to those of us who are now engaged in nonscientific
accounting. Consider both the content and language of the following
quotation which is from an *engineering* text:

> A material balance of an industrial process is an exact *accounting* of
> all the materials that enter, leave, accumulate, or are depleted in the

6. For a contrasting view and a lucid discussion of the responsibility for statements,
see Miller, "Audited Statements." For an elaboration of my view on the issue, see
Sterling, "Glimpse of the Forest."

course of a given time interval of operation. The material balance is
thus an expression of the law of conservation of mass in *accounting*
terms. If direct measurements were made of the weight and composition
of each stream entering or leaving a process during a given time interval
and of the change in material inventory in the system during that
time interval, no calculations would be required. Seldom is this feasible,
and hence calculation of the unknowns becomes indispensable. (HOUGEN,
ET AL., *Chemical Process*, p. 196, italics added)

Sterling's law, assuming that it is confirmed, could be used in the
same way as the law of conservation of mass. As the quotation says,
direct measurements could be made which would be a substitute
for the calculations of the law. In the same way, instead of applying
Sterling's law we could make direct measurements of the exit values
of the automobiles at the end of each year. The quotation continues
to say that such direct measurements are not feasible and thus the
calculations become indispensable. In this context "feasible" refers
to the relative costs. Obviously, it is "feasible" in the sense of "possible"
to directly measure the mass; however, it is much less expensive
to make calculations. It is the excessive cost of direct measurements
that makes the calculations "indispensable." Direct measurements of
the exit value would be more expensive than calculations.

The "calculations" mentioned in the quotation are "predictions"
in scientific parlance. The law allows one to anticipate unobserved
phenomena by inputting observations and making logical manipula-
tions. That anticipation is a prediction in the scientific sense despite
the fact that it refers to the present instead of the future. This point
is important to accountants. We seem to think that the empirical test
of a law is its ability to forecast the future. We have erroneously
equated "prediction" to "forecast." As a consequence, we impose
a too stringent requirement on accounting laws—a requirement that
many scientific laws could not meet. For example, the law of conservation of mass will allow one to predict the *present* material inventory.
(The prediction is simply the "algebraic" sum of the previous measurements of the streams of mass into and out of the process.) The
comparison of a separate measurement of the material inventory to
the prediction is a scientific verification of the law although it is
not a forecast. The law will allow us to forecast the future material
inventory if and only if we can also forecast the mass entering and
leaving the process. Since it is impossible to forecast the mass entering
and leaving the process, the law would fail the accounting requirement
of forecasting the future material inventory. However, the failure is
due to the inability to forecast the inputs to the law, not a failure
of the law.

Consider Sterling's law. It would pass the predictive ability test in the scientific sense. Its very purpose is to predict the present exit value, and that prediction is capable of verification. However, it would fail the forecast test. It would certainly not be capable of forecasting the future income of the firm. It could not forecast the future depreciation because additional automobiles may be purchased or the present automobiles may be sold. In addition, the law may not even be able to forecast next year's exit value.[7] However, if we are willing to utilize a law that will predict the present, that is, if we are willing to accept scientific criteria, the law will meet the test.

This analogy, like most analogies, is far from perfect. The law of conservation of mass is much more general and much more powerful than Sterling's law. The generality is evidenced by the fact that engineering textbooks, such as Hougen et al. (*Chemical Process*), are a series of explanations of the various applications of the laws of conservation of energy and mass. Such texts begin with a brief description of the general laws of conservation and then proceed to discuss a large variety of specific applications. Often the applications require more specialized laws. For example, when discussing the application of the general laws to gaseous mixtures, they present Dalton's law; and when discussing the application in regard to vapor pressures, they present Raoult's law. Both Dalton's law and Raoult's law are much more specialized than Newton's laws of conservation. The general laws of conservation provide the unifying theme, the synthesis of the various specialized laws.

Sterling's law is much more specialized than Dalton's or Raoult's,

---

7. At the present time we do not know enough about prices to enable forecasts to be made with any degree of assurance. Therefore, I stated the proposed law in terms of this year's exit values. It is likely that we will be forced to change the law—either the functional form or the rate of decline—in future years. Many accountants will be inclined to reject the law for this reason. They will continue to think that our subject matter is inherently more difficult because it is less stable than the physical world. In truth, scientists face the same problem. In regard to science in general, Whitehead (*Science*, p. 5) writes: "Obviously, the main recurrences of life are too insistent to escape the notice of the least rational of humans . . . but there is a complementary fact which is equally true and equally obvious:—nothing ever really recurs in exact detail. No two days are identical, no two winters." Thus, the physical world is also unstable and it presents a problem for scientists. But this has not prevented them from searching for laws which they must periodically alter.

We could do the same with Sterling's law. Academics or the research arm of the AICPA or FASB could periodically test and revise such laws. Practitioners could then use the results in their yearly accounting and auditing.

A complementary approach is for practitioners to make direct measurements periodically while relying on predictions in the interim. Sprouse and Moonitz (*Broad Accounting Principles*, p. 34) suggested that the productive assets should be measured directly every five years. In the intervening years they thought that predictions would suffice.

let alone Newton's. I would like to be able to present a set of general, powerful laws for your consideration. Unfortunately, I cannot do that. My feeble, specialized law is the best that I can do at the present time. My objective is to persuade you that accounting laws are *possible*, that it is *not* necessary that accounting be based on conventions. If I can persuade you that accounting laws are possible, then we can be on our way toward a science. We can begin seeking other specialized laws. Once we have presented a collection of specialized laws, perhaps a Newton will appear to provide an accounting synthesis—to provide a general, powerful set of laws for accounting. If we continue to define accounting as necessarily unscientific, we prohibit the possibility of a Newton making an appearance.

In short, I think that it would be much more productive if our researchers would try to establish specialized, simplified laws rather than continuing to argue about which conventional allocation is better "matching" or continuing to provide evidence that competing sources of information allow the market to adjust for differences in conventions. As long as depreciation is defined as a conventional allocation, there is no possibility of deciding between accelerated and straight line—the issue will remain unresolved because it is in principle unresolvable. The proposed law has the advantage of being a resolvable issue. It certainly will not solve the global problems of accounting, but I would prefer to simplify and try to resolve one issue, however small, than to continue the debate for another century. The law has all the characteristics of any other scientific law. Despite its feebleness, it has all the advantages of a scientific law, and none of the disadvantages of an accounting convention.

7

The Relevance Test

> Such a [scientific] method, which takes advantage of
> the objective connections in the world around us,
> should be found reasonable not because of its appeal
> to the idiosyncrasies of a selected few individuals, but
> because it can be tested repeatedly and by all men.
> COHEN and NAGEL, *Logic and Scientific Method*, p. 195

My previous experience leads me to believe that many readers will
not like the law I proposed in Section 6.3. Some readers will say
that the law is concerned with values, while accounting is based
on costs. This is a definitional question. We now account for costs
because we have defined "accounting" as a process of allocating costs.
We could define it some other way.

The problem with continuing to define "accounting" as a process
of allocating costs is, in the words of Cohen and Nagel, that accounting
will continue to depend upon "the idiosyncrasies of a selected few
individuals."[1] On the other hand, if we are willing to redefine
accounting so that we account for some measurable attribute, the
propositions of accounting can be tested repeatedly and by all men.
Such testing will allow us to resolve our problems instead of continuing
to debate them. We can adjudicate our disputes by appealing to
scientific tests instead of appealing to a legislature or court.[2]

1. The selected few individuals upon whose idiosyncrasies accounting has depended
in the past have been mainly managements and accountants. Most of the proposals
for reform have been to make accounting depend upon the idiosyncrasies of a different
set of individuals. That is, in my view, the proposals to make accounting depend
upon the deliberations of the CAP, APB, FASB, or SEC are arguments about *whose*
idiosyncrasies it ought to depend. I do not think that these kinds of proposals for
reform get to the root of the problem.
2. I have previously tried to draw the distinction between legalistic and scientific
accounting in, for example, Sterling, "Accounting at the Crossroads." I have also tried
to forecast the outcome of legalistic accounting in, for example, Sterling, "Accounting
in the 1980s." Evidently, I did not make myself clear because a number of people
have misinterpreted my remarks. The misinterpretation seems to stem from different

Thus, in moving toward a science we must first decide to account for measurable attributes. We now turn to the question of which measurable attribute(s) we should measure and report.

7.1 Selecting the Attribute(s)

> No science deals with its objects of study in their full concreteness. It selects certain of their properties and attempts to establish relations among them.
>
> LAZARSFELD, "Evidence and Inference," p. 100

After we have decided to measure (as opposed to conventionally allocate), we still must make difficult choices—we must decide which one or which collection of measurable attributes that we wish to account for. In the previous chapter I argued that exit values were measurable. But the measurability of exit values does not ipso facto mean that we should account for them. Measurability is a necessary but not a sufficient condition.

This problem of selecting the attribute(s) is not peculiar to accounting. It pervades all of science as Lazarsfeld indicates. For example, in engineering one can account for either mass or energy. Both mass and energy are measurable attributes—neither are conventions. Both are subsumed under general, powerful laws. A material balance is based on the law of conservation of mass, and an energy balance is based on the law of the conservation of energy. Both laws are subject to empirical tests and therefore the choice cannot be made on the basis of empirical testability. Thus, the engineer is faced with a choice of accounting for either mass or energy—the choice of a

---

perceptions of the alternatives. Most accountants perceive governmental regulation as the alternative to our present situation. They argue that the standard-setting function should be performed in the private sector (by the APB, FASB or some other private legislative body) not in the public sector (by the CASB, SEC or some other public legislative body). I think that standard-setting by the private sector is a lost cause. If accounting is going to continue to be based upon legislation, I think that the forces of the political process will eventually move it to the public sector. The final result will be that some governmental body, probably a body more like the CASB than the SEC, will legislate accounting rules.

This melancholy conclusion has been misinterpreted as *advocating* the outcome. That was not my intention. Instead, my intention was to *forecast* the outcome of the current drift in accounting thought. If we continue to conceive of accounting as being based upon conventions (which require legislation), I think that the eventual outcome will be governmental legislation.

My main point is to present scientific testing as an alternative to legislation. I prefer scientific testing to private or public legislation. Thus, I think if we move toward a science, we can move away from the need for legislation; and thus we can discontinue the arguments about the *source* of the legislation.

material balance or an energy balance. Since neither measurability of the attribute nor empirical testability of the law will allow engineers to choose which attribute to account for, an additional criterion is required. We face the same problem in accounting. For example, we could measure and report entry values. Since entry values are equally as measurable as exit values, measurability will not allow us to choose between them.

Some avoid making such choices by adopting a policy of data expansion. Instead of choosing between, say, entry values and exit values they would expand the data by presenting both in a multicolumn report. (See Revsine, "Data Expansion," for background and analysis. I had previously discussed the issue under the imprecise headings of "additional disclosure" and "different incomes for different purposes." Revsine's terminology—and analysis—is better.) There have been many proposals to expand the data in order to avoid the choice, some of which have been put into effect. The most obvious example is the SEC's requirement to report replacement costs in addition to historic costs.

I have previously argued that data expansion is not a solution because it overlooks two constraints: (1) the additional cost of providing the additional channel capacity; (2) the possibility of overwhelming the receivers with too much data. (See, e.g., *Enterprise Income*, p. 51ff and "ASOBAT Review.") These constraints are now known as "cost-benefit analysis" and "information overload." Despite exhortation that information must be cost beneficial and a considerable amount of behavioral evidence that too much data result in less efficient decisions, the movement toward data expansion continues. The FASB is apparently going to require three valuation bases: replacement costs and price-level adjusted historic costs in addition to unadjusted historic costs. But even this is not sufficient for many of the more enthusiastic proponents of data expansion. Their answer to all questions is to add more data in more columns in more detail at lower levels of aggregation with more explanatory footnotes.

The problem now goes beyond cost benefit and information overload. Adoption of a policy of unconstrained data expansion is, in effect, an abdication of formulating a theory of reporting; it prohibits the move to a science of accounting. Those who see data expansion as a solution are, in effect, attempting to deal with the objects of study in their full concreteness instead of selecting certain attributes. As Lazarsfeld indicates, no science can do that. Boulding (*Economics*, p. 3) states the problems in terms that are particularly appropriate for accountants: "It is a very fundamental principle indeed that knowledge is always gained by the orderly loss of information, that is, by condensing and abstracting and indexing the great buzzing confusion of information that comes from the world around us into a form which we can appreciate and comprehend." Thus, we must adopt the objective of an orderly loss of information, not unconstrained data expansion.

In short, we cannot avoid making such choices. The question, then, is how we should make such choices. In science the answer is clear. The choice between accounting for mass and energy, for example, is made on the basis of relevance, on the basis of how the information is to be used. Scientists do not report material balances when the decision requires information about energy. We have done the same. We all agree that we should not report the length or color of assets. The basis of that judgment is that length and color are irrelevant to the kinds of problems faced by users. Thus, we have already implicitly adopted the criterion of relevance. The remaining task is to make the adoption explicit, define the concept, and begin to apply it rigorously.

7.2 Relevance Defined

> The scientist looks for laws or connections among facts in order to explain and to predict phenomena. Speaking loosely, we may "explain" the fact that Jones makes more money than Smith by pointing to Jones' superior education. But a man from Mars or anyone else may well wonder why we cite Jones' education rather than, say, his height. Speaking more strictly, we then expand our explanation. To cite a cause as an explanation of an event is, implicity at least, to cite an instance of a law. Jones' education, rather than his height is *relevant* to his income because we know a law or generalization connecting education with income, but no such law connects height with income.
>
> BRODBECK, *Readings*, p. 9, italics added

As Brodbeck says, in science the notion of relevance means that one fact or attribute is connected to another by means of a law. Without laws all facts would appear to be equally relevant or irrelevant. The world would be a bewildering array of unconnected facts. Laws permit us to separate the relevant from the irrelevant. If we want to predict or explain x, we must look for a law that has x as its output and then we must examine the law to determine the relevant inputs.

Thus, in science it is clear that one cannot determine relevance in isolation. The term must be used in a prepositional phrase, the object of which is a particular law. A fact or attribute may be relevant to law x but irrelevant to law y.

Defining relevance in accounting must follow the scientific lead. We cannot define relevance in isolation. We must specify that a fact or attribute is relevant to *something*. For reasons which will be discussed in the next section, I have previously suggested that relevance be defined in relation to decision models as follows:

> A measure of an attribute is "relevant" to a decision model if and only if that attribute is specified by that decision model.

In accounting, there are many other views of the relevance or usefulness criterion. My main objection to these other views is not that I disagree with them but rather that they do not provide explicit definitions. I cannot know whether I agree or disagree with the other views because their lack of definition prohibits me from knowing what they mean with any reasonable degree of precision. In order to avoid the problem of others not knowing what I mean, I will discuss the role of decision models at some length.

7.3 Decision Models

> The essence of decision making is the formulation of alternatives and the subsequent choices between them. The manner in which this choice can be achieved [includes the] . . . construction of a model of the problem situation based upon the relationship of the factors and parameters involved. . . .
>
> RADFORD, *Complex Decision Problems*, p. 1

A "decision model," as I use the term, is merely a special kind of scientific law. It is a goal-oriented, economic, empirical generalization. Its purpose is to permit one to make scientific-type predictions—to permit one to make "if . . . then . . ." statements. The following is the general structure of decision models:

> If measure x has some relation to measure y, then z will be the case.

There are many exceptionally complicated decision models. An indication of the complexity is given by the fact that entire textbooks are written about a single model. The complexity of such decision models has caused some accountants to despair. Rather than despair, I think that we need to simplify and learn from the simplifications.

My favorite simple example is the comparison of densities in order to predict whether or not an object will float. If one needs a life raft, for example, one must decide which of the available objects should be selected. Thus, there exists a problematic situation requiring a decision. The type of problem faced specifies the type of decision model needed. In this case, one needs to know which of the available objects will float on water. A well-confirmed decision model is at hand. This decision model specifies two attributes—weight and volume—to be measured, and one concept—density, the quotient of weight and volume—to be calculated. Then it specifies that one compare the density of the available objects to the density of water. It says:

> If the density of object x is less than the density of fluid y, then x will float on y.

Despite the simplicity of this decision model, it has been a very fruitful one in science; but it will not solve all problems. Even in building a life raft, there are other relevant factors which are not supplied by this specialized model. Thus, for the purpose of building a life raft, the model is incomplete. Many accountants would reject the model because it is incomplete. Moreover, one must make a host of other decisions that have nothing to do with whether an object will float on a fluid. For that host of decisions, this decision model is inapplicable. Many accountants would reject this decision model as a basis for reporting because it is specialized and, therefore, more often inapplicable than applicable.

These are unreasonable requirements. Although we prefer more complete and more general models—models encompassing more factors relevant to a specific problem and models applicable to a wider variety of problematic situations—we must recognize that not even in the millennium are we likely to discover a single decision model that is both complete and applicable to many different kinds of decisions. Therefore, we must accept the fact that all decision models will be limited to a given class of decisions.[3] Other decision

---

3. Acceptance of this fact is merely a specific case of accepting scientific simplifications. The float-on decision model is a highly useful scientific simplification. It does not take much imagination to make it so complicated that we become so confused that we despair. Unfortunately, we accountants seem to have a propensity to do just that. When I previously presented the example of the float-on decision model (Sterling, "Relevant Financial Reporting"), I received a number of lengthy letters that correctly pointed out the incompleteness and specialized nature of the model. The problem was that the critics so complicated the model that the issue became highly confused. By the time they added a large number of other *desirable* characteristics to the model (such as color, to make the life raft more visible), the *indispensable* characteristic of whether or not the life raft would float was obscured in a morass of complexity.

models will be required for other classes of decisions.

If we accept that premise, then we can concentrate on the benefits to be derived from examining a specialized model. Within the limited context of float-on decisions, the above decision model is quite helpful. A major benefit is that the model precisely specifies what to measure, and thus, by implication, it also specifies what *not* to measure. It separates the almost limitless number of attributes into two classes: relevant and irrelevant. The relevant attributes are weight and volume. All other attributes (for example, color, area, and age) are irrelevant. When faced with a very complex set—a set of attributes with an almost infinite number of elements—the decision model allows us to partition that complex set into a simple subset of relevant attributes and its complement of irrelevant attributes.

One long unresolved issue of accounting has been what we ought to account for. It seems that this basic question has been with us since Pacioli. As with our other issues, we have been unable to reach a resolution. I think that the examination of decision models is a promising approach to resolving that issue, to providing an answer to what we ought to account for. Indeed, I cannot think of any other scientific[4] approach that has any hope of resolving this particular issue. Given the need to predict floating, if scientists had a choice between density and area, the approach that they would use to provide an answer is clear: since the decision model specifies density and does not specify area, they would choose to calculate and report density. It is as simple as that. The same criterion should be applied in accounting. We should examine economic decision models in order to discover what attributes are specified by those models.

There are a great many objections to the decision-model approach. One objection is the complexity of "real" decision models as opposed to my simple examples. An immediate reply that occurs to me is that float-on decisions are real. There are a good many real decisions that require the ability to predict floating. More generally, I think that the answer is to simplify. Since we cannot solve all of the problems of the complex, real world at once, I think our choice is either to simplify or to be mystified by the complexities. I chose to simplify.

A second objection has been put in terms of "dictatorship versus democracy." Many accountants recommend that we survey the decision makers to find out what they want to know or test what capital market agents react to and then use the results of such surveys and tests

---

4. There is a plethora of nonscientific approaches, for example, legislation by the FASB, SEC, or CASB. Even so, if legislation is to provide useful information, it must ultimately be based on decision models.

as a basis for reporting. The survey or test approach is alleged to be "democratic," while the decision-model approach is alleged to be "dictatorial" or "paternalistic."[5] Scientists would not fall into this trap. Even if they discovered that a majority of the decision makers thought that, say, color was relevant to whether a body would float on a fluid, they would not reinforce that error by reporting color in the context of making decisions about floating. It is the possibility of errors of this kind, among other reasons, that causes me to define relevance on the basis of decision *models* instead of decision *makers*. Even if I had the power, I would not "dictate" that a decision maker could not select a colorful, solid-metal ball to be used as a life raft. However, I would try to convince him that he had erred. If that is being a "dictator," then I plead guilty. I would try to convince him that density is relevant and color is irrelevant to a float-on decision. If that is "information paternalism," then I plead guilty. If his ship were sinking, I would send him a signal about density instead of

---

5. A variant of this objection is an unqualified faith in empiricism and a disdain for the a priori or normative. Opponents argued that the choice should be made by the users, not accountants, and the survey or test results would reveal the users' choice. At the height of the debate, my priors were that "sophisticated" (e.g., bankers and financial analysts) users would have been conditioned to ask for a continuation of what they had been getting, that is, historic costs (*Enterprise Income*, p. 55n) and that "naive" (the general public) users, not having been subjected to such conditioning, would want current values (*Enterprise Income*, pp. 268, 278, 314ff). Surveys have confirmed my priors: Tweedie's ("Cash Flow") results indicate that naive users want cash flows and exit values; Benston and Krasney's ("DAAM") results indicate that sophisticated users want a continuation of historic costs. Benston and Krasney's results are such that one can infer intermediate conditioning points since less sophisticated (less experienced) investment officers had less desire for historic costs than the more sophisticated (more experienced) investment officers.

We still face the choice. The survey results merely shift the argument to whether we should be responsive to the wants of sophisticated or naive users. Empiricism will not allow accountants to avoid making the choice.

Note that these survey results are also pertinent to those who argue that we cannot change from historic costs to current values because it would be too disruptive and confusing. Those who make that argument are focusing only on the current generation of sophisticated users, overlooking future generations who are now naive and a subset of those who will go through the disruptive and confusing process of becoming sophisticated. We teachers have direct evidence of the process. In the elementary course we face naive accountants and have some difficulty hammering home the idea that the balance sheet is a statement of unexpired costs, not values. The elementary students have their thinking disrupted and are often confused. In graduate seminars we face sophisticated accountants and have some difficulty hammering home the idea that the balance sheet could be a statement of values, not unexpired costs. The graduate students also have their thinking disrupted and are often confused. We can avoid the second disruption by not teaching current values to graduate students or, for future generations, we can avoid both disruptions by not teaching unexpired costs to elementary students. If the objective is to minimize disruption, the latter is clearly preferable.

color even though I recognize that as a consumer of information he has a right to buy any information he wants. If that is "not responding to market demand," if that is "violating consumer sovereignty," then I plead guilty.[6]

A third objection is based on a confusion between "normative" and "descriptive" science. People often remind me that science is descriptive and that I have criticized others for trying to deduce the "ought" (normative) from the "is" (descriptive). They say that if accounting is to be a science, then it cannot establish the goals that people *ought* to pursue, that it cannot contain normative propositions.[7] The answer to this criticism is to point out that the float-on decision model is purely descriptive. It is not normative. The confusion between normative and descriptive arises when a goal is stated. The point can be illustrated by expanding the example. Suppose that a decision maker is faced with choosing between object x_1 and object x_2. Suppose further that we have found object x_1 to be less dense than fluid y and object x_2 to be more dense than fluid y. If the decision maker is willing to specify his goal, it is properly within the realm of science to make "ought" statements. If the goal is to find an object that will float on fluid y, we can properly say that the decision maker ought to choose object x_1. If the goal is to find an object that will sink, we may properly say that he ought to choose object x_2. Thus, decision models per se are not normative. They do not specify a goal. Instead, they aid in achieving the goal specified by the decision maker.

6. If the example of using a solid-metal ball as a life raft seems too far fetched, consider Minard's report ("Cheerful Days") that some great businessmen consult their astrologers before making a major decision. If we adopt the position of responding to the wants of decision makers, we must begin to supply astrology reports to that group of businessmen. Since astrology reports are not specified by any decision model, I would have no hesitancy in refusing to supply such reports. When I present such examples to my opponents, they usually reply that we are a "service profession" and therefore we must respond to the market demand without regard to our own "value judgments." Although there is much to be said for giving the customers what they want, it does not correspond to the usual notion of a profession.

The judgments that I am asking the profession to make are scientific judgments, not value judgments. Other professions make such judgments regularly. Physicians, for example, refuse to meet the market demand for Laetrile on the basis of scientific evidence. No profession, except the oldest profession, adopts an unqualified policy of giving the customers what they want.

7. See Pap (*Introduction*, p. 410) for a lucid discussion of the " . . . misleading formulations of this essentially correct insight" in general and, in particular, for his conclusion that the nonnormative nature of science ". . . does not mean that factual [descriptive] investigations are irrelevant to normative conclusions, for a nontrivial normative conclusion can be derived from a normative major premise only with the help of a factual [descriptive] premise" (p. 411).

Fourth, some accountants criticize the decision-model approach because of the variety of decision situations. They correctly note that when we broadcast our information to the general public, we cannot know all of the decision situations. From this observation they correctly conclude that we cannot supply the decision maker with *all* of the needed information. We can avoid despair by distinguishing the necessary from the sufficient. Although we cannot supply sufficient information, we can supply necessary information. Suppose object x is in our possession, but we do not know the locations of the various decision makers. One decision maker may be faced with a float-on decision at the Great Salt Lake, while another may be at Lake Superior. The densities of the two bodies of water vary. If we give them only the information about the density of object x, we have not supplied all of the information needed by the two decision makers. However, we have supplied information that is necessary for the decision. Although we might prefer to provide sufficient information, we may have to settle for providing only necessary information. As will be explained more generally in section 8.1, the decision maker must supply part of the information himself. In this case, the decision maker would have to measure the density of the particular fluid in his particular decision situation and then compare the result to the information that we supplied about the density of object x.

A fifth objection has been that economic decisions require forecasts, while my simplified physics decisions do not. We need to distinguish between the forecasts of two things: outputs and inputs. The output of the model is a prediction—it allows one to anticipate whether or not an object will float on a fluid. The inputs to the model are measurements—the weight and volume are measured and then put into the model. The difference is that most, if not all, economic decision models require forecasts of one or more of the inputs. Usually, we are required to forecast the cash flows and compare the discounted value of those flows to the required sacrifice as follows:

> If the (measured) required sacrifice to acquire project i is less than the discounted value of the (forecasted) cash flows from project i, then (it is forecasted that) one will accumulate more money by acquiring project i than by investing the required sacrifice at the discount rate.

The same situation may arise in the float-on decision. Suppose that the decision maker is planning a future trip to the Great Salt Lake and has no way to measure its density. He must forecast one input.

If the (measured) density of object x is less than the (forecasted) density of the water in the Great Salt Lake, then (it is forecasted that) x will float on the Great Salt Lake.

Forecasting an input is a significant problem. Among other things, it makes it necessary to distinguish good decisions from good outcomes. That is, given the forecast, the decision may have been a good one but the forecast may be wrong, resulting in a bad outcome. Alternatively, we may get a good outcome by chance even though we made a bad decision. Despite these problems, the *structure* is the same—the model still specifies the inputs that we need to measure and/or forecast, and thus it provides us with a means of distinguishing the relevant inputs from the irrelevant inputs.

There are other objections to the decision-model approach. It would be tedious to try to reply to all of them. My hope is merely that I have said enough to indicate the nature of the problem and the promise of the approach. If we are willing to simplify and look for the benefits that can be derived from the decision-model approach, we can make great progress. If we continue to look at all of the complexities, we are apt to despair. I do not think that decision models will supply answers to all problems nor even easy answers to some problems, but I do believe that they will allow us to distinguish the relevant attributes from the irrelevant attributes. Decision models will allow us to decide what we ought to account for. If they can make a contribution to the resolution of that long-unresolved issue, it will be a most significant advancement for accounting.

7.4 Irrelevancies

> Objection, your honor. Irrelevant.
> PERRY MASON

In most cases when we deem an attribute to be irrelevant, it means only that it is not specified by a particular decision model. That same attribute may be specified by other models. For example, area is irrelevant to the float-on decision model, but area is relevant to other decision models.

In addition to directly measurable attributes, there are calculated attributes, sometimes called "derived measurements" or "theoretical terms." Density—the quotient of weight and volume—and area—the product of length and width—are examples. Although such calculated attributes do not have to be subject to direct empirical verification, they must lead to a prediction that *is* subject to empirical verification. For example, density need not be directly measurable since it leads to a float-on prediction that can be empirically verified.

The purpose of this requirement is to prohibit the proliferation of calculated attributes. It is one application of "Ockham's razor"; it is the desire to keep science as simple as possible. Without the requirement, it would be possible to invent an infinite number of calculated attributes. More important, science is intended to produce useful concepts, and this requirement is an attempt to eliminate useless concepts.

Scientists often present counterexamples to try to clarify the criterion as well as to indicate its indispensability. Hempel (*Fundamentals,* p. 46) does this by inventing a concept called "hage" which he defines as the product of a person's height and age. As Hempel says, hage has many qualities. In his terms, it "would have relatively high precision and uniformity of usage." However, it lacks the quality of theoretical import or, as Hempel says, "We have no general laws connecting the hage of a person with other characteristics." Hage is irrelevant to *all* decision models; there are no known if . . . then . . . statements that specify hage as an input.

Hempel invented the fictional concept of hage. The cephalic index is a factual example. At one time, certain scientists calculated and reported caphalic indexes in accord with a hypothesis that they were theoretically important. Brodbeck (*Readings,* p. 8, italics altered), employing "useful" and "significance" as synonyms for "theoretical import" writes:

> The concept cephalic index can be quite adequately defined in terms of the ratio of the width of a person's head to its length, with the method of measurement precisely stated. Yet, for the psychologist at least, a person's cephalic index is an uninteresting fact. It is not interesting because a person's cephalic index has *no connection*, as far as we know, with any of his behavior. There are, in other words, no laws *connecting* it with behavioral concepts. It is, therefore, not a *useful* concept. Because caphalic index does not enter into laws, the concept is *useless* for predicting or explaining behavior. It lacks "meaning" in the sense of significance.

The concept of cephalic index has many qualities (adequate definition and precision), but it lacks the indispensable quality of usefulness or relevance. The hypothesis was not accepted because no one discovered any if . . . then . . . statements that specify a cephalic index.

The purpose of Hempel and Brodbeck in presenting their counterexamples was to demonstrate that relevance to at least one model is indispensable. A concept may have all sorts of other qualities—it may meet a host of other criteria—but without relevance to at least one model, it will be summarily eliminated from the store of scientific concepts.

The need for the application of this criterion to accounting should be obvious. As Chambers ("Financial Information," p. 15) originally demonstrated and as Grady (*Inventory*, p. 379) subsequently confirmed, the "variety of possibilities in accounting, if viewed in the aggregate mathematical scale of combinations, would be an astronomical figure." The very fact that such an astronomical number of possibilities exists in accounting provides some evidence that the relevance criterion has not been applied because, as Hempel (*Fundamentals,* p. 46) says, irrelevancies such as hage "can be readily defined in any number."

The truth of the ability to readily define such notions in any number is demonstrated by the fact that we continue to add such definitions. We have recently seen proposals to allocate inventories in a fashion similar to depreciation as well as proposals to apply a LIFO-type allocation to depreciable assets. Such proposals are conclusive proof of our ability to define an infinite number of such notions.

Thus, the problem is not our ability to add such notions. The problem is our inability to eliminate such notions. In accounting the need for elimination is usually discussed under the heading of uniformity. But the issue is much deeper. In science, the need for elimination is called "parsimony." As William of Ockham (Moody, *Philosophy,* p. 307) put it, "What can be done with fewer [concepts] is done in vain with more." We accountants are in rather desperate need of a close shave with Ockham's razor. We need to eliminate notions rather than to continue to add them.

The way to eliminate notions is to subject them to the relevance test. As I will discuss more fully in the following chapters, the notion of depreciation as presently defined lacks theoretical import or significance. I believe that the notion is useless because, like hage and the cephalic index, it is irrelevant to all decision models. My belief about that notion, however, is of much less importance than the acceptance and rigorous application of the relevance test. In accounting, as in science, demonstrable relevance to at least one decision model must be the primary criterion for concepts. After a concept passes the relevance test, then we can subject it to secondary tests. But no matter how many other tests a concept passes, if it is not relevant to any decision model, then it ought to be eliminated from the store of accounting concepts.

Application of
the Relevance Test

Almost all accountants agree with the usefulness or relevance criterion in the abstract. The problem arises in the application of that criterion. There are many rather vague assertions that this or that figure is relevant, but rarely is there a demonstration of relevance. My plea is that we begin to rigorously apply the relevance criterion—that we begin to provide demonstrations that others can assimilate, validate, corroborate, and verify.

8.1 The Decision Process

I will begin the application of the relevance test by providing a general outline of the decision process. Although such a generalization, like all other generalizations, leaves out many important details, it presents an overview of the process.

All decision models require information about:

(1) Alternatives = $A = \{a_1, a_2, \ldots, a_n\}$
(2) Consequences = $C = \{c_1, c_2, \ldots, c_n\}$
(3) Preferences = P = a function for ordering consequences.

A schematic of the decision process is shown in Exhibit 8.1-1.

8.1.1 Alternatives. The first thing the decision maker must do in

Exhibit 8.1-1
The Decision Process

Step 1	Step 2	Step 3	Step 4
Determine Alternatives	Forecast Consequences	Select Preferred Consequence	Take Action

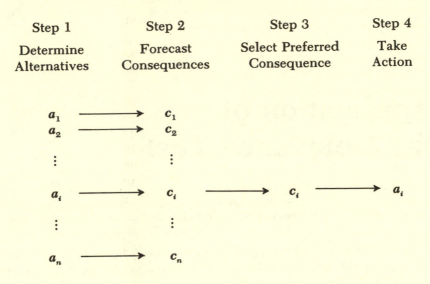

any decision situation is to determine the available alternatives. They are sometimes called "possible courses of action" or "feasible rival acts." Modifiers such as "available," "possible," and "feasible" are used to emphasize that the decision maker must first determine the kinds of choices he faces. He must segregate the possible from the impossible or the available from the unavailable. There is no point in considering the consequences of an action which is not available to the decision maker.

Many factors are pertinent to this determination, most of which are peculiar to the decision maker or to the type of decision. One factor common to all decisions is that the alternatives must be available at the moment of choice—they must be *presently* available. The decision maker may plan what he may do when he faces future alternatives or he may ruminate about past alternatives, but the choice is always restricted to the alternatives that are available at the time of the decision—the present.

Another common factor is that the alternatives must be competing in the sense that the selection of one obviates the selection of another. If alternatives are not competing, no decision is required. The decision maker need not choose between i and j if he can select both i and j.

It would be best to have a complete specification of all of the alternatives because if the list is not complete, one may not know about the existence of an alternative with a preferred consequence. A complete specification of all alternatives, however, is often impossible because even in a simple decision situation, there may be an infinite number of available alternatives. Even if it is possible—even if the number of available alternatives is finite—specifying all alternatives is likely to be too costly. The decision maker then is confronted with a dilemma at the very beginning of the decision process. Specifying additional alternatives is costly and should not be done unless the expected benefit exceeds the cost. But the expected benefit of specifying an additional alternative is the possibility of finding a preferred consequence, and one cannot forecast the consequence of an alternative until that alternative has been specified. Thus, he needs to forecast the consequence before specifying the alternative, and he needs to specify the alternative before forecasting the consequence. The dilemma is revealed. We usually say that the decision maker is forced to "satisfice" (select the best from an incomplete list of alternatives) as opposed to "maximize" (select the best from a complete list of alternatives), but this terminology only describes the process. It does not resolve the dilemma.

This difficulty is not pertinent to the present discussion. Instead, we merely need to recognize that the decision process is the choice of presently available, mutually exclusive alternatives.

8.1.2 Consequences. The second thing that the decision maker must do is to forecast the consequences or outcomes or payoffs of each of the alternatives. Since the consequences lie in the future, the decision maker faces a formidable forecasting problem. Because choosing an alternative depends upon the consequence of that alternative, the decision maker must set a one-to-one correspondence of alternatives to consequences. He must be able to say, "If I choose alternative a_i, the consequence will be c_i."

Of course, many refinements are possible. One refinement is to associate various payoffs with various states of nature. In such analysis, the consequence is a vector. One way to convert the vector to a single number is to weight the payoffs by the probability of the associated state of nature which makes the consequence an "expected value." Another common refinement is to adjust the payoffs to reflect time value. The payoff (perhaps an expected value) is reduced by an interest factor which makes the consequence a "discounted value."

The forecasting difficulties and the methods of refinement are not pertinent to this discussion. Instead, we merely need to recognize that the essence of the decision situation is that a forecasted consequence must be associated with every alternative.

8.1.3 Preferences. The third thing that the decision maker must do is to select the preferred consequence—he must choose the "best" consequence. What is best is a personal determination of the decision maker. At the present time we do not know much about how such choices are made. Behavioral research on the decision process is inconclusive. Theoretical research has not yet been able to identify a general optimal strategy. Thus, the most we can say at the present time is that preferences are personal.

The process of determining the preferred consequence is not pertinent to this discussion. Instead, we merely need to recognize that the decision maker must select a consequence, that he must choose what he thinks is best. The choice of the consequence determines the choice of the alternative. That is, the one-to-one correspondence of alternatives and consequences means that selecting a given consequence uniquely determines the alternative.

8.1.4 Information. Decision models are abstractions which are separate and apart from decision makers. For example, the capital budgeting model can be considered separately from the persons who use that model. The decision *model* requires information about alternatives, consequences, and preferences. The decision maker can be considered as a supplier of information to the decision model. Consider Exhibit 8.1-2.

The accounting system is also a supplier of information, but it

Exhibit 8.1-2
The Information System

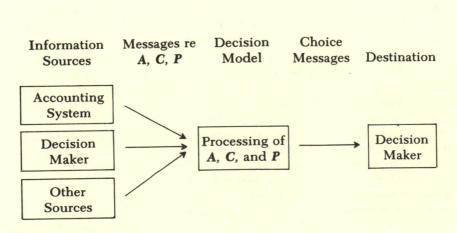

is not necessary for the system to supply all of the information required by the model. In nonfeedback situations, such as providing financial statements to investors, it is impossible for the accounting system to provide information about the preferences of the decision makers. Since the decision makers already know their preferences, the point may seem unimportant. However, many accountants have become bogged down in their efforts to design an information system because they were unable to specify the decision maker's utility function or because they were unable to aggregate utility functions of different decision makers. If we view the decision maker as the supplier of this kind of information to the decision model, this problem is bypassed, if not solved.

A similar point may be made in regard to consequences. Scholars who have carefully examined the decision process have argued that consequences are "imagined" by the decision maker and are "in the highest degree a 'personal' or 'subjective' thing" (Shackle, *Decision,* pp. 9–12). For this reason, we may have to face the possibility of requiring the decision maker to supply the forecasted consequences. To put it negatively, it may be impossible for the accounting system to supply the forecasted consequences.

The same words can be used to describe the process of satisficing. What is "satisfactory" to a decision maker is a personal or subjective thing. Therefore, only the decision maker can determine when the list of alternatives is sufficient to permit the choice to be made. To put it negatively, the accounting system cannot be expected to supply the complete list of alternatives since the cost of that list is likely to be prohibitive.

These considerations have the effect of limiting the kinds of information that the accounting system can supply. This limitation may result in less information than many accountants would like to supply. But what is impossible today may become possible tomorrow. Thus, I am not attempting to prejudge the case. Instead, my point is that we should examine the information system to determine which source is best equipped to supply various kinds of information. It is not reasonable to expect a single source to supply all information. I think that one reason for the widespread despair in accounting is that the goal has been overly ambitious. Some accountants have set out to establish a "complete" information system—one that would specify all alternatives, forecast all consequences, and then select the preferred consequence. Although I admire their ambition and I have been instructed by their research results, I think that a more modest goal would yield more positive research results.[1] The more modest goal that I have in mind is to view the decision maker as one source of information and the accounting system as another. There may be still other sources of which we should be cognizant. We can then turn our attention to specifying the kinds of information which the accounting system is best equipped to supply.

8.2 Market Decisions

> In a minute there is time
> For decisions and revisions which a minute will reverse.
> ELIOT, "Prufrock"

The second step in applying the relevance test is to consider a given class of decisions. I will apply it here to those decisions involving the market. In a market economy such as ours this is probably the most important class of economic decisions. Although there are many decisions that do not involve the market, in a market economy a great many decisions are of the buy versus not-buy or sell versus not-sell type.

8.2.1 Market Alternatives. The set of feasible market alternatives is determined by comparing the required sacrifice to the available funds. It may be stated as a general principle.

Alternative Principle: If $s_{it} \le F_t$, then the purchase of i is a feasible alternative at time t (8.2-1)

where

s_{it} = the required sacrifice for asset i at time t
F_t = the available funds at time t

The available funds are a function of three interrelated variables.

$$F_t = f(x_{1t}, x_{2t}, ..., x_{nt}, \Delta \text{Debt}, \Delta \text{Capital})$$ (8.2-2)

where

x_{it} = exit value of asset i at time t

1. Most of the research results to date have been negative—proofs that it is impossible to set up an optimal information system. Although to prove the impossibility of something is an important research result in general, these particular proofs in accounting have not come as a surprise. If one examines the specifications of the information system the researchers set out to establish, it is obvious that it is impossible. For example, we have witnessed researchers specifying such things as the utility functions of *all* receivers, the probability distributions of *all* consequences of *all* alternatives, and so forth. Given these specifications, I for one do not need a proof of an impossibility theorem. I will grant a priori that it cannot be done.

Normally (i.e., excluding gifts, inheritances, and the like) the available funds come from these three sources. Many recurring exchanges are limited by the size of the cash balance, in which case the exit value (face value) of cash is relevant. If the cash balance is not adequate for a desired acquisition, then there are three choices: (1) borrow, (2) raise equity capital, or (3) sell a noncash asset. If we desire an unowned asset more than a currently owned asset, we can sell the owned asset and use the proceeds to purchase the unowned asset. Or, we can make the exchange directly (barter) without going through the medium of cash. Thus, exit values are relevant to the determination of the available funds, and the total available funds are relevant to the determination of goods that one can command. The various combinations of goods that one can command are the market alternatives.

We cannot specify the precise functional form of the total available funds since the ability to borrow may depend upon the values of the owned assets as well as the current debt-equity structure. The ability to borrow may also depend upon the potential lender's forecast of the cash flows from the project. The same is true of the ability to raise equity capital. Despite our inability to express the relationship precisely, we can be certain that the available funds come from these three sources.

The sacrifice required to obtain an asset is specified by the entry value (immediate purchase price) of that asset. That is,

$$s_{it} = n_{it} \text{ if } i \text{ is unowned} \tag{8.2-3}$$

where

$$n_{it} = \text{the entry value of asset } i \text{ at time } t$$

The sacrifice required to obtain a project is the sum of the entry values of the various assets involved in the project. Thus, entry values of unowned assets are relevant to the determination of alternatives. Specifically, if $n_{it} \leq F_t$ then the purchase of asset i is an available alternative.

The sacrifice required to keep an owned asset is specified by the exit value (immediate selling price) of that asset. That is,

$$s_{it} = x_{it} \text{ if } i \text{ is owned} \tag{8.2-4}$$

Owning an asset requires a sacrifice equal to the amount of the exit value. The decision not to disinvest is structurally identical to the decision to invest; therefore, the sacrifice required for keeping an asset is the amount of cash that was not received by not disinvesting. Of course, continuing to own an asset is always a feasible market alternative since the required sacrifice is equal to the available funds from selling that asset. That is, x_{it} is the required sacrifice, and x_{it} is a component of F_t. Therefore, $x_{it} \leq F_t$ in all cases.

In short, for a market exchange to be classified as a feasible alternative, the entry value of unowned assets must be less than or equal to the available funds. Exit values of owned assets are components of the available funds.

Of course, this is perfectly obvious. We all know from ordinary experience that we cannot purchase an asset unless we have funds equal to or greater than the purchase price of the asset. Although this fact is obvious, I have never seen it discussed in the accounting literature. The purpose of elaborating the obvious is to try to get us to focus on first principles. I think that part of our difficulty in accounting has been that we often begin our reasoning in the middle of the problem instead of at the beginning. When I ask colleagues to specify the decision process of purchasing an asset, they always begin with some elaborate (and impressive) discussion of probability distributions, utility functions, systematic risk, and other factors that have to do with consequences. No one has ever begun with a specification of the alternatives. No one has even started with the obvious question of whether or not the purchase is possible— whether or not the available funds equal or exceed the purchase price.

Perhaps the reason for neglecting alternative specifications is that it is too simple and obvious to require mention. Another possible reason is that we take different approaches to the problem. I have taken the "capital rationing" approach, that is, a strict limitation on available funds including a limitation on additional debt. The other approach is to assume that the amount of additional debt is unlimited and the cost of the additional debt causes decision makers to reject alternatives. Under this approach, one calculates the marginal cost of obtaining the marginal debt necessary to obtain the marginal alternative. That marginal cost is added to other marginal costs, and one continues to accept alternatives as long as marginal revenues exceed marginal costs. Under this approach, all market alternatives are available. One can purchase all of GM plus all of GE plus all of IBM and so on. The factor that limits such purchases is that the cost of debt increases until the purchases are unprofitable.

The advantage of this approach is that it reminds us that the more the debt, the higher the cost of debt. It also has the advantage of permitting us to draw continuous curves when we try to represent the decision situation. The disadvantage is that it does not accurately represent the action of lenders. Sometimes lenders refuse to make loans even when offered very high rates of interest. Equity Funding and Penn Central could not obtain a loan from a loan shark, much less from a bank. Of course they were troubled businesses, but their difficulty does illustrate the point that some loans will not be made no matter how high the rate of interest. Thus, there is a limit on additional debt. Their difficulty also illustrates the point that additional debt depends upon extant (net) assets. Ordinarily, lenders will not make a loan without some extant assets—without a "down payment" in the terms of personal finance or a "cushion of safety" in the terms of corporate finance. These extant assets plus the asset purchased from the loan constitute the total collateral to the lender. As one continues to make additional purchases from additional loans, one will eventually exhaust the extant assets. Eventually one will not have enough assets to make the down payment or to provide the cushion of safety. Equity Funding had reached this point; therefore, it could not obtain additional loans. Thus, the amount of additional debt available to a particular borrower depends upon the extant net assets of that borrower. Since those extant assets are finite and since they are exhausted by the process of obtaining additional debt, the available additional debt is strictly limited.

For these reasons, I take the capital rationing approach. I have no fundamental quarrel with the other approach since it highlights the increasing cost of debt and since it satisfies our desire for continuous functions. However, I think that the capital rationing approach is a more accurate description of the actions of lenders. In addition, the capital rationing approach allows a sharp separation of alternative specification from profitability analysis. (It also highlights the role of extant assets, and that is what we accountants account for.) Profitability is concerned with the consequence of an alternative. Forecasting consequences is the *second* step in the decision process. The first step is to determine the available alternatives.

8.2.2 Market Consequences.

The market consequences of undertaking a new project or maintaining an existing project are the forecasted future cash flows that result from that project. There may be nonmarket consequences that the decision maker should consider (for example, one may be sent to jail for engaging in an illegal project, or one may get satisfaction from beating the competition), but I will concentrate on the market consequences. These consequences may also be stated as a general principle.

Profitability Principle: If $s_{it} < d_{it}$, then i is expected to be more profitable than investing s_{it} at the discount rate.[2]

where

d_{it} = discounted value of asset or project i at time t

The future cash inflows come from selling the output of the project as well as selling the inputs at termination or abandonment of the project. Thus, one must forecast the future selling prices of the outputs as well as the future exit values (salvage values) of the inputs. The future cash outflows are the purchases that must be made in order to continue the project. They include the replacement of productive assets as well as the purchase of supplies and labor. Thus, the future entry values of the required inputs are also relevant. Once one has made all these forecasts of future prices (as well as the future quantities to be purchased and sold), the various forecasted magnitudes are arithmetically adjusted to get the discounted value.

The resulting discounted value is then compared to the required sacrifice. The comparison may be stated as a difference

$$d_{it} - s_{it} = \text{net discounted value of } i$$

If the net is positive, i is expected to be more profitable than investing s_{it} at the discount rate. Of course, this is the familiar capital budgeting model.[3] However, the capital budgeting model is almost invariably stated in terms of engaging in a new project. In those cases the discounted value is compared to the amount of cash that must be sacrificed in order to purchase the assets necessary for the new project. That is,

$$d_{it} - n_{it} = \text{net discounted value for } \textit{unowned} \text{ assets}$$

Since it is stated this way, one tends to forget that this decision

2. The more general form was given in Section 7.3: "If the (measured) required sacrifice to acquire project i is less than the discounted value of the (forecasted) cash flows from project i, then (it is forecasted that) one will accumulate more money by acquiring project i than by investing the required sacrifice at the discount rate." Stating the principle in this way makes it clear that we are comparing the consequences of two alternatives. One alternative is to obtain or maintain project i, and the other is to invest the required sacrifice at the discount rate. Thus, "profitable" in this context is a short-hand expression for accumulating more money.

3. The model is stated here in its "net present value" form as opposed to its "internal rate of return" form in order to avoid confusing the process of allocating with the process of discounting. Also, I use "discounted" instead of "present" in order to avoid confusing a temporal location with the discounting process.

model is also applicable to existing projects. Since it is possible to alter or abandon an existing project, the projects should also be reevaluated periodically. In this reevaluation, the decision model specifies the comparison of the *updated* discounted value to the *present* required sacrifice. The updated discounted value may come from an alteration in the forecast or from a different discount rate. The present required sacrifice is given by the exit value of the owned assets. That is,

$$d_{it} - x_{it} = \text{net discounted value for } owned \text{ assets}$$

If one wishes to maximize, one should discontinue the project and sell the assets if the discounted value of the future cash flows is less than the sum of the exit values. As in the case of a new project, a maximizer should not commit the required sacrifice if the sacrifice is greater than the discounted value of the forecasted cash flows. In the case of an existing project, the required sacrifice is the exit value(s) of the owned asset(s).

The symmetry of the two decisions seems to be difficult to grasp. Perhaps it can be clarified by considering Exhibit 8.2-1. If the decision maker does not want to use an unowned asset, the amount of cash that *is* available for investing is the amount that was *not* paid by *not* purchasing. In the same way, when one uses an owned asset, the amount that is *not* available for investing is the amount that was *not* received from *not* selling. To state it the other way, if the decision maker wants to use an unowned asset, the amount that is *not* available for investing is the amount that *is* paid by purchasing. If the decision maker does not want to use an owned asset, then the amount that *is* available for investing is the amount that *is* received from selling.

Thus, n_{it} can be viewed as the required sacrifice from purchasing or as the amount of cash available to invest from not purchasing. Also, x_{it} can be viewed as the required sacrifice from not selling

Exhibit 8.2-1

Alternative Ownership	Use	Invest at the Discount Rate
Unowned	Purchase	Not Purchase
Owned	Not Sell	Sell

or as the amount of cash available to invest from selling. Whichever way one views it the relevant variables are d_{it}, n_{it}, and x_{it} as shown in Exhibit 8.2-2.

8.2.3 Market Risk. The profitability principle specifies the comparison of the discounted value of project i to the sacrifice required to obtain or maintain project i. Other things equal, a maximizing decision maker will select the most profitable projects. However, the decision maker may assess the relative riskiness of the projects and decide to reject the most profitable project on the basis of a higher assessed risk.

Risk assessment is a most difficult task. It is easy to identify the root cause: the future is unknown. Anything that depends on the future is risky because of the simple, straightforward fact that the future is unknown. The question is how does one assess an unknown; that is, how does one assess risk?

The first demarcation is between the unknown future flows and the known, present stocks. The future flows are risky; one purpose of accumulating present stocks is to reduce the risk. As Staubus (*Accounting Decisions*, p. 378) puts it: "Risk and uncertainty in business operations are related to the timing and amounts of inflows and outflows of assets. . . . One method of providing for uncertainty is to carry a stock of an asset, such as cash or inventory, to buffer temporarily unequal inflows and outflows."

The economics-finance approach to risk assessment is to calculate the variance of the future flows. In effect, the decision maker is asked to refine his forecast. Instead of forecasting a single payoff, he is asked to forecast several possible payoffs and assign a subjective probability to each payoff. From the forecast he calculates the expected value and the variance. The variance (or the standard deviation) is taken to be a risk indicator. An expected value with a greater variance is taken to be more risky than one with a smaller variance.

Exhibit 8.2-2

Alternative Ownership	Use	Invest at the Discount Rate
Unowned	d_{it}	n_{it}
Owned	d_{it}	x_{it}

The variance focuses exclusively on the future flows, neglecting the present stocks. On the basis of risk, one would always prefer a present stock to a future flow. But decision makers regularly sacrifice present, known, riskless stocks for future, unknown, risky flows. They deliberately take risks in order to obtain more expected profits. This action suggests that an additional approach to risk assessment is to consider the relationship of present stocks to future flows. Since the root cause of risk is the unknown future, the less that one is dependent upon the future the less the risk. Thus, the degree of dependency upon the future is an indication of risk. Since stocks lie in the present, the greater the stocks the less the risk.

Exit valuation is a measure of the present stock of cash that an owned asset will command. It is the "current cash equivalent," in Chambers's apposite phrase. One can convert an asset into a present, riskless stock of cash, or one can use the asset in order to obtain the future, risky flows. To hold an asset, the discounted value must be greater than the exit value. But events may cause the owner to alter his forecast. If the forecast is changed so that the discounted value is less than the exit value or if it is changed so that the variance becomes intolerably large, the owner can sell for the exit value. This means that the exit value is a measure of the downside risk. It is the amount that can be recovered if the expectations are lowered. The greater the exit value the less the downside risk. Thus, a report of exit values is ipso facto a report of the downside risk.

A decline in exit value means that one has less present, riskless stocks, that one is more dependent upon the future, risky flows. Thus, the greater the decline in exit values the greater the risk. This notion of risk is applicable to the purchase decision and can be illustrated by considering that decision.

Let us consider the market forces that affect the values relevant to the purchase decision. Since the proffered law was concerned with depreciation, let us consider the relative risk and return in the purchase of depreciable assets. We know that, in general, the more specialized the depreciable assets, the greater the risk of purchasing or owning that asset. But we also know that the more specialized the asset, the more efficient it is in accomplishing its specialized task and therefore the more profitable it is to purchase or own that asset. To put it negatively, the more flexible or adaptable an asset—the more uses to which it can be put—the less efficient it is in any given use. Thus, the more flexible the asset, the less the expected return from purchasing or owning that asset. But flexible assets are also less risky.

The relative differences between the various values are indicators of both the return and the risk. When contemplating a profitable purchase, the values will be ordered as follows:

$$d_{it} > n_{it} > x_{it} \qquad (8.2\text{-}5)$$

and there are market forces which tend to increase the differences for specialized assets and to decrease the differences for flexible assets.

The demand for a depreciable asset—producer good—is derived from the demand for the consumer good(s) which it will produce. Thus, the price—both entry and exit—of a depreciable asset is partially determined by the consumer good(s) which it will produce. The price is also partially determined by the supply curve which depends on the cost functions of the manufacturers of the producer good. Looking at the demand side, the process is that each producer forecasts his cash flows from selling the consumer good. The resultant discounted value is the basis for each producer's bid on the depreciable asset. It provides a ceiling on the price the producer is willing to pay; that is, if $d_{it} < n_{it}$ then the producer will not purchase. Only when $d_{it} > n_{it}$ will the purchase be made and $d_{it} - n_{it}$ = producer's surplus in the language of price theory.[4]

One meaning of "specialized" in this context is the relative number of consumer goods that can be produced by a given depreciable asset. A depreciable asset that can produce consumer goods A, B, and C is less specialized than one that can produce only A. If the producer decides to produce A, he must also decide which depreciable asset to purchase. The specialized depreciable asset is more risky because if the demand for A declines, he has no alternatives. He is solely dependent upon continued sales of A. The less specialized depreciable asset can be put to producing B or C if the demand for A declines. Thus, the less specialized asset is less risky since it has alternative uses. But the specialized asset is also likely to have a greater discounted value. The reason for specialization is to gain greater efficiency of production. The more specialized the asset, the lower the cost of production, other things equal. Translating this into value terms, "efficiency" means that there will be less future cash outflows required

---

4. In price theory the explanation is that P^* is the highest price the producer would be willing to pay and P is the market price. Then $P^* - P$ is the producer's surplus. Price theory is an instantaneous analysis. When we add the time factor, the discounted value is the price the producer is willing to pay, hence $d_{it} = P^*$.

Also, price theory assumes infinite divisibility of producer goods which permits profit maximization to be at the point where marginal costs equal marginal revenues. I am not assuming infinite divisibility; therefore, I have stated the decision rule as an inequality.

to operate the depreciable asset. Given the same future cash inflows from selling the consumer good, the lower future cash outflows result in a higher discounted value.

It is often the case that the more specialized the asset, the higher the entry values. In order to gain greater efficiency, we are usually required to make a greater initial investment. "Up front" costs are incurred in order to lower the required future cash outflows. Part of this is due to the breadth of the market. Specialized assets have fewer potential purchasers. Hence the suppliers of specialized assets have a smaller market with the attendant higher costs. Certainly, in the case of an asset that is so specialized that only one is produced (a made-to-specification asset), the cost of production will be much higher than that of a standard, mass produced asset. But only less specialized assets have enough potential purchasers to permit the manufacturer to engage in mass production. Thus, the more specialized the asset, the greater the cost of manufacturing that asset, other things equal. This will raise the supply curve for specialized assets resulting in a higher offering price, that is, a higher entry value to the producer.

In short, the more specialized the asset, the higher the discounted value and the higher the entry value. Both values tend to increase with specialization.

We also noted that when contemplating a purchase, the entry value will be greater than the exit value. If one purchases an asset and resells it immediately, there will be a loss. "I bought a car, and it depreciated $1,600 as soon as I drove it off the lot" is a common expression which illustrates this difference. The amount of the depreciation (decline in exit value) is the car dealer's margin plus twice the transaction costs. The dealer earns a margin—he sells at retail and buys wholesale—which means that the producer buys at retail, and if he resells to the dealer he must sell at wholesale. Thus, $n_{it} > x_{it}$.

In the language of price theory, $n_{it} - x_{it} =$ sunk cost. The cost is "sunk" because it cannot be recovered from the asset. Its recovery depends solely on the future cash flows from the outputs of that asset, that is, on d_{it}. For this reason, the purchase of a depreciable asset, regardless of the degree of specialization, puts the purchaser in a higher risk position. He is exchanging the present for the future. He is sacrificing a *present* value in the amount of n_{it} and receiving a (time adjusted) *future* value in the amount of d_{it}. Since the future is uncertain, he is in a higher risk position. But x_{it} is a present value that can be immediately recovered. Hence the net present value that is sacrificed is the sunk cost. The greater the sunk cost, the greater the risk since the recovery of the sunk cost depends on an uncertain future.

The same result is obtained from looking at the alternatives. In general, the greater the number of alternatives, the smaller the risk. The less specialized asset can produce consumer goods A, B, or C. The purchase of the less specialized asset is tantamount to purchasing a "portfolio" of consumer goods. The less specialized the asset, the greater the "diversification" of that portfolio. The more specialized asset is a higher risk because it is less diversified—it results in putting all of your eggs in one basket. Thus, the greater the number of production alternatives, the lower the risk. In addition to the production alternatives, there are market alternatives. The asset can be sold, and the proceeds used to buy bonds or to buy another depreciable asset. Prior to the purchase the market alternatives, the ability to command goods, are limited by n_{it}. After the purchase the market alternatives are limited by x_{it}. Since $n_{it} > x_{it}$, the market alternatives have decreased. The sunk cost is a measure of the decrease in the market alternatives. The fewer the total (production and market) alternatives, the greater the risk. Thus, the greater the sunk cost, the greater the risk.

Obviously, the producer would prefer to minimize his risk. Thus, he would prefer to minimize his sunk costs. To illustrate assume $d_{1t} = d_{2t} = \$125$ and $n_{1t} = n_{2t} = \$100$. At this point the producer is indifferent. The assets are equally profitable. However, if we add $x_{1t} = \$90$ and $x_{2t} = \$20$, the producer is no longer indifferent. He would clearly prefer asset 1. If he alters his forecast after the purchase, he can recover $90 from the asset. Thus, only $10 depends on the future. He has sacrificed $10 of presently available value in return for $125 of time adjusted future value. Thus, for asset 1, $10 is the amount *put at risk*. For asset 2, he can recover $20 if he alters his forecast after the purchase. Thus, $80 depends on the future—$80 is the amount put at risk. Clearly, one would prefer to sacrifice the smaller amount of presently available value if the future values are equal. That is, the producer would prefer to minimize his sunk costs.

Indeed, the producer would prefer $n_{it} < x_{it}$. If the producer could find such a situation, he would be inclined to become a marketer and abandon his producer role. If he could purchase assets and *immediately* resell them at a greater amount, he could increase his wealth without limit. Since the turnover time is zero, he could sell an unlimited number of assets, and thus no matter how small the margin, the increase in wealth is unlimited. Such happy situations are seldom found because, given freedom of entry into the market, competitors would attempt to do the same thing, with the result of driving n_{it} up and driving x_{it} down until $n_{it} > x_{it}$. Even in near perfect markets, there is a difference amounting to twice the broker's commission. (The price plus the commission is n_{it} and the price minus the commission is x_{it}; $n_{it} - x_{it} =$ twice the commission.) In other markets where the dealer takes title to the goods, there is a delay, sometimes lengthy, between purchase and resale. The dealer cannot immediately resell his goods for a greater amount because of the same market forces.[5] Thus, dealers face a market in which $n_{it} > x_{it}$. The producer faces the same situation. If the producer purchases from a dealer and then immediately resells to the dealer, the difference between the producer's n_{it} and x_{it} is the dealer's margin plus twice the transaction costs.

Given that the market prohibits the producer from avoiding sunk costs, the best that he can do is to minimize them. But the minimization of sunk costs is likely to come at the expense of the maximization of producer's surplus. The producer would prefer the more efficient, specialized asset because of its greater producer's surplus. Unfortunately, the more specialized assets have a tendency to have lower

---

5. An unfortunate implicit distinction in my previous work has caused some misunderstanding in what I mean by "exit values of inventories." The terms "wholesale" and "retail" should clarify what I meant. A retailer purchases in the wholesale market. For illustration, assume that he purchases in carload lots. The retailer's entry value is the wholesale purchase price of carload lots, plus incidental costs such as transportation. The retailer's exit value is the wholesale selling price of carload lots, less incidentals. Thus, the retailer's entry value is greater than his exit value at least by the amount of the incidentals. It may be greater than the amount of the incidentals since he may be forced to sell carload lots (to wholesalers) at less than the price he pays for carload lots (from wholesalers). That is, the retailer may be forced to make up the wholesaler's margin by selling to the wholesaler at the wholesaler's normal purchase price. If the wholesaler permits returns of merchandise for "full credit," the only difference is the incidentals. If the incidentals are zero and returns for full credit are permitted, $n_{it} = x_{it}$ for inventories.

In general, $n_{it} \geq x_{it}$ for inventories and in most cases $n_{it} > x_{it}$. The retailer prefers $n_{it} = x_{it}$ because it puts him in a zero risk situation. If he cannot sell the goods at the retail price, he can return them to the wholesalers without loss. Thus, $n_{it} - x_{it}$ is also a risk indicator for inventories.

The implicit distinction that I am now attempting to make explicit is to differentiate "inventory" and "units." The retailer buys inventory in the wholesale market and sells units in the retail market. He buys carload lots and breaks them down into units. In the language of economics he adds *time* and place utility. The retailer cannot *immediately* sell the units at the retail price. There is a delay between purchase and sale. Hence, the retail prices lie in the future, and, therefore, they are a component of d_{it}, not x_{it}.

A number of people have criticized me for "realizing a profit at purchase" because "exit value of inventory" was interpreted as the retail price of units. I apologize for not making the distinction explicit. I agree with my critics that it is an error to value inventory at retail prices.

exit values and therefore greater sunk costs.

The less specialized the depreciable asset, the more orderly the market for that asset. Certain standard types of depreciable assets are regularly traded in volume, and their exit values are easily determinable. Since these standard types will produce a number of consumer goods, there is a broad base of price support. If the demand for consumer good A declines, the producer can switch to B or C. The producer's discounted values of B and C provide a floor for his asking price. Other producers of B and C are potential purchasers of the asset. The discounted values that other producers assign to B and C provide a basis for their bid price. Thus, from both the supply and demand sides, the ability to produce B and C will support the price of the less specialized asset. For this reason, the exit values of the less specialized assets tend to be higher than those of more specialized assets, other things equal. The breadth of the market will also attract more dealers and better price information. The increased competition among dealers and the better price information tends to decrease the dealer's margin—the difference between the dealer's wholesale purchase price and his retail selling price. Since the producer buys retail and sells wholesale, the decreased margin decreases the difference between his entry and exit values.

The specialized asset has less support for its exit value. If it will produce only one consumer good, the only potential purchasers are other producers of that one good. There is less breadth in the market, less volume, less price information, and less competition among dealers. Therefore, the spread between entry and exit values tends to be greater. In extreme cases of specialization the spread is also extreme. For example, a unique depreciable asset which is built to the specifications of a given producer is likely to have an extreme spread. The entry value of such a unique asset will be higher than that of a standardized, mass produced asset. The exit value will be zero, since no other producer will have the same specifications, and therefore there are no other potential purchasers. Thus, the spread is between a higher entry value and a zero exit value. In such extreme cases the risk is also extreme because the venture depends upon the continuation of the demand for the one consumer good and also upon the continuation of the one type of production process. A change in *either* consumer tastes or in the technology of production may render the asset useless.

In summary, the market forces are such that we can expect n_{it} and d_{it} to increase with specialization and for x_{it} to decrease with specialization. Therefore, the market forces dictate that the more specialized the asset, the greater the difference between n_{it} and x_{it}, that is, the greater the sunk cost. Since both d_{it} and n_{it} tend to increase with specialization, we cannot say that the market forces dictate that the difference between d_{it} and n_{it} increases with specialization. However, we can say that a decision maker will require a greater difference for specialized assets in order to compensate for the increased risk.

The amount put at risk can be stated as an index.

$$(n_{it} - x_{it})/n_{it} = \gamma \qquad (8.2\text{-}6)$$

Gamma will ordinarily vary from 0 to 1 with 1 indicating the highest risk ($x_{it} = 0$) and 0 the lowest risk ($n_{it} = x_{it}$). In general, the more specialized the asset the greater the value of gamma.

The decision analysis to this point has focused on the purchase of a depreciable asset. The choice has been to purchase a more or less specialized asset. Therefore, the n_{it}'s have been relevant to the assessment of risk. To complete the analysis we must also look at the sacrifice. The purchase of an unowned asset requires the sacrifice of an owned asset. Thus, $n_{ut} = x_{ot}$ where u indicates unowned and o indicates owned. The owned asset may be idle cash, cash obtained from additional debt, or cash obtained from selling another asset, that is, the replacement of one asset with another. Or it could be a barter or a partial barter (trade-in). Regardless of the asset given in exchange, its exit value is equal to the entry value of the purchased asset. This allows us to restate the value ordering of an unexpected profitable purchase as

$$d_{ut} > x_{ot} > x_{ut} \qquad (8.2\text{-}5 \text{ restated})$$

as well as allowing us to restate gamma on the basis of a change in exit values.

$$(x_{ot} - x_{ut})/x_{ot} = \gamma \qquad (8.2\text{-}6 \text{ restated})$$

Actually we are comparing exit values over time in (8.2-6 restated). That is, the exchange requires time for it to be effected so that to be complete we should note that x_o is at time t while x_u is at time $t + \varepsilon$ where ε is a small unit of time. Gamma is also useful in assessing risks of holding an asset over time. It is the decline in exit values that measures the amount put at risk whether that decline be occasioned by an exchange or by passage of time. Thus, gamma can be restated again in terms of owned assets declining over time.

$$(x_{ot} - x_{ot+1})/x_{ot} = \gamma \qquad (8.2\text{-}7)$$

The sharper the decline in exit values the more that is being put at risk during the time period. Gamma is useful for comparing the relative decline in exit values. Since the exit values of depreciable assets usually decline over time, $0 \geq \gamma \geq 1$ is the usual case. Occasionally exit values of depreciable assets increase over time. (Perhaps they should be called "appreciable assets.") Such a situation would be indicated by a negative gamma.

In summary, exit values directly display an indication of downside risks since they are measures of stocks of equivalent (riskless) cash. Gamma is an index of the amount put at risk by exchange or by passage of time. These are indications of risk given by the *market*. The variance is a calculation of *individuals'* forecasts of the variability of the payoffs. A major difference between gamma and the variance as risk indicators is that the former is obtained from observations in the market while the latter is obtained from individualistic expectations. Another difference is that the former focuses on present stocks while the latter focuses on future flows. Thus, the risk indicators are different but they are not competing. Just as an individual may assign a (discounted) value to an asset different from the (entry or exit) value assigned by the market, an individual may assess the risk of an asset differently from the assessment by the market. Perhaps the two kinds of risk indicators will be found to be complementary. Even if they are found to be complementary, their combination is likely to be deficient. It appears that risk is a vastly complicated concept that cannot be captured by any single indicator or any combination of known indicators.[6] For the nonce, I will conclude

---

6. To illustrate the complexity of risk analysis, consider a naive application of the variance. Suppose that a decision maker were faced with the choice of the i, j, and k, given the following forecasted outcomes and probabilities:

i: $\$1,000(0.5) + \$2,000(0.5) = \$1,500$
j: $\$1,000(0.5) + \$3,000(0.5) = \$2,000$
k: $\$1,000(0.5) + \$4,000(0.5) = \$2,500$

In order to avoid the arithmetic of discounting, all of the flows are forecasted to occur at the same time. On the basis of discounted values a maximizer would clearly prefer k. That is, $d_{kt} > d_{jt} > d_{it}$. Equally clear on the basis of variances, a risk avoider would prefer i. That is, $V(d_{kt}) > V(d_{jt}) > V(d_{it})$.

Thus, it appears that we have an indeterminate choice. It appears that it depends on the personal reference of the decision maker in regard to maximization versus risk. However, closer inspection reveals that the risks are the same. Only the discounted values differ. More specifically, the worst outcome is the same in all three systems; the probabilities are also the same. The only difference is the payoffs of the best outcome. For this reason, the clear choice ought to be k—it has a greater discounted value with equal risks.

To illustrate the equality of risk, assume that i, j, and k are three casinos. The gamble is to bet on the flip of a fair coin. For a bet of $\$1,000$, the payoff on tails is $\$1,000$ at all three casinos. If heads, the payoff is $\$2,000$, $\$3,000$, and $\$4,000$ at i, j, and k, respectively. This is a case of heads I win and tails I do not lose. Thus,

that exit values are relevant to risk assessment but they are not sufficient for a complete assessment.

8.2.4 Summary. A market decision model specifies the following prices:

(1) The present exit values of owned assets because
    (a) when compared to the entry value of unowned assets, they assist in defining the available market alternatives;
    (b) they completely define the sacrifice required to maintain ownership of the asset;
    (c) when compared to exit values of unowned assets, or compared over time, they provide a market risk assessment occasioned by exchange or the passage of time; and
    (d) they provide an indication of downside risk.

(2) The present entry values of unowned assets because
    (a) when compared to the exit value of owned assets, they assist in defining the available market alternatives; and
    (b) they completely define the sacrifice required to acquire unowned assets.

(3) The present exit values of unowned assets because when compared to the exit value of owned assets, they provide a market risk assessment occasioned by exchange.

(4) The forecasted future entry and exit values associated with the use or operation of a given asset because
    (a) when discounted and compared to the required sacrifice [(1b) or (2b)], they permit a decision in regard to expected profitability; and
    (b) their variance provides a risk indicator.

---

there is *zero risk* at all three casinos. The only difference is that casino k gives the best payoff and casino i gives the worst payoff. For this reason there is no rational reason to select casino i. The problem is that the variance risk indicator shows casino i to be the least risky—it yields an erroneous signal.

The basis for the error seems to spring from the idea that the ability to forecast a specific outcome is associated with riskiness of the expected value. The more peaked the distribution, the more likely the expected value to the payoff. And vice versa, the flatter the distribution. But the ability to forecast the specific outcome is not the sole, nor even the primary, meaning of risk. The notion of risk contains some elusive properties. Part, but only part, of the notion of risk is captured by the variance.

I am indebted to Professor E. E. Williams for discussions of risk and uncertainty. He is of the view that we face uncertainty, not risk, in the market and that therefore all risk analysis is deeply flawed.

9

The Valuation Methods

> Having accepted the principle that the original valuation of assets should not exceed the cost price . . . there remains the more important question as to subsequent revaluations of assets. Should they be put down at the original acquisition price or at some other valuation? If at some other value, shall it be the current market price, the present value to the concern or the price they would bring in liquidation?
>
> HATFIELD, *Modern Accounting*, p. 80

The question of valuation has been with us for a long time. Hatfield's question was published in 1919, and he was not the first to raise it. Our inability to resolve the question has been, in the main, due to our application of criteria peculiar to accounting. We have employed criteria such as matching, conservatism, going concern, and diversity among entities. I propose that we apply the more general, time-tested criteria of science: namely, the interrelated criteria of empirical testability and relevance. In this chapter, I will apply the relevance test to each of the valuation methods that are prevalent in the literature.

9.1 Exit Values

> There is no gain so certain as that which arises from sparing what you have.
>
> PUBLIUS SYRUS

I mean by "exit values" or "exit valuation method" the process of valuing assets at their immediate market selling price. "Depreciation" is the difference between such exit values at two dates. The depreciation for the first period is the difference between the entry value (equal to the exit value of the cash or other asset sacrificed) of the new asset and its exit value at the end of the first period.

From the outline of the decision process presented in Section 8.2, it is clear that exit values are relevant to (1) the determination of the set of available alternatives, (2) the determination of the profitability of existing projects, and (3) the assessment of risks.[1]

9.1.1 Alternatives. Since the consideration of alternatives is so often overlooked in the accounting literature, perhaps it would be well to posit a general law.

> Iron Law of the Market: Asset i can be exchanged for asset j if and only if the exit value of i is greater than or equal to the entry value of j.

The law is simplistic in the sense that it does not tell you anything that you did not already know. In one sense it is a definition. It helps to clarify the meaning of market exchange, exit value, entry value, and asset. In another sense it is a tautology and, as such, is not possible to falsify. In still another sense, the law is quite vulnerable to falsification since it implies that it holds in *all* cases. Given a definition of entry and exit values, one can observe market exchanges to determine whether the definition is violated. If it were found to be violated, we would have to decide whether to change the definition of entry and exit values or to discard or alter the law.

In all of these senses, the law is similar to the general scientific laws. The law of conservation of mass, for example, simply says that within a closed, isolated system, the sum of the changes in mass equals zero. In ordinary experience, this means that if I move my desk from the west wall of my study to the east wall, the total mass in my study does not change—the sum of the increment and decrement is zero. Could anything be more simplistic? It is also definitional in that it helps to clarify the concept of mass as well as the concept of a closed, isolated system. It is tautological in the sense that if something is *not* conserved, either it is *not* mass or the system is not closed and isolated. From this tautology, we could deduce (with the help of a factual premise) that ideas are not mass because they are not conserved. If we move the desk to the bedroom, we could

---

1. It is equally as important here to note what I did *not* say as it is to note what I did say. I have been misinterpreted as having claimed that exit values are relevant to *all* economic decisions. Obviously, exit values are not relevant to all economic decisions. The only thing that I have claimed is that exit values are relevant to *some* economic decisions. I have also been misinterpreted as having claimed that exit values are the *only* values needed to make the various decisions. Obviously, one cannot make a decision by considering exit values alone. My analysis of the decision process specifies *comparison* of exit values to other values.

observe that mass was not conserved in the study and deduce that the study is not a closed, isolated system. In the final sense, the law is quite vulnerable to falsification and has been tested many times. Einstein's work caused some fundamental rethinking about the definition of mass and about discarding the law or altering it from a general to a special case, that is, to restrict its empirical domain to low velocities.[2]

In short, the Iron Law of the Market has the same characteristics as other general scientific laws. It will also serve the same purpose as other scientific laws, namely, to remind us of the nature of the market. In the same way that the law of conservation of mass continues to remind us of the nature of mass, the Iron Law should continue to remind us of the nature of markets.

Another requirement of general scientific laws is that they be logically fertile—that they entail a variety of consequences (see Margenau, *Physical Reality*, pp. 81–84). If we keep the Iron Law before us, perhaps it will prove to be logically fertile for accounting. Let us take a first feeble step by deriving two principles:

Exchange Principle 1: The exit value of any *owned* asset is relevant to all decisions regarding actual or potential exchanges of that asset.

Exchange Principle 2: The entry value of any *unowned* asset is relevant to all decisions regarding actual or potential exchanges of that asset.

Since these principles are nothing more than an elaboration of the obvious, I believe them to be incontrovertible. To put it another way, I believe that they constitute a demonstration of the relevance of exit values of owned assets—a demonstration that others can assimilate, validate, and corroborate.

9.1.2 Profitability. Recall that the profitability principle specifies that the required sacrifice for project i must be less than the discounted value of project i in order to classify project i as a profitable alternative. To make this principle more concrete, let us consider three examples of profitability decisions that specify exit values.

The most general decision regarding an asset is whether to keep

---

2. See Kuhn (*Scientific Revolution*) for a general discussion and specific examples, for example, pp. 131–32 for the tautological nature of Dalton's atomic theory in chemistry. See Caws (*Philosophy*, pp. 82–89) for a discussion of how a law may serve different roles at different times.

it and use it or to sell it and invest the proceeds in some other asset.

Keep versus sell: $d_{it} \gtreqless x_{it}$
  If $>$ keep i
  If $<$ sell i

Observe that this decision model is concerned exclusively with the choice of using an asset versus selling it. It specifies the comparison of the exit value from selling to the discounted value from using. It says that exit values are necessary but not sufficient to make the decision. Obviously, there are a host of other decisions that this model is not applicable to. In addition, there are many more complex decisions. For example, if one were contemplating using the asset to produce product A versus product B, the above decision model is not adequate. In that case, one would need to compare the discounted value of the forecasted cash flows from product A to those from product B. Ceteris paribus, if the discounted value of A is greater than B, one should produce A; and, in a significant sense, the cost of producing A is the foregone discounted value of B. This is the well-known opportunity cost notion. However, comparing the discounted values of A to B assumes that at least one of the discounted values is greater than the exit value of the asset. If the exit value is greater than both discounted values, the asset should be sold.

Consider the objection to reporting exit values, particularly for depreciable assets, because the assets are intended to be used, not sold. Many people then conclude that exit values are "obviously irrelevant." The error in that conclusion is that one cannot decide whether one ought to use an asset or sell it until he has compared the exit value to the discounted value.

Observe also that the decision model is stated in a normative form. It implicitly assumes a profit-maximizing goal. In the unlikely event that the goal is to minimize profits, the inequality signs should be reversed. The model will aid in achieving either goal.

A common variant of the keep versus sell decision is the keep versus replace decision. It can be stated in general terms.

Keep versus replace: $(d_{ut} - n_{ut}) \gtreqless (d_{ot} - x_{ot})$
  If $>$ purchase u
  If $<$ keep o

Here, we are deciding whether to replace the owned asset with an unowned asset. Of course, a prior requirement is to determine that replacement is an available alternative, that is, that $n_{ut} \leq x_{ot}$ or that additional financing is available in the amount of $n_{ut} - x_{ot}$ if n_{ut}

$> x_{ot}$. In case additional financing is required, d_{ut} will have to be adjusted to reflect the cash outflows from servicing the debt. The exit value of the owned asset is relevant to the determination of the additional financing required; or, in more general terms, it is relevant to the determination of whether replacement is an available alternative, as well as to the determination of the relative profitability of replacement.

In addition, the market risk from replacement specifies the exit value. The amount put at risk is $x_{ot} + \Delta\text{Debt} - x_{ut}$. Since x_{ut} is the amount immediately recoverable upon replacement, the difference is the amount that depends solely on the future—the amount depends on d_{ut} for its recovery.

This decision model shows again the error of blindly assuming that owned assets are intended to be used, not sold. Firms regularly replace their owned assets. I have great difficulty understanding the strident assertion "assets are intended to be used and therefore exit values are irrelevant" that is so often encountered in the literature. People who make that assertion must be overlooking the fact that firms adapt to changing technology, changing consumer tastes, and changing prices. If the demand for the consumer good being produced changes, an owned asset may have to be replaced with an unowned asset in order to serve the customers.

If the technology of production changes, an owned asset may have to be replaced with an unowned asset in order to meet the competition. If relative prices change, an owned asset may have to be replaced with an unowned asset in order to minimize costs, that is, to substitute one kind of capital for another kind or even to substitute labor for capital. These decisions are not merely theoretical niceties. Firms regularly make such decisions since they must adapt to changing conditions. In the apt phraseology of Chambers (*Accounting, Evaluation*, p. 81), exit values are a measure of the firm's "adaptive capacity."

I have similar difficulty with the notion that exit valuation "violates the going concern assumption." Even if we accept a strict interpretation of the going concern assumption, it does not mean that firms cannot replace assets. Indeed, if a firm does not replace its assets, it cannot continue—it will cease being a going concern after the present assets are sold (inventory), or wear out, or become obsolete (depreciable asset). Since exit values of owned assets are necessary for the replacement decision and since replacement is necessary for the continuity of the firm, exit values are necessary for the going concern. Exit valuation does not imply liquidation of the firm.

Another variant of the keep versus sell decision is the keep versus rent or lease decision. It also can be stated in general terms:

Keep versus rent: $(d_{ot} - x_{ot}) \gtreqless d_{rt}$
If > keep o
If < rent r

Here, we are deciding whether to keep the $o$wned asset or to sell it and $r$ent an unowned asset. Both d_{ot} and d_{rt} include the cash inflows from using the asset. Since the cash outflows to make the rental payments lie in the future, no present sacrifice is required to obtain the rental asset. Hence, d_{rt} is the net discounted value of renting. For the owned asset d_{ot} includes the future cash outflows for maintenance and upkeep. Thus, $d_{ot} - x_{ot}$ is the net discounted value. As before, we select the largest net discounted value, given a profit-maximization goal.[3]

This decision shows again the error in blindly assuming that the asset is intended to be used instead of sold. The objection to exit valuation is often put in terms of "essential assets." It is said that essential assets cannot be sold; therefore, their exit values are clearly irrelevant—to report them is absurd. There are three errors in this rationale.

First, if the asset is essential to the operation of the firm, it is not essential that it be owned; it could be rented or leased. Firms often lease assets. Exit values are demonstrably relevant to the rent versus keep decision.

Second, if the asset is essential and it is more profitable to own it than to rent it, its exit value should be compared to the discounted value of the forecasted cash flows of the firm as a whole. In most cases, the exit value of an individual asset will be less than the discounted value of the firm. However, this is a marginal analysis; the sum of the exit values of the individual essential assets may be greater than the discounted value of the firm. Moreover, although relatively rare, the exit value of an individual essential asset may be greater than the discounted value of the firm. This situation has often occurred when population shifts have caused large increases in the exit value of owned land. It sometimes happens to firms; it

---

3. Many textbooks present the rental decision as a cost-minimization problem instead of a net discounted-value maximization problem. If the assets are identical so that the cash inflows from renting are the same as those from owning, the results are equivalent. Denoting inflows and outflows by superscripts + and −, we have $d^{+}_{ot} = d^{+}_{rt}$; therefore, we want to compare d^{-}_{ot} to d^{-}_{rt}. But one cannot neglect x_{ot}. An additional cost of owning is the foregone earnings from not investing x_{ot} at the discount rate.

often happens to farms. The reason farmers sell their *essential* land is that its exit value is greater than the discounted value of operating the farm.

Third, in a very real sense, no asset is essential. One can always substitute one kind of asset for another. It is possible to substitute escalators for elevators or to substitute land for both by constructing a one-story building. It is possible to substitute conveyor belts for forklift trucks or to substitute labor for both by moving the goods manually. It is possible to substitute on-the-job trained bookkeepers for college-educated bookkeepers or to substitute capital for both by purchasing a computer. Those who talk about essential assets overlook the substitution effect occasioned by changes in relative prices. Exit values are prices that must be considered in relation to other prices in order to make the substitution decision.

There are a great many other decision models which specify exit values.[4] Indeed, as asserted in Exchange Principle 1, exit values of owned assets are relevant to all decisions regarding actual or potential market exchanges of those assets. The above decision models are merely examples of such actual or potential market exchanges. Instead of continuing to present examples, I ask the reader to assist in the generalization of this analysis by performing the following experiment: (1) Select any managerial accounting textbook which considers "normative" (i.e., profit-maximizing) decision models. (2) Select any decision in that text which requires the purchase of an unowned asset. (3) Reverse the situation so that the asset is owned but the decision is the same. (4) Substitute "exit value" for "purchase price" or "investment" every place that it appears. (5) Determine if a rational decision is possible without the substitution in (4) under the condition of (3).

For example, when you encounter the discussions of the "make or buy" decision in regard to subassemblies, you will notice that one relevant variable is the "investment in the machines" or the "cost [entry value] of the machines." The viewpoint of the decision is whether to purchase the machines necessary to make the subassembly or to buy the subassembly from an outside supplier. To perform the experiment, reverse the situation so that the machines are owned.

---

4. There are also a great many decision models which do *not* specify exit values. The existence of a great variety of decision models caused me (in *Enterprise Income*) to rank the various values. On the basis of the admittedly limited number of decision models examined there, I came to the conclusion that exit values were highest in rank. For this reason, I concluded that they are the last values that should be eliminated when we begin to encounter constraints.

Now consider the same decision of making the subassembly or buying it from an outside supplier. Then substitute "exit value of the machines" for "cost [entry value] of the machines." I think you will find that you cannot make a rational decision without that substitution in this case. I think you will find the same to be true of all other cases. If you find it to be true, you will have provided a corroboration or verification. If not, you will have provided a falsification.

9.2 Entry Values

> Not to be covetous, is money; not to be a purchaser, is a revenue.
>
> CICERO

I mean by "entry values" the process of valuing assets at their current purchase price and defining depreciation as the difference between such market prices. This is Johnson and Bell's ("Current Replacement Costs") recent proposal.

Entry values are equally as measurable as exit values. We can make the same kind of inferences regarding entry values as were discussed in Section 6.2 regarding exit values. Thus, entry values meet the first criterion of being a measurable attribute. As discussed in Chapter 5, I consider this to be a criterion of great importance. Since entry values refer to empirical phenomena, they are much superior to the conventional allocations that we presently report.

I do not, however, understand the relevance of entry values. As noted in Exchange Principle 2, the entry values of all unowned assets are relevant to all contemplated purchases of those assets. But it seems obvious that entry values of owned assets are irrelevant to their sale (since one must sell them for their exit value) and to their purchase (since they are already owned). Thus, the relevance of entry values of owned assets escapes me.

Perhaps the fault is in my inability to understand. Colleagues have been kind enough to try to explain the relevance of entry values of owned assets. Despite their excellent tutelage and despite my sincere attempts to understand, I must confess that the relevance of entry values still seems to be based more on intuition than on a demonstration. I look forward to a demonstration that others can assimilate, validate, and corroborate. When others agree that they have received such a demonstration, it will be clear that the fault lies in my inability to understand. Until then I must conclude that the relevance of entry values is yet to be demonstrated.

9.3 Discounted Values and Forecasting

> If we could reduce the future cash flows to a single
> number at various times through an appropriate dis-
> counting process, earnings for a period could be deter-
> mined by comparing changes in present value, as long
> as changes in the monetary unit were adequately
> considered. This *ideal* is unobtainable by any present
> direct measurement process.
> TRUEBLOOD COMMITTEE, *Financial Statements*, p. 32,
> italics supplied

It has long been held that the discounted valuation method is the
"ideal" toward which accounting should strive.[5] (I use "discounted
value" instead of "present value" to avoid confusing the process of
discounting with the present temporal location.) The proposal is to
forecast the future cash flows, discount those flows by some appropriate
interest rate, and then report assets at the resulting discounted value.
The difference between the discounted values of the firm at two
dates is defined as the income for the period. In regard to depreciable
assets, the difference between the discounted values of the asset at
two dates is defined as the depreciation for the period.

The accounting literature discusses two fundamentally different
kinds of discounted values. Unfortunately, both sometimes go by the
same name. The two can be distinguished by identifying the dependent
and independent variables in the discounting equation. In the first
case, the purchase price and forecasted cash flows are the independent
variables, while the discount rate is the dependent variable. That
is, a discount rate is selected which makes the discounted value equal
to the purchase price. I call this the "dependent-rate" method. In
the second case, the forecasted cash flows and the interest rate are
independent variables. From these independent variables, one calculates the discounted value. I call this the "independent-rate" method.

The dependent-rate method reverts to historic costs. The asset is
initially recorded at its purchase price, and the discounting process
is nothing more than another method of allocating the purchase price.
Thus, the dependent-rate method is properly subsumed under the
discussion of historic costs.

---

5. The Trueblood Committee (*Financial Statements*, p. 32) was quite specific in
conceiving the problem to be one of measurement and urging the adoption of the
ideal if those problems can be overcome: "It may be asked whether periodic earnings
in terms of present value changes can be approximated, acknowledging that presently
known methods do not permit precise measurement. If they can, an advance could
be made toward the ideal."

The independent-rate method results in recording a gain at the time of purchase. We can reasonably assume that a profit maximizer would not incur the risk of purchasing a depreciable asset unless the discounted value is greater than the purchase price. Hence, the asset is initially recorded at its independently determined discounted value which is greater than the cash sacrificed, and the difference is the profit from purchase. If expectations remain constant, this independently determined discounted value is allocated as a function of time. If expectations change, the process is repeated—the different forecast and/or different discount rate is used to calculate a new discounted value. The difference between this new discounted value and the old discounted value results in another gain or loss to be recorded at the time the forecast or rate is changed.

The independent-rate method is under consideration in this section. Also, I will discuss forecasts in the same context, since most of the same points apply to both discounted values and to forecasts.

There is no question about the relevance of discounted values. As we noted in the outline of the decision process in Chapter 8, discounted values are specified by a great many decision models. Every decision requires a forecast. We noted that the profitability principle requires comparing the required sacrifice for project i to the discounted value of project i. Despite this immediate concession that discounted values are relevant, we must inquire further and draw some distinctions. We must ask *whose* discounted values are relevant.

We have already noted that discounted values are not measurements. Instead, they are mathematically adjusted forecasts.[6] As such, they have no present empirical referent—they are "subjective." Opponents usually argue that the subjectivity of discounted values is a sufficient reason for rejection. Proponents readily admit that discounted values are subjective, but they go on to argue that their relevance overshadows their subjectivity. In effect, they argue that relevance is a more important criterion than objectivity.

The basis for the relevance of discounted values is also the basis for their subjectivity—they are forecasts. Proponents correctly note

---

6. The distinction between measurements and forecasts cannot be overemphasized. The literature sometimes speaks of "measuring present [discounted] values," and this unfortunate locution has a tendency to confuse the issues. As Margenau (*Physical Reality*, p. 374) says, the "outcome of a measurement characterizes the state of the observed system at the time at which the observation was made. . . . But never do we say that we are measuring the value of a quantity at a future time."

The point is that the words "measurement" and "forecast" refer to different kinds of operations or different kinds of processes as well as to different temporal locations. To use the same term to refer to such differences is productive of error.

that all decision making requires choosing forecasted consequences. Thus, they say that since forecasting is indispensable to decision making, its relevance is thereby demonstrated. They often go on to speak of the "value" of such information. They allege that knowledge of the future is the most valuable kind of information.[7]

I believe that this formulation is correct. However, I disagree with the proponents when they use this correct formulation as a premise from which to conclude that we ought to report forecasts. I think the conclusion is in error and the source of the error is the failure to make two crucial distinctions: (1) knowledge of the future (i.e., certainty) versus forecasting the future (i.e., uncertainty—the requirement that one makes one's best guess as to what the future holds); and (2) private versus public knowledge or forecasts.

9.3.1 Certainty. Let us first consider knowledge of the future as opposed to forecasts of the future. Suppose that I were fortunate enough to receive daily delivery of *tomorrow's Wall Street Journal.* The knowledge of the future prices of all stocks and commodities reported therein would enable me to increase my wealth almost without limit. Thus, the proponents are correct: the information would be exceptionally valuable. To put it another way, tomorrow's *Wall Street Journal* would fetch an exceptionally high price.

It seems that the proponents of reporting forecasts have some such analogous model in mind. In reading between the lines of some of the pleas presented by financial analysts, they appear to yearn for knowledge of the future because such knowledge would give them a competitive advantage. Their yearning for this valuable knowledge causes them to urge accountants to report such knowledge. Some accountants seem to reason similarly. They set themselves the commendable goal of aiding users by providing the "most valuable" information. They correctly note that the most valuable information is knowledge of the future. They then conclude that we ought to strive to report such knowledge.

The fault in this reasoning is their failure to distinguish private from public knowledge. The exceptionally high value of tomorrow's

---

7. Some of the more extreme proponents say that knowledge of the future is the *only* information that has value. They claim that measurements are irrelevant or valueless to decision making since one must select from forecasted consequences. They overlook the fact that measurements serve as explanations of the past and that such explanations aid in formulating forecasts. They also overlook the role that measurements play in delimiting the alternatives. One must first determine the set of feasible alternatives and *then* forecast the outcomes or consequences of those alternatives. Measurement is indispensable to determining the alternatives.

Wall Street Journal is due to the privacy of the knowledge, not to its futurity. If everyone had access to a daily delivery of tomorrow's *Wall Street Journal,* no one would have a competitive advantage. Since tomorrow's prices would be publicly known with certainty, today's prices would be adjusted (bid up or down) to equal tomorrow's prices less one day's interest at the risk-free rate. Hence, public knowledge of tomorrow's prices would allow one to earn no more than the risk-free rate. As a result, the value of knowing tomorrow's prices would be the same as the value of knowing today's prices. To put it another way, the subscription price to tomorrow's *Wall Street Journal* would be the same as the subscription price to today's *Wall Street Journal.*

The moral for accounting should be clear. If we had knowledge of the future—if we could display future financial statements—then the public reporting of such information would not achieve the objective of providing the "most valuable" kind of information.

We must also consider the motivation to conceal knowledge of the future. Private access to tomorrow's *Wall Street Journal* provides a high motivation to conceal it and no motivation to reveal it. Since keeping it secret would allow one to increase one's wealth almost without limit, the possessor would have no motivation to sell the knowledge. Since making the knowledge public would dramatically decrease its value, potential purchasers would not be willing to pay a high price. Therefore, there would be no economic mechanism to cause it to be publicly reported. In the absence of an economic motivation, we would have to rely on coercion. It is difficult to conceive of an effective way to coerce the possessors of such knowledge to reveal it. Since the knowledge would be private, it would be impossible to identify the possessors of the knowledge. Thus, it would be impossible to know whom to try to coerce. Even if we could identify the possessors, we could not be sure that they had revealed their knowledge: they could lie. They could always claim that they were forecasters instead of possessors of knowledge, and this would provide them with an ironclad defense—we could not punish someone for making an erroneous forecast. The only way that we could know that they had not lied is to possess the knowledge ourselves. But then *we* would be motivated to conceal our knowledge, and the problem of coercing us to reveal it would be shifted to someone else.

The moral for accounting and auditing should be clear. If an auditor assumes the duty of requiring disclosure of private future knowledge, he will have the impossible task of identifying those clients who possess such knowledge. If he could identify such clients, the auditor would have to resort to coercion to get them to reveal the knowledge. But the auditor could not be certain that the clients had revealed the true state of their knowledge. The auditor could not verify the future knowledge unless he also possessed that knowledge. But if the auditor possessed the knowledge, it would be to his economic advantage to conceal it. We would now be faced with the problem of coercing the auditor to reveal the knowledge.

Another point that can be gleaned from the example is that uncertainty is a necessary ingredient for the operation of the market. To put it negatively, public knowledge of the future would spoil the market. If everyone had access to tomorrow's *Wall Street Journal,* then no one would "trade the market" on the basis of tomorrow's prices. Since tomorrow's prices would be publicly known with certainty, the only thing that one could earn would be the risk-free interest rate. Purchasing stock would be equivalent to depositing money in the bank. Thus, knowledge of the future would eliminate the risk of trading the market; and once the risk had been eliminated, the returns for bearing that risk would also have been eliminated. This is what I mean when I say that knowledge of the future "spoils the market." Such knowledge completely changes the character of the market.

Of course, I am speaking only of earning the risk-free rate of return for one day. If there were public knowledge of tomorrow's prices today, we would still trade the market on the basis of forecasts of the uncertain prices at the day after tomorrow and beyond. The result of having knowledge of tomorrow's prices would simply shift everything one day forward. That is, tomorrow's prices would be based on forecasts of an unknown future—only today's prices would be affected by knowledge of tomorrow's prices. Hence, the net effect of public knowledge of tomorrow's prices would be to require traders to forecast from tomorrow into the unknown future instead of forecasting from today into the unknown future. Such a situation would undoubtedly result in calls for the public reporting of day after tomorrow's prices which, if accomplished, would shift everything two days forward and thus would result in calls for the public reporting of the prices three days hence, and so forth indefinitely.

The moral for accounting is that people who desire knowledge of the future cannot be satisfied. If we were able to supply knowledge of the near future, the need for forecasting the distant future would still exist. The people who feel uncomfortable with the uncertainty of the near future would still feel uncomfortable with the uncertainty of the distant future. Indeed, supplying them with knowledge of the near future may create even more discomfort because it is more difficult to forecast the distant future than it is to forecast the near future. Thus, we cannot relieve their discomfort until we can supply knowledge of the future extending to eternity. If we could accomplish that, all market activity would cease. I do not know what kind of world it would be in such a situation, but I do know that it would be quite different from the world in which we now live.

Finally, there is the impossibility of obtaining future knowledge. I have discussed some of the things that would result *if* we had such knowledge. The reason for that discussion was to provide another perspective for those accountants who have long held the belief that all our reporting problems would be solved if we knew the future. I believe that those accountants are correct in the sense that such future knowledge would eliminate the need for accounting. As Shackle (*Decision,* p. 4) says, "Perfect foresight would render decision *empty*." Therefore, the task of providing information relevant to decisions would also be empty. That is, if we had knowledge of the future, we would have no need for decisions and no need for accounting. We would all be unemployed. Before everyone bolts for the unemployment office, let me hasten to repeat that it is impossible to obtain future knowledge. The moral to be drawn from that is we cannot satisfy users who want future knowledge and we should not try. People will continue to yearn for future knowledge, and they will even continue to err in their belief that publicly reported future knowledge will provide them with a competitive advantage. They will continue to be uncomfortable in the face of uncertainty. Accountants may be able to provide them with some sympathy, but we cannot provide them with future knowledge. Therefore, we cannot succumb to the plea that the objective of accounting should be the provision of future knowledge.

9.3.2 Uncertainty. Let us now turn to a consideration of reporting forecasts (one's best guess of an uncertain future state) as opposed to reporting knowledge of the future. We noted above that uncertainty is a necessary ingredient for market operation. Let us inquire further into the nature of that uncertainty.

A market is, in one sense, like a horse race. Not only must the outcome of the race to be uncertain, there also must be disagreement about that outcome. If everyone knew which horse would win—had knowledge of the future—no one would be interested in running the race. Thus, public knowledge of the future "spoils horse racing" in the same way that it "spoils the market." Moreover, in the absence of such knowledge, under conditions of uncertainty, different forecasts are necessary to the running of the race. If everyone agreed which horse would win, the race would not be run. The race is run because different people have different views—different forecasts—about the outcome. To put it another way, if everyone forecasted that horse H_1 would win, no one would be willing to bet on horses H_2, H_3, . . ., H_n. Thus, different forecasts are necessary for the race to be run as well as for bets to be placed.

The market is similar. Not only is an uncertain future necessary for market operation, different forecasts of that uncertain future are necessary. The point can be illustrated by considering a barter.[8] Suppose that person A now owns General Motors stock and person B owns General Electric stock. Suppose that they decide to trade their stocks. From the observation of this exchange, we can infer with certainty that A prefers General Electric to General Motors and B prefers General Motors to General Electric.

If we are willing to assume that the traders are rational—that they prefer profits to losses and more profits to less profits—we can also infer that each person forecasts greater returns from the stock that he has acquired. Thus, from the observation of the exchange and from the reasonable assumption of rationality, we confidently infer three things:

(1) Person A forecasts greater returns from GE than from GM, else he would not have been willing to exchange.

(2) Person B forecasts greater returns from GM than from GE, else he would not have been willing to exchange.

(3) The market price of GM is equal to the market price of GE, else the exchange would not have occurred. That is, if the market price of the two stocks had diverged, it would have profited either A or B to sell his stock for cash and then to purchase the other stock for cash. Since neither did that, since there was a barter, we can infer that the price is equal.

We can convert these forecasts to discounted values.

---

8. The point is even more vivid when one considers short selling. In that case, the long buyer forecasts a price increase while the short seller forecasts a price decrease. Since there must be a long buyer for every short seller, every exchange is made on the basis of diametrically opposed forecasts. Despite the vividness of this example, it is not considered in the text for two reasons: (1) it was discussed at length in *Enterprise Income;* and (2) critics have deemed it to be a unique case—they have not recognized that the same conclusions apply to other situations.

$$(1) \quad GM_A < GE_A$$
$$(2) \quad GM_B > GE_B$$
$$(3) \quad GM_M = GE_M$$

The symbols represent the discounted values assigned by A, B and the market M. Person A must assign a discounted value to GE which is greater than the discounted value that he assigns to GM in order to be willing to exchange. The reverse is true for person B. Likewise, the market price may be considered to be a discounted value—a weighted average of the discounted values of all the traders in the market. Since the current market prices are equal, the market discounted values are equal.

In terms of discounted values, three different, apparently contradictory, expressions are required to describe this simple exchange. Upon reflection, however, the apparent contradiction disappears. In the same way that different people must forecast different outcomes of horse races in order to induce them to bet on different horses, different people must forecast different outcomes of the stock market in order to induce them to bet on different stocks. Thus, different discounted values must exist in order to induce people to hold different stocks or in order to induce people to exchange one stock for another.

The moral for accounting is that the existence of different discounted values tarnishes this "ideal" toward which accounting should strive. I believe that many of the past proposals to report discounted values have overlooked the fact that such values will necessarily vary from person to person and from firm to firm. Many of those proposals read as if the authors thought that there was some single, true discounted value and that the only problem was the practical or empirical one of determining that single, true discounted value. The fact is that there is no single, true discounted value. Instead, there are many true discounted values—probably as many true discounted values as there are participants in the market. Thus, the problem of determining a single, true discounted value is a conceptual one, not an empirical one.[9]

These comments also apply to those who propose that this or that valuation method be used because "it better approximates discounted

9. Alternatively, the proponents of reporting the single, true discounted value may be thinking of the one discounted value that is based on an accurate forecast. That is, they are looking for a discounted value that will turn out to be true when the future becomes the present. If this is what they mean, they are striving to report future knowledge. If they find such a single, true discounted value, the previous discussion about reporting future knowledge is applicable.

values." I have often wondered just how one would test for such an approximation. That is, since these authors admit that they do not know what the discounted value is, how can they know which method best approximates that unknown discounted value? In addition, we need to ask whose discounted value they are trying to approximate. Since the discounted values necessarily vary from person to person and firm to firm, it is impossible to find a single method which would approximate all discounted values. Therefore, we must ask whose discounted value they are trying to approximate.

The moral for auditing is that if we adopt the "ideal," we will be presented with a cruel dilemma. On the one hand, we could perform the audit by preparing an independent discounted value from an independent forecast. Then we could compare our independent discounted value to the one prepared by the client. But what will such a comparison tell us? Unless we possess future knowledge (in which case the problem reverts to the previous discussion), the only thing that we have accomplished by this procedure is to add one more different discounted value to the already large stock of different discounted values. The fact that our independently determined discounted value differed from the client's would not provide justification for denying a certificate. Similarly, if by chance our independently determined discounted value agreed with the client's, this agreement would not be justification for providing a certificate. To put it negatively, suppose that we were fortunate enough to have both A and B as clients. If our independently determined discounted value happened to agree with A's discounted value, it would necessarily disagree with B's discounted value. If we thought that such an agreement provided justification for certifying A's discounted value, we would be forced to deny a certificate to B. This action would be strange since we know that the very nature of the market requires B's discounted value to be different from A's.[10]

---

10. Again, the point is even more vivid when one considers short selling. Suppose that we were auditing both the long buyer and the short seller. Since the long buyer profits if and only if the price increases and the short seller profits if and only if the price decreases, how would we go about auditing them? If we decide to certify one and deny certification to the other, we have, in effect, announced to the world that our ability to forecast the future is better than that of the participants in the market. I doubt that anyone would believe us, but this would not prevent them from suing us when we were wrong. On the other hand, we could not very well certify to both since one *must* be wrong. I originally ran into this problem when I was writing *Enterprise Income*. Since I could not see a solution to the problem, I asked the proponents of reporting discounted values to solve it. I am still waiting for that solution.

It would be terribly high-handed, as well as the assumption of an awesome responsibility, if we appointed ourselves as the final arbiter of the correctness of such exchanges. Thus, we would find ourselves in an untenable position: our independently prepared discounted values would not provide sufficient justification to either grant or deny a certificate. We must then conclude that we cannot perform the audit by comparing the client's figures to our independently prepared discounted value. What is the alternative? Without an independently prepared discounted value to compare to the client's, the only thing that I know that we could do is to check the arithmetic. That is, we cannot verify the forecasted cash flows since our independently prepared forecasts would be no better than the client's and since such forecasts will vary from client to client. We cannot determine the appropriate discount rate since it is also an individual matter reflecting the client's preferences for future consumption over present consumption or reflecting a target rate of return below which the client will not go. As I go through the list of things that we cannot do in verifying discounted values, I always come to the sad conclusion that we can only check the arithmetic. The British have evidently reached the same sad conclusion. Accountants there are limited to checking "the accounting bases and calculations for the forecasts" (Rule 15 of the City Code of London, quoted by Stamp and Marley, *Accounting Principles,* p. 196). If that is all we can do, the auditing process is rendered vacuous.

Perhaps there is another alternative that I have not been able to identify. As I see it, however, the cruel dilemma is (1) to prepare an independent discounted value which does not provide justification for either granting or denying a certificate or (2) to only check the arithmetic, which renders the auditing process vacuous.

The existence of differences in discounted values raises serious questions about their relevance. Of course, it is clear that *A*'s discounted values are relevant to *A*'s decisions, but it is not at all clear that *B*'s discounted values are relevant to *A*'s decisions. First, *A* knows that the inequality signs must be reversed in order for the exchange to occur. That is, *A* knows that *B* expects GM to outperform GE from the very fact that *B* is willing to exchange GE for GM. And *B* knows the same thing about *A*'s forecasts. Thus, the act of exchange (or the refusal to exchange) *is* public reporting of the direction of the expectations of the participants. Since this information is publicly known and since the exchange occurs despite the public knowledge, it is clear that each participant considers his forecast to be superior to the other's forecast. *A* must consider his forecast to be better than

B's because if *A* thought that *B*'s forecast were better, *B*'s willingness to exchange would cause *A* to be unwilling to exchange. The same is true for *B*.

The horse race analogy still fits. If GM and GE are the names of the only two horses in the race and if *A* and *B* agree to a wager, each knows that the other forecasts a different outcome. *A* knows that *B* expects GM to outperform GE from the very fact that *B* is willing to bet on GM. Since *A* bets on GE despite his knowledge of *B*'s forecast, *A* must think that his forecast is superior to *B*'s. If *A* thought that *B* had a superior ability to forecast the outcome, *B*'s willingness to bet on GM would cause *A* to refuse to bet on GE.

The conclusion is clear: *A*'s forecasts, or discounted values, are relevant to *A*'s decisions, while *B*'s forecasts, or discounted values, are irrelevant to *A*'s decision. And vice versa for *B*. More generally, one's *private* forecasts are relevant to one's decisions. *Public* forecasts of others are not relevant.

On another level of analysis, others' forecasts are quite relevant. When knowledge of others' forecasts would yield a competitive advantage, the information would obviously be relevant. In a higgling situation, for example, it would be to *A*'s advantage to have knowledge of *B*'s forecasts or discounted values. But since *A*'s knowledge would be to *B*'s disadvantage, *B* would be unwilling to reveal it. And vice versa.

Some have suggested that we force both *A* and *B* to reveal such information. Two points are in opposition to this suggestion: (1) as discussed supra there are grave problems in attempting to coerce people to reveal such information; and (2) if both revealed it, then neither would have a competitive advantage—both would be in the same competitive position as they would have been without the revelation.

To illustrate the second point, consider the discounted values in Exhibit 9.3-1. As before, *A* owns GM and *B* owns GE. There are

Exhibit 9.3-1

Trader \ Stocks	GE	GM
A	$150	$100
B	$100	$125

no established market prices; instead they are higgling over the prices. With our Olympian knowledge of their assigned discounted values, we know that the price range for GE is between $100 and $150. B would be unwilling to sell GE for less than $100, and A would be unwilling to pay more than $150. We cannot specify the price they will agree to, but we can specify the range. Similarly, we know that the range for GM is between $100 and $125.

If A knows B's discounted values and B does not know A's, A has a competitive advantage. He can offer to purchase GE for $101 and to sell GM for $124, knowing that B would be inclined to accept. And vice versa for B. However, if both have knowledge of the other's discounted values, they revert to the same position as before—they higgle over the prices with the range being between $100 and $150 for GE and between $100 and $125 for GM. Neither is better off.

Given that neither is better off, we can question the wisdom of attempting to coerce people to reveal such information. It seems especially unwise since publicly reporting this kind of information is directly contrary to the tradition of the market system under which we operate. The entire fabric of our market system—from high-level economic theory to the folklore of the eastern "yankee trader" and the western "horse trader"—is based on *shrewd* trading. We have made a virtue out of the wily horse trader's ability to conceal his true estimate of the horse's value. From the notion of the self-interest invisible hand of Adam Smith to the present day abstruse theorems of information economics, we see economists elaborating the obvious: the present owner is motivated to conceal or minimize bad news about the asset he is attempting to sell, while the potential purchaser is motivated to conceal or minimize good news about the asset he is attempting to purchase. To overcome this motivation in regard to *news* is extremely difficult; to overcome this motivation in regard to *forecasts* would require that we change the economic system from one of self-interest to one of altruism. I do not assign a high probability to that prospect.

9.3.3 Extensions. The problem of reporting forecasts or discounted values goes beyond the simple trading situation illustrated. The major oil companies have taken diametrically opposed positions on various sources of energy. Since some oil companies have invested heavily in coal gasification and eschewed investment in oil shale while others have done exactly the opposite, their respective forecasts or discounted values must have been different. Since automobile manufacturers have employed opposite strategies in the production of small automobiles, their forecasts or discounted values must have been different. We can infer the direction, but not the details, of their discounted values from observing the actions that they take. Thus, the actions taken *are* a public reporting of forecasts albeit not quantified forecasts. We can also infer that each company thinks that its forecasting ability is better than the other's. If Shell thought that Exxon's forecasting ability was better, Shell would employ the same strategy as Exxon. Thus, Exxon's forecasts are not relevant to Shell's decisions. And vice versa.

On another level of analysis, if access to Exxon's forecasts gave Shell a competitive advantage, those forecasts would be relevant to Shell's decisions. And vice versa for Exxon. But since neither firm would want to give the other a competitive advantage, both would be unwilling to reveal the details of their forecasts. Both have incurred substantial costs to gather the information necessary to make the forecasts and to do the analysis, and both feel that they have a proprietary interest in that analysis. In such cases it seems to be (1) impossible to get the firms to voluntarily report such information and (2) inappropriate for accountants to try to coerce them to report it.

We must also face the problem of trying to audit such figures. Only time will tell which forecasts are correct. Remember that Ford Motor Company produced both the Mustang and the Edsel—the Mustang being the most successful automobile model in the post-World War II era and the Edsel being the most unsuccessful model in that era. Ford forecasted that both models would be successful, else they would not have undertaken to produce both. Given such wide variations in the consequences of such undertakings, the problems of trying to audit their forecasts or discounted values seem totally insurmountable.

9.3.4 Summary. Knowledge of the future would be relevant to decision making if it were available. Private knowledge of the future would be extremely valuable to the possessor. However, public reporting of such knowledge would dramatically decrease its value—it would not be the most valuable kind of information that we could report. Instead, the ability to report future prices would be equally as valuable as the ability to report present prices. Regardless of considerations of value, it is impossible to obtain knowledge of the future; therefore, it is impossible to report it.

One's private forecasts of an uncertain future are relevant to all decisions. Indeed such forecasts are indispensable to the decision process. However, forecasts prepared by others are not relevant to one's decisions. Different forecasts are necessary to the operation of the market; and each participant can infer the direction, but not the details, of other participants' forecasts from the action that they take. Further information about the details of others' forecasts might give one a competitive advantage; but if all forecasts were publicly reported, all participants would be in about the same position as they were prior to the report. Thus, there are serious questions about the relevance of publicly reported forecasts.

9.3.5 Different Discount Rates.

Up to this point we have examined the reporting problems caused by different forecasted outcomes—"heterogeneous expectations" in the language of finance. Another source of reporting problems is the application of different discount rates. Even if all decision makers forecasted identical outcomes—had homogeneous expectations[11]—their discounted values would differ if they applied different discount rates.

Empirical evidence for the variation of discount rates is given by Hausman ("Individual Discount Rates"), for example. In the purchase of energy-saving consumer durables, Hausman found that the discount rate was quite sensitive to income levels. Hausman's findings are given in Columns 2 and 3 of Exhibit 9.3-2. In Column 4, I have assumed that each investor forecasts a net cash inflow of $125 one year hence. Column 5 displays the discounted value of these homogeneous expectations. The point of Column 5 is to show that identical assets and identical forecasts have dramatically different discounted values.

These differences raise questions about the relevance of *reported* discounted values. It is clear that A's discounted value is relevant to A's decision, but it is equally clear that B's discounted value is irrelevant to A's decision. Therefore, we must ask why we would want to report B's discounted value to A. The discount rate is personal to each individual decision maker. (The rates displayed in Exhibit 9.3-2 are actually means for the income class. Hausman found that the rates were different for each individual.) Since the rates are personal,

---

11. The finance literature often *assumes* homogeneous expectations. Some accountants have taken this assumption to be an accurate description of the expectations of decision makers. There is ample evidence that expectations are heterogeneous. Careful examination of the finance literature which assumes homogeneous expectations reveals that the reason for making the assumption was to make the model tractable, not to accurately describe the expectations of decision makers. Other researchers, for example, Lintner ("The Aggregation"), in the area of finance have included heterogeneous expectations in their models.

Exhibit 9.3-2

(1) Person	(2) Income Class*	(3) Discount Rate*	(4) Forecasted Outcome	(5) Discounted Value
A	$ 6,000	89%	$125	$ 66
B	$10,000	39%	$125	$ 90
C	$15,000	27%	$125	$ 98
D	$25,000	17%	$125	$107
E	$35,000	8.9%	$125	$115
F	$50,000	5.1%	$125	$119

*Source: Hausman ("Individual Discount Rates," table 8)

then the discounted values are personal. Reporting these personal discounted values would not allow receivers to discriminate among assets. At best, it would allow receivers to discriminate among people who own the asset. If the objective is to report something about assets, then it is absurd to report different values for identical assets with identical forecasts.

Those who advocate reporting discounted values think that they can resolve these problems by using "the market rate of discount." Staubus (*Accounting Decisions,* p. 208) writes: "The answer to this reasoning is that the accountant must use the market discount rate, not that of any one investor, and that the investor's personal choice of rate for the type of asset or liability in question cannot be significantly higher than the market's or he will have no investment." The "market rate of interest" is undefined. There are two broad interpretations: dependent rate and independent rate.

One interpretation is that rate which sets the present price equal to the discounted value, analogous to the "yield rate" or "effective rate" for bonds. Staubus (p. 209) suggests this analogy: "In fact, in cases in which both [market prices and discounted values] are readily available, such as quoted bonds, discounted future cash flow equals current market value." If this is the proper interpretation of the market discount rate, then I have no objection to reporting discounted values because the discounted value is *by definition* the current market price. To illustrate, assume that the current market price of the asset is $100 and that it yields a cash flow of $125 one year hence. Then the market discount rate is $(125/100) - 1 = 25\%$. The discounted value is $125/1.25 = \$100$, the current market price.

In general, the yield rate or effective rate is a dependent variable. The price and the future cash flows are the independent variables. In order to calculate the effective rate for a given bond issue, we must first obtain the current market price from the market and the future cash flows from the document. Once the two independent variables have been obtained, the yield rate is a straightforward calculation. If we now discount the future cash flows by the yield rate, we obtain the current market price. Therefore, employing "the market rate of discount" under this interpretation is unnecessary. Why should we go to the trouble of (1) observing the market price, (2) calculating the yield rate, and (3) calculating the discounted value when the results of Step (3) are necessarily equal to the observation of Step (1)?

Another interpretation of "the market rate of discount" is that it is an independent variable, such as the prime or risk-free rate. If the prime rate were 10 percent, the discounted value of $125 one year hence is $114. The arithmetic is easy but I do not know why we would want to report this figure. It would not be relevant to anyone's decision. It would not be relevant to A's decision to buy or keep the asset; and if A reported it, B would also find it irrelevant.

In the bond market we now observe different prices for bonds that have the same terms. A low-grade corporate will have a higher yield rate (lower price) than a high-grade corporate with the same coupon rate and same maturity date. If we discount both the high grade and the low grade by the same (prime) rate, we will obtain the same discounted value. This would conceal the differences in risk. It would report sameness where difference exists. Therefore, it would be at best irrelevant and at worst misleading.

In summary, I find the dependent-rate discounted value to be unnecessary and the independent rate to be irrelevant. The dependent rate is relevant because the discounted value is equal to the market price, but it is also unnecessary for that same reason. The independent prime or risk-free rate results in a discounted value that is irrelevant to the potential purchaser's decision to purchase or the potential seller's decision to sell, as well as being irrelevant to the receivers of the reports. The independent personal rate results in a discounted value that is relevant to that individual but irrelevant to the receivers of the reports. In addition, the discounted values obtained from independent personal rates are not empirically testable. Therefore, I conclude that discounted values should not be reported.

There is, however, one application of the discounting process that I would like to encourage, namely, to estimate a market price. Consider, for example, a noninterest-bearing receivable with a known due date and known amount but no readily observable market price. Practice has been to report the face amount of that receivable and this has resulted in abuses and scandals. Real estate developers, for example, reported the face amount of long-term, high-risk receivables, and this practice became known as "front-end loading" of income. My suggestion at the time of that scandal was to report the exit value of those receivables, that is, the amount that would be received from factoring them. Since their exit value was about 10 percent of their face value, no front-end loading would have occurred. Staubus is concerned about this problem, but his suggested solution is to discount the receivables at the "market rate." If his objective is to estimate the market price (exit value) of those receivables, I agree and applaud his efforts. Under this interpretation, the application of the discounting process has the same objective as the application of Sterling's law—the prediction of an exit value.

9.4 Conventionally Allocated Past Purchase Prices

> We are not talking of truth, but of meaning: meaning which is the antecedent condition of both truth and falsehood, whose antithesis is not error but nonesense.
> LEWIS, *Rehabilitation*, p. 157

I use the rather long phrase, conventionally allocated past purchase prices, to refer to what is usually called "historic costs," that is, the various figures that we report on financial statements. The attempt is to clearly distinguish historic costs qua unallocated past purchase prices from historic costs qua allocated past purchase prices. When I use "historic costs," I am referring to the latter meaning.

I must confess that I do not know the meaning of historic costs. Of course, I can cite the definitions given in the literature, but these are internal definitions, viciously circular. The clearest example is the definition of an asset as anything with a debit balance after the books are closed. Other definitions are equally circular. For example, "unexpired costs" is defined as the amount of the purchase price that has not yet been expensed. But "expense" is defined as cost that is expired, and therefore to say "not expensed" is to say "not expired." Since "un" and "not" are synonyms, the definition says that an unexpired cost is an unexpired cost. Caws (*Philosophy*, p. 46) draws the distinction and states the problem: "Definitions of terms by reference to other terms belonging to the same language system (for example, the language of physics) are *internal* definitions, and one might, by using this kind of definition alone, build a whole ingrown language whose terms referred to each other but to nothing else. Definitions which go outside the language system to something else—perception, for instance—are *external* definitions, and they are required if the whole system is to mean anything." Since I am unable to find any external definitions for such terms as expired and unexpired costs, I am unable to determine the meaning of such terms. This absence of meaning is probably the reason that "truth" has been expunged from the accounting vocabulary, since the antecedent condition of truth and falsehood is meaning. Since the antithesis of meaning is nonsense, I must reluctantly conclude that historic costs are nonsense.

Historic costs also fail to meet the criterion of relevance. In previous applications of the relevance test, I was unable to discover any decision models which specified historic costs. There are some decision models that specify past purchase prices, usually in a series, but I did not find any decision models which specified conventionally allocated past purchase prices. Despite a diligent search, I did not discover any propositions that said, "If the book value (or depreciation) of asset x is greater than . . ., then . . ." Since I was unable to examine all of the decision models in the world, I could not prove conclusively that historic costs are irrelevant to all models. For that reason I asked for assistance from other accountants by asserting that historic costs are irrelevant to all decision models and then challenged the readers to prove me wrong (Sterling, "ASOBAT Review," p. 110–11). I deliberately stated the proposition in universal form so that it would be easy to prove it false. Only *one* example of relevancy is required to prove the proposition false because it says that historic costs are irrelevant to *all* decision models.

People have responded to my challenge in various ways. Professor Roman Weil has correctly pointed out that income taxes are based on historic costs. (See footnote 13 infra.) The most common response, however, is to reverse the burden of proof. Respondents have said that since historic costs are currently in use[12] and since I am the one arguing for change, it is my duty to prove that historic costs are irrelevant instead of their duty to prove that historic costs are relevant. That is an excellent strategy for them to employ because I cannot possibly supply such a proof.

---

12. Some respondents cite the fact that historic costs are used as prima facie evidence of their usefulness. They fail to distinguish between decision models and decision makers. See Section 8.1 supra.

I cannot supply a proof because of the structure of the two competing propositions. Compare the following analogous propositions: "all swans are white" and "there exist some green swans." The first proposition is easy to falsify—one must discover only one nonwhite swan. The second proposition is impossible to falsify. If I examined as many as one million swans and found them all to be white, I would not have disproved the second statement because if I examined another million swans, I might discover a green swan. Even if I examined the second million and found all them also to be white, it possible that I would find a green swan in the third million, and so forth indefinitely. Thus, the structure of the two propositions is such that one is highly vulnerable to falsification while the other is impossible to falsify.

Scientists are aware of the differences in the structure of such statements. It is such differences that cause Popper (see esp. *Logic*) and others to argue that falsification, as opposed to verification, should be the major empirical criterion of science. Laws are stated in their universal form—they include or imply the word "all." It is impossible to verify universal propositions. As noted above, the proposition "all swans are white" cannot ever be completely verified. Although one can never completely verify the proposition, its universal form makes it peculiarly vulnerable to falsification. It requires the discovery of only one nonwhite swan to falsify it. For this reason, scientists would be receptive to propositions such as, "Cephalic indexes are irrelevant to all decision models." They would recognize the ease of falsification. They would also recognize the impossibility of falsifying propositions such as, "Cephalic indexes are relevant to some (at least one) decision model." Since it is impossible to falsify that proposition and since its verification requires only one instance, they would require the person who believes the proposition to be true to come forth with a demonstration of its truth.

It is for this reason that I repeat the assertion and the challenge: historic costs are irrelevant to all decision models.[13] If it is true that

---

13. I, of course, freely admit that historic costs are specified by various statutes, notably the internal revenue code. There are many reasons for excluding legal specifications from scientific inquiry. The most general reason is that statutes may be at variance with scientific laws, such as the anti-evolution ("monkey law") statute or the attempt to legally define the value of π as 3.0. More specifically, taxes can be based on a great variety of things. Compare, for example, our present tax statutes to the ancient French tax statute which based the tax liability on the number of windows in the owner's house. We would agree that in such a situation the number of windows is relevant to paying taxes and that taxes are relevant to economic decisions. However, the number of windows per se is not relevant to any known economic decision model.

historic costs are relevant, it is easy to falsify my assertion. If it cannot be falsified, we must conclude that, on the basis of presently available knowledge, historic costs do not meet the scientific test of theoretical import or relevance. To scientists the failure to meet this test was sufficient reason for them to cease calculating and reporting cephalic indexes. I think that it ought also to be sufficient reason for accountants to cease calculating and reporting historic costs.

Thomas (SAR #9, p. 114–15n) has reached the identical conclusion by a different route. After considering the allocation problem in painstaking detail, he concluded that historic costs are "nonsense" and asked: "Is it simplistic to suggest that, in the long run, the least dangerous way to stop reporting nonsense is just to stop reporting nonsense?" A long time has passed since Thomas reached that conclusion and asked that question.[14] The conclusion has not been refuted, and the question has not been answered. If the discipline of accounting is to make progress, if it is not to become completely stagnant and sterile, we must answer such questions. We must *demonstrate* that our figures are not nonsense. If we cannot, we must stop reporting nonsense.

9.5 Conventionally Allocated Current Purchase Prices

> Things that are done, it is needless to speak about
> . . . things that are past, it is needless to blame.
>
> CONFUCIUS

I refer here to what usually goes under the name of "replacement costs," that is, the various allocation and reporting procedures suggested by Edwards and Bell (*Theory and Measurement*), Revsine (*Replacement Cost Accounting*), the SEC, and others. The thing common to such proposals is that they are allocations of current purchase prices instead of allocations of past purchase prices. Thus, replacement costs in this sense are quite similar to historic costs. (The other sense of replacement costs is the measurement and reporting of unallocated current purchase prices which was discussed in Section 9.2.)

In the same way, historic costs are relevant to taxes, and taxes are relevant to decisions; but historic costs per se are not relevant to any known economic decision model.

14. In reply to Thomas, I would answer in the affirmative. The question *is* simplistic. But I would hasten to refer him to similar questions in the history of science. "The hardest part is not to answer but to conceive the question. The genius of men like Newton and Einstein lies in that: they ask transparent, innocent questions which turn out to have catastrophic answers" (Bronowski, *The Ascent of Man*, p. 247).

Since replacement costs are identical to historic costs except for the temporal location of the purchase price, almost all of the criticism that has been leveled against historic costs can also be leveled against replacement costs. We previously (Section 6.1) noted that allocated figures are not measurements. Thus, replacement costs fail the first criterion of empirical testability. In regard to the relevance test, I have never seen anyone display a decision model that specifies replacement costs as inputs. It seems that the main thrust of replacement-cost proponents is a desire to update accounting reports. They want to present current data instead of past data. They have not been directly concerned with the relevance test. Although I applaud their efforts in this direction—I would much prefer current information to outdated information—I think their lack of attention to the relevance test is a fundamental flaw in an otherwise noble effort. To put it in Brodbeck's (*Readings*) terms, a current cephalic index is no better than a past cephalic index. To put it in Thomas's (SAR #9) terms, current nonsense is no better than outdated nonsense. Perhaps I am wrong about the relevancy of replacement costs. Obviously, the proponents believe that they are relevant. But this belief seems to be based on intuition. Since I do not share that intuition and since I have not been able to discover any well-formed decision models which specify replacement costs, I must conclude that at the present time the relevancy of replacement costs has not been demonstrated.

There is one interesting hypothesis which can be interpreted as an attempt to demonstrate the relevancy of replacement costs. Revsine (*Replacement Cost Accounting*) believes that replacement-cost income may be used to forecast distributable operating flows. If this hypothesis is found to be true, replacement-cost depreciation will be relevant to the forecast of distributable operating flows (net cash inflows less cost of replacing the equivalent productive capacity). It will also become empirically testable albeit in a slightly different sense.

The distinction is between "theoretical terms" and "empirical terms." The latter are directly empirically testable, being subject to direct observation or measurement. The former are not directly measurable. Instead, they are indirectly empirically testable since they lead to an outcome that is directly observable or measurable. Density can be used to illustrate a theoretical term. Since it leads to the ability to predict an observable outcome—objects floating or not floating—it is both relevant and empirically testable. If someone proposed that density be calculated as, say, the product instead of the quotient of weight and volume, we could empirically test which method of calculation is the better predictor of floating. Similarly, different methods of allocating the current purchase price of new assets could be subjected to the empirical test of the best predictor of distributable operating flows.

This is an interesting hypothesis that has some careful reasoning behind it, but at the present moment, that is all it is—an interesting hypothesis. We must await the outcome of the tests before we decide whether it ought to be discarded (as the cephalic index was discarded) or added (as density was added) to the store of scientific concepts.

9.6 Physical Capacity

> There is no less merit in keeping what we have got, than in first acquiring it. Chance has something to do with the one, while the other will always be the effect of skill.
>
> OVID

Some entry-value and replacement-cost proponents utilize the value measures as an indication of physical capacity of the firm. They argue, in effect, that monetary measures are nothing more than a measure of the firm's ability to command physical goods and that one should look through the monetary veil to see the physical goods that can be commanded.

The proposal has been with us, in one form or another, for a long time. Many price-level adjustment proposals were based on the ability to maintain physical capacity. Inflation was seen to be eroding the capacity of the firm, and the solution was to adjust the monetary measures to reflect the real (that is, physical) measures. In the great LIFO-FIFO debate, physical capacity was a major factor. Many LIFO proponents based their argument on the ability to maintain physical capacity. "Fool's profit" was a monetary measure which exceeded the firm's capacity to replace its inventory. A partial solution was LIFO, and the natural progression was from LIFO to NIFO—next in first out—which was permitted in some special cases. NIFO is, of course, merely another name for the entry value or replacement cost of inventory.

Physical capacity measurement is still championed by many accountants at the present time. The argument has been stated in several ways. One is based on the capital maintenance concept. The argument is that the firm must maintain its physical capacity. If it does not, it will dwindle and eventually die. Thus, the firm's revenues must be directed toward replacing physical capacity before dividends are paid. The firm's ability to pay dividends—its distributable operating flows—is given by the revenue left after provision for replacing physical capacity. Another way is based on the opportunity cost concept. If a firm takes a unit out of stock to sell it, the opportunity cost of selling that unit is the purchase price necessary to replace it.

A third way is based on the entity concept. One looks to the income of the entity as opposed to the income of the proprietors. The entity is "better off" if and only if it increases its physical capacity. If it increases its money but that money will not purchase any additional physical capacity, the entity is no better off. From this concept came the proposals for price indices specific to the entity. The kinds of goods purchased by a particular entity formed the "market basket" from which the price index for that entity was calculated. This is considered to be the relevant index because it reflects the actual purchases of the entity. To put it negatively, the consumer price index is considered to be irrelevant to the entity because the entity does not purchase consumer goods. The GNP implicit deflator is irrelevant because it is too general. The market basket of the GNP implicit deflator includes all goods, and the entity does not purchase all goods. The wholesale price index is better, but it is also too general. Thus, one forms a price index specific to the entity and uses that index to adjust monetary measures to reflect physical capacity. Such adjustments result in income only to the extent that they reveal increases in physical capacity.

The argument for inventory can be clearly stated. Assume that a firm buys 100 units for $1.00 each and sells them for $1.50 each. The monetary measure is $150 − $100 = $50. That is, the firm started with $100, ended with $150, and the monetary profit is the difference. But suppose that the purchase price (wholesale) had increased to $1.20 per unit. The physical capacity measure is 125 − 100 = 25 units. That is, the firm started with the ability to command 100 units, ended with the ability to command 125 units, and the physical profit is the difference. In order to reflect the change in physical capacity in monetary terms, one needs to deduct the replacement cost of the inventory from the revenue. Thus, the physical capacity measure expressed in money is $150 − $120 = $30. Dividing $30 by the $1.20 replacement cost per unit yields the ability to command an additional 25 units, which is equivalent to the direct measure of physical profit obtained by subtracting 100 units from 125 units.

The same result is obtained from a price level adjustment by an entity specific index. In this case there is only one good; therefore, we can calculate an index that perfectly reflects the entity's purchases.

It is the price relative, p_1/p_0, where p_1 is the purchase price at time of sale and p_0 is the purchase price at the time of the original purchase. Denoting the quantity sold by q, the historic cost of goods sold is $p_0 q$. Adjusting by this perfect index is accomplished by multiplying $p_0 q$ by p_1/p_0 which yields $p_1 q$, the replacement cost. Thus, the same physical measure is achieved by specific indices as by replacement costs.

It is clear that units of inventory are a measurable attribute. There is no difficulty in counting the inventory purchased, nor is there any difficulty in determining the inventory purchasable. Thus, physical capacity meets the first criterion of empirical testibility. In addition, the ability to replace inventory is relevant. In the terms used in this essay, one thing that we need to know is the available alternatives. Ability to replace the inventory is another way of stating whether or not replacement is an available alternative. The problem is that the physical capacity method specifies one available alternative; it does not specify the available alternatives. To put it another way, it assumes that the firm will replace the units sold with *identical* units. It also assumes a *markup-turnover firm model;* that is, the firm purchases in one market (e.g., the wholesale market), and sells in a different market (e.g., the retail market). If either of these apparent assumptions are violated, the measure of physical capacity runs into serious problems.

9.6.1 The Firm Model.

Instead of a markup-turnover model, consider a firm that buys and sells in the same market, for example, a trader in the stock or commodity market. Suppose a trader buys 100 shares of GM for $1.00 per share at time 0 and sells them for $1.50 per share at time 1. The physical capacity measure will show a zero profit. The firm started with the ability to command 100 shares and ended with the ability to command 100 shares, and its physical capacity profit is the difference of zero. That is, if we apply the same concepts and same terms that we applied to the inventory case, we reach a profit of zero despite the increase in price. Indeed, even if the price decreases, we reach a profit of zero. Any positive price will yield a zero profit because the cost of replacing *identical* units in this kind of firm is always equal to the revenues from selling.[15] The only occasion in which there will be a physical capacity profit is when the price goes to zero. With a zero price, the number of units purchasable

---

15. Or if one takes the difference between entry and exit values into account, there is always a loss equal to twice the commission regardless of whether the price increases or decreases.

increases; therefore, shares purchasable at time 1 are greater than shares purchased at time 0. Otherwise shares purchasable at time 1 will always equal shares purchased at time 0; therefore, the physical profit will always be zero.

The same result is obtained from the specific price index. The retail sale price per unit is not separate from the wholesale price per unit. Therefore, the monetary profit is $p_1 q - p_0 q$. Adjusting the cost by the specific price index of p_1/p_0 yields $p_1 q - (p_1/p_0)p_0 q$ which reduces to $p_1 q - p_1 q = 0$ in *all* cases.

The consequent of a zero profit in all cases is absurd. The consequent of a positive profit only when the price goes to zero is absurd. Thus, physical capacity measures are not applicable to firms that buy and sell in the same market.

The reason we consider physical capacity measures to be absurd in such cases is that they are irrelevant to decisions. The decision to sell 100 shares of GM was based on the trader's comparison of GM's discounted value to its exit value. If he found GM's discounted value to be less than its exit value, he would sell and invest the proceeds at the discount rate. Or he may purchase GE if its discounted value is greater than that of GM even though GM's discounted value is greater than its exit value. Or he may sell GM and purchase bread and meat if he desires consumption more than investment. As we run through the variables relevant to the decision, we do not find the specification of the number of shares of GM that can be replaced. In such markets the replacement of number of shares is irrelevant because one does not replace *identical* units. The desire for identical units is satisfied by deciding not to sell rather than deciding to sell and repurchase. Thus, physical capacity measures are irrelevant for this type of firm.

9.6.2 Different Units. Consider the replacement of units in a firm that buys wholesale and sells retail. As long as the firm replaces identical units, we can calculate an empirically testable physical profit as demonstrated above. But what happens if the firm changes the kind of units that it purchases? A change in the kind of units purchased does not violate the going concern assumption. It is a regular occurrence in long-established firms. Macy's and Gimbels purchase and sell mini skirts one year and then purchase and sell maxi skirts the next year. Both have been going concerns for a long time. How does one employ a measure of physical capacity when the units are minis in one year and maxis in the next year? It is easy enough to subtract minis from minis or maxis from maxis, but grave problems arise when the firms switch from minis to maxis. For example, Macy's purchases 100 minis for $1.00 each and sells them for $1.50 each. The purchase price for maxis is $1.20 each. The arithmetic is the same as before: $150 − $100 = $50 monetary profit; 125 units (maxis) − 100 units (minis) = 25 units of physical profit; in monetary terms physical profit is $150 − $120 = $30 which, when divided by $1.20, yields 25 units.

Thus, there is no difficulty with the arithmetic. But what does the arithmetic tell us about the physical capacity of the firm? Is the capacity greater or smaller or equal? Since the units are not commensurable, there is no unambiguous answer. We may be willing to accept the ambiguity in this case because the units are similar—both are skirts—and the small difference makes it seem reasonable. But at some point this measure will yield such absurd results that we will be forced to seriously examine the nature of the ambiguity. For example, suppose that after selling the mini skirts, Macy's decides to replenish its inventory by purchasing coats at $75.00 each. The units are similar—both are clothing—but the difference is great. The capacity for purchasing minis was 100 units; the $150 revenue will purchase 2 coats; the loss in capacity is 98 units. Expressed in money $150 − $7,500 = −$7,350 which when divided by $75 replacement cost per unit yields the same result of −98 units.

The same problem arises in attempting to adjust by an entity specific price index. The price of minis was p_0 at time 0, but at time 1 there are no minis to be purchased; therefore, p_1 does not exist. The price of maxis is p_1 at time 1, but at time 0 there were no maxis to be purchased; therefore, p_0 does not exist. Thus, there is no specific price index because the price index for minis lacks a numerator and the price index for maxis lacks a denominator. We can overlook the fact that the units are incommensurable and form a specific price index of the ratio of the price of minis to the price of maxis. The resulting profit will be the same as above. We can also prepare a specific price index of the ratio of the price of coats to the price of minis. This will also yield the same results—a loss of $7,350 or 98 units.

The results are absurd. The problem is that the units are not identical. It is impossible to obtain an unambiguous measure in any firm that does not replace with identical units. A large number of firms, perhaps most firms, are thus excluded. Car dealers purchase and sell 1978 models in 1978, while they purchase and sell 1979 models in 1979. Toy dealers purchase and sell hula hoops one year, while they purchase and sell skateboards the next year. Last year's propellers are this year's jet fans in firms that sell airplane parts, and last year's slide rules are this year's hand-held electronic calculators in firms that sell office and engineering supplies. Last week's fresh strawberries are this week's fresh cherries at the grocery. And so on for a great number of firms.

In general, physical capacity measures are not applicable to firms that adapt to a changing market. Some markets change relatively slowly; thus, there may be some firms which can utilize physical capacity measures in the short run. Eventually, however, the market will change, causing either a discontinuity in the measure or ambiguous results. Abrupt changes in the units will cause absurd results.

9.6.3 Inventory Adjustment—Increasing Costs.

Up to this point we have considered the problem after the units have been sold. Under these conditions the adjustment is made to cost of goods sold. Let us now consider the case in which the units have not been sold. Under these conditions the adjustment is made to the inventory. I will continue with the same example. The firm has purchased 100 units at $1.00 each and the replacement cost of identical units is $1.20 each at the end of the period. The proposal is to write up the inventory from $100 to $120. The incremental $20 is a monetary adjustment that does not reflect a change in the physical capacity of the firm. The firm started with 100 units and ends with 100 units, so the number of units has not changed. Thus, the firm is no better off in physical capacity. For this reason the increment in the monetary measure is not income to the firm. Instead, it is an adjustment to the owners' contributed capital. The comparative balance sheets are shown in Exhibit 9.6-1. All of the previously stated arguments apply. If the firm sells these units, it will have to pay $120 to replace them, so the revenue in excess of $120 is the amount of distributable operating flows.

Exhibit 9.6-1

	t_0	t_1
Cash	$ -0-	$ -0-
Inventory	100	120
Total Assets	$100	$120
Contributed Capital	$100	$120
Retained Earnings	-0-	-0-
Total Equities	$100	$120

A major benefit of this method of reporting is said to be that it will assist management in establishing prices. The markup should be based on the replacement cost in order to put the firm in the same physical capacity position. Thus, the retail price should be set at $1.20(150%) = $1.80. This price is expected to yield total revenues of $180. These total revenues will permit the purchase of 150 units ($180/$1.20). Had there been no increase in replacement cost, the expected total revenues would have been $150 [= $1.00(150%)100 units]. That revenue would permit the purchase of 150 units (= $150/$1.00). In short, applying the same markup rate to replacement costs leaves the firm in the same physical capacity position as it would have been if there had been no price increases. If the firm does not apply the markup rate to replacement cost, if it unthinkingly applies the rates to historic cost, it will be better off by only 25 units (= $150/$1.20). Thus, the firm ought to apply the markup rate to replacement cost in order to maintain the same physical capacity. Moreover, the firm should be able to sell the units at that price because their competitors who are just now purchasing the units will have to pay the replacement cost, and the competitors will be forced to base their markup on that figure. The firm can meet the competition at the higher retail price.

This discussion is intended to show that the *firm* is equally as well off from following this pricing policy. The *owner* is not equally as well off. The distributable operating flows will be $60 (= $180 − $120) if the replacement cost increases, while the flows would have been $50 (= $150 − $100) had the purchase price remained constant. Thus, if the profit is distributed, the owner will receive $10 more as a result of the replacement-cost increase.

The owner is more interested in his capacity to purchase bread and meat than he is in his capacity to purchase units of inventory. Thus, the better-offness of the owner is more accurately reflected by the consumer price index than by the specific price index. But the owner will always prefer $60 to $50. In the consumer goods market, the owner is a price taker. Regardless of where the consumer price index stands at a given moment in time, $60 will always purchase more consumer goods then $50. Thus, the owner would always be better off from constant markups on increasing replacement costs. This would be a Utopian method of accounting: The firm would be equally as well off and the owner would be better off. Many physical capacity proponents seem to have this situation in mind. They want to assist management in its pricing policy by revealing the replacement cost necessary to maintain physical capacity. This will result in the markup being based on replacement cost. They want to assist owners in earning greater profits since a constant markup rate applied to a large base results in greater profits. Needless to say, many managers and owners are strong supporters of this method of accounting.[16]

9.6.4 Inventory Adjustment—Decreasing Costs.

To date all of the arguments for measuring physical capacity that I have seen have been couched in terms of increasing replacement costs. In times of inflation it is rather natural to think exclusively about increasing prices. Even in times of inflation, however, some prices decrease. Dealers in electronic calculators provide a ready example since their prices have decreased dramatically in the recent past.

Let us consider the case. The firm has purchased 100 calculators at $1.00 each, and the replacement cost of identical units is $0.60 each at the end of the period. Applying symmetrical concepts, the proposal is to write down the inventory from $100 to $60. The decremental $40 is a monetary adjustment that does not reflect a change in the physical capacity of the firm. That is, the firm started and ended with 100 units, so the firm is no worse off in physical capacity. For this reason, the decrement in the monetary measure

---

16. They are particularly enthusiastic in regulated industries. Since I am known as a current-value advocate and since most managers do not know that there are different kinds of current values, I have received a number of requests to act as consultant in the installation of replacement-cost/physical-capacity systems. What the managers and owners want to do is to write up the assets to replacement cost and use that figure in calculating their selling prices. Since the public utility commissions allow them to earn a "fair rate of return," the application of that rate to an increased asset base results in higher selling prices. Since the write-up is taken to capital instead of income, the same result is achieved if the public utility commission figures the return on equity rather than assets.

The managers and owners also want to deduct the increased replacement costs from the increased revenues in order to report an acceptable profit to the public and the public utility commission. In addition, they and other nonregulated firms hope to eventually convince the Congress to levy the income tax (but not the property tax) on the basis of replacement costs. The argument is that the present tax law is confiscating capital instead of taxing income since the firms cannot maintain their physical capacity.

This would be a truly Utopian system. Managers would be happy because they could increase their reported assets without an accompanying sacrifice and they could increase their selling prices. Owners would be happy because they could increase their reported equity without an accompanying reported or taxed profit and they could increase their dividends. Both would be happy with the prospect of paying lower taxes. Accounting practitioners and consultants would be happy with the prospect of the increased fees from installing such systems. Accounting theoreticians would be happy because of the rarely received support of owners, managers, and practitioners for their theoretical proposals. Perhaps consumers and taxpayers would not find this system Utopian, but you cannot please everyone.

is not a loss to the firm. Instead, it is an adjustment to the owner's contributed capital. The comparative balance sheets are shown in Exhibit 9.6-2. All of the previously stated arguments about profits apply. If the firm sells the units, it will have to pay $60 to replace them; so the revenue in excess of $60 is the amount of the distributable operating flows.

The same is true of the pricing policy arguments. The markup should be based on the replacement cost in order to put this firm in the same physical capacity position. Thus, the retail price should be set at $0.90 [= $0.60(150%)]. This price is expected to yield total revenues of $90. These revenues will permit the purchase of 150 units (= $90/$0.60). Had there been no decrease in replacement cost, the expected total revenue would have been $150 [= $1.00(150%)100 units]. That revenue would permit the purchase of 150 units (= $150/$1.00). In short, applying the same markup rate to replacement costs leaves the firm in the same physical capacity position as it would have been had there been no price decrease. Thus, the firm ought to apply the markup rate to replacement cost in order to maintain the same physical capacity. Moreover, the firm will probably be forced to sell at that decreased price because their competitors who are just now purchasing will be able to acquire the units for $0.60 and will base their markup on that figure. Thus, the firm will have to sell at the decreased price in order to meet the competition.

All of this discussion is intended to show that the firm is equally as well off from following this pricing policy. Thus, the arguments are symmetrical—they result in the same conclusions whether it be

Exhibit 9.6-2

	t_0	t_1
Cash	$-0-	$-0-
Inventory	100	60
Total Assets	$100	$60
Contributed Capital	$100	$60
Retained Earnings	-0-	-0-
Total Equities	$100	$60

a replacement-cost increase or decrease.[17] Once again, the owner is not equally as well off. The distributable operating flows will be $30 (= $90 − $60) if the replacement cost decreases, while they would have been $50 (= $150 − $100) had the replacement cost remained constant. Thus, if the profit is distributed, the owner will receive $20 less as a result of the replacement-cost decrease. Since $50 will always purchase more consumer goods than $30 regardless of what changes have occurred in the CPI, the owner will always prefer $50 to $30 in distributable operating flows. Thus, the owner will always be worse off from constant markup rates on decreasing replacement costs.

9.6.5 Firms Versus Owners. This reveals a fundamental choice that we accountants face: Whose wealth and income should we attempt to measure? The concepts of wealth and income must refer to a specific person or a specific group.

These concepts are indicated by ordinary linguistics when we speak of the wealth and income *of* the nation or the wealth and income *of* GM or the wealth and income *of* Sterling. Obviously, we cannot speak meaningfully of wealth and income unless we have a specific object for the preposition *of*. Until we supply the object for that preposition, we cannot begin to measure wealth and income. The choice revealed here is the firm versus the owner. Should we measure the wealth and income of the firm or the wealth and income of the owner? The firm, at least in its corporate form, is known to be a

---

17. This should not come as a surprise. It is simply a recognition of the fact that price changes of goods owned do not affect the quantity of goods owned. One has the same physical capacity (number of units) before and after the price change. The only case in which physical capacity is changed is when the price goes to zero.

Although rare, there are actual cases of prices going to zero. Recall the sharp decline in prices of hula hoops after that fad had peaked. At the end of the fad the price of hula hoops was zero—they were free. There were literally millions of hula hoops that could not be sold at a price greater than zero. Suppliers offered hula hoops to retail toy stores at a zero replacement cost. One retail chain store with which I am familiar had an inventory of hula hoops at the time the price went to zero. It decided to increase its inventory by "buying" additional hula hoops at a zero replacement cost. The supplier was happy to get rid of them. The retailer's idea was to resell them at a zero retail price, that is, to give them away as a promotion.

This firm was in fact able to increase its physical capacity because the replacement cost went to zero. However, it also gave away its inventory which it had previously purchased for a price greater than zero. Physical capacity proponents would be forced to argue that the firm had made a profit since it had increased its capacity. The owners thought they suffered a loss since they gave away their previously acquired inventory. I side with the owners.

fictitious person. We can postulate that this fictitious person's maximand is physical capacity. Since this fictitious person is not a consumer, we can conclude that ability to command consumer goods is irrelevant. Since it does not consume the goods that it deals in, it has no declining marginal utility for those goods. Its utility is a linear function of the quantity of goods. The prices of those goods are not pertinent except insofar as the prices affect the quantity that it can command when it holds cash. It is indifferent to price changes of goods that it holds in inventory since those changes do not affect the quantity. Its pertinent price index is the price relative of the good that it deals in since it is only interested in its ability to command that particular good.

This does not describe the owner. The owner is a real person, a consumer. For any particular good, the marginal utility declines with the quantity owned. The owner qua consumer will get less satisfaction from owning the second calculator than he gets from owning the first; the hundredth calculator will provide minimal marginal utility. Thus, the owner qua consumer would be quite happy to exchange the hundredth calculator for a pound of meat. The consumer prefers a variety of goods. The way to obtain a variety of goods in a market economy is via exchange. The medium of exchange is money, and the ratio of exchange is price.

Just as the firm is indifferent to price changes, the owner is indifferent to quantity changes. It makes no difference to the owner whether it is 100 units that can be sold for $1.50 each or 2 units that can be sold for $75 each since both yield $150. The command over consumer goods is equal; therefore, the owner is indifferent to the quantities held by the firm.

If the owner qua consumer owns a good and its price goes up relative to the prices of other goods, the owner is better off because he can command a greater quantity of *other* goods, and vice versa if the price of an owned good declines. The best available measure is money. The owner prefers a monetary measure of the firm to a physical measure of the firm because the monetary measure better reflects his ability to command a variety of goods. Of course, if the price *level*, as opposed to the price *relative*, changes, we need to adjust the monetary measure to more accurately reflect the changes in his ability to command the variety of goods. But since it is a variety of goods that is of interest, it is clear that the pertinent price index is not specific to the firm's normal purchases but rather a general index that reflects the owner's normal purchases. This seems to me to imply the use of the CPI. It certainly does not imply a specific price index.

9.6.6 Summary. The measurement of physical capacity has severely limited applicability. The measure is applicable only when prices are increasing, the firm replaces identical units, and the firm buys in one market and sells at a markup in another market. If the firm buys and sells in the same market, the measure yields absurd results. If the firm replaces with different units, the calculation yields incommensurable results. If the prices are decreasing, the measure does not reflect the owner's loss in command over consumer goods. Therefore, measuring physical capacity is a special case that cannot be generally applied to the measurement of wealth and income.

10

Financial Statements:
The Balance Sheet

> The basic objective of financial statements is to provide
> information useful for making economic decisions.
> TRUEBLOOD COMMITTEE, *Financial Statements*, p. 13

We now turn to the question of the form and content of financial
statements. I agree with the Trueblood Committee that the basic
objective of financial statements is to provide information useful for
making economic decisions. In my terminology, the objective is to
provide information relevant to decision models.

10.1 The Firm Model

> The price of the employment of models is eternal
> vigilance.
> BRAITHWAITE, *Scientific Explanation*, p. 93

Since the proffered law was concerned with depreciation and since
I still believe that working through specific, simplified firm models
offers great promise (see *Enterprise Income*, pp. viii–ix), I will sharply
restrict the range of consideration. The firm that I will consider has
only two assets—cash and a depreciable asset—and no debt.[1] It sells
an immediately perishable good for cash; hence, there is no inventory
to account for. Since all sales are for cash, there are no problems

---

1. I am assuming debt to be zero to simplify the case and to make the exposition
easier. However, since there has been some misunderstanding of how I would report
debt on an exit value balance sheet, I will state my view without going into detail
on my reasons. I have proposed that debt be treated as a negative asset, as a deduction
in COG. Thus, debt should be recorded at time *t* at the amount that would be required
to discharge that debt at time *t*. For example, if outstanding bonds can be purchased
at less than their face value at time *t*, I would report the debt at the market value
of the bonds. If the bonds can be called at less than their market value, I would

in accounting for receivables. For the same reason, by assumption, there are no problems in accounting for revenues. Depreciation is the major expense. Other expenses, such as wages, are paid in cash and, by assumption, offer no complications. Examples of real world counterparts of this firm are an airline, a taxi company, a car rental agency, and a building-rental trust. An airline, for example, sells a seat on a flight. If the seat is not sold, it perishes upon takeoff. The airline, therefore, maintains no inventory. Its major assets are cash and airplanes. Its major expenses are depreciation and wages. The same is true of a taxi company. If time passes without acquiring a passenger, the service perishes. It, therefore, maintains no inventory. Its major assets are cash and automobiles. Its major expenses are depreciation and wages. The point is that although this is a simplified case, it is not an unrealistic case—there are real world firms of this type.

The purpose of such a simplification is to permit us to focus tightly on the question of the value, and changes in value, of the depreciable asset. Since the quantity of cash and its increments (revenues) and decrements (wages) present no problems, the only problematic asset is the depreciable asset and the only problematic expense is depreciation. In addition, the simplification allows us to be quite specific as the occasion demands. We can discuss the general characteristics of the firm model as well as present particular figures when they assist in the exposition.

The final simplification is to assume a stable price level. The process of accounting for exit values is separable from the process of adjusting for price-level changes. Although both are needed, price-level adjustments are straightforward mechanics once the objective of the reports has been established. A general discussion of my views on price-level adjustments is in *Enterprise Income* (pp. 331–50). A less detailed discussion is given in "Relevant Financial Reporting." The reasons and mechanics presented in these sources are also applicable to this firm model. Chambers's "capital maintenance adjustment" ("NOD, COG and PuPU") is a short-cut technique that yields identical results.

---

report the debt as the call value. In general, debt should be reported at its "discharge value," and the arguments for that reporting method are almost identical to the arguments for reporting exit values of assets. See Vickrey ("Two Views" and "Realizable Market Value") for further discussion of discharge values.

10.2 Assets—Items of Wealth

> The war waged between practical men and theorists
> has arisen in large measure from the ambiguity of the
> word *wealth* in ordinary speech, and the confusion
> which has continued to obtain between the fixed,
> definite idea of *value in exchange,* and the ideas of
> utility which everyone estimates in his own way,
> because there is no fixed standard for the utility of
> things.
>
> COURNOT, *Mathematical Principles*, p. 8

The left hand side of the balance sheet is an array of the categories of assets, their values and their sum. Define

$$X_{ft} = \sum_{i \in f} x_{it} \qquad (10.2\text{-}1)$$

where X_{ft} is the total assets of firm f at time t. It is the sum of the exit values of all assets that are an element, ε, of firm f. In the case at hand, we have

Cash	x_{1t}
Depreciable Asset	x_{2t}
Total Assets	X_{ft}

Cash presents no problem. As demonstrated in the previous chapters, the exit value of the depreciable asset is (1) empirically testable and (2) relevant to a number of decision models. Thus, the only additional question to be considered is the sum, X_{ft}.

It is surprising and distressing to find so little discussion of the total asset figure in the accounting literature. Since total assets is one of the central concepts of accounting, one would expect to find a good deal of explanation and interpretation. The fact is that there is practically none. The literature does contain a large number of disclaimers. We are often told what the total assets is *not* intended to represent, but we are seldom told what it *is* intended to represent. It is this lacuna in the literature that causes me to want to be quite explicit about what I propose to measure and report.

The attribute that I seek to measure and report is Command Over Goods (COG), that is, value in exchange. Obviously, the quantity of cash is a measure of COG. The exit value of the depreciable asset is also a measure of COG, as was discussed in Section 8.2. When the two are added, the sum is intended to be a measure of the firm's total COG. That is, if the exit value of a depreciable asset is added to the cash on hand, the sum is intended to represent the firm's total ability to command goods in the market, neglecting additional financing. The legitimacy of such an addition is an empirical question and will be discussed below.

COG is relevant to all decisions regarding actual or potential market exchanges. When compared to entry values of goods offered in the market, COG specifies the goods that could be acquired—it determines the available market alternatives. It is also relevant to the determination of the profitability of owned assets as well as the determination of relative risk. This relevance was demonstrated for individual assets in Section 8.2. The question of the relevance of total COG will be discussed below.

10.3 Empirical Testability—Additivity

> The answer to the problem of determining descriptive validity lies in Campbell's argument that calculations such as addition and subtraction are acceptable only upon empirical verification. That is, the additivity of the property under examination must be empirically verified before similar calculations can be attributed any descriptive validity. The general character of such empirical verification involves an independent measurement of the quantity of property exhibited by the combination of systems which possess that property. . . . We conclude that verification of descriptive validity necessarily requires empirical operations in the form of independent measurements that prove the additive nature of the property being measured.
>
> LARSON, "Descriptive Validity," pp. 487–88

The first criterion to be applied is the empirical testability of X. (I will omit the subscripts unless we are talking about different firms or different times.) The common name for this criterion is "additivity." Speaking loosely, the question is whether it is legitimate to add the exit values of the assets.

In regard to exit values, this question has been examined by Larson and Schattke ("Current Cash Equivalent"), Chambers ("Continuously Contemporary Accounting"), Vickrey ("Measurement Discipline" and "A Comment"), McKeown ("Additivity"), and others. I also discussed the issue in *Enterprise Income*, pp. 360–61. The problem is, in essence, that exit values are market prices and they have all the characterisitcs of any market price. One characterisitic is a downward-sloping demand curve under conditions of imperfect competition. This means that within a commodity class, the quantity offered affects the price. For example, the exit value of two units of inventory (sold together) is not equal to twice the exit value of one unit. The same problem is encountered when we consider sales of different commodity classes. For example, the exit value of an inventory plus the exit value of a warehouse (sold separately) is not necessarily equal to the exit value of the inventory and warehouse (sold together). The exit value of the firm as a whole (all assets sold together) is not necessarily equal to the sum of the exit values of the individual assets sold separately.

Empirical testability is the root of the additivity question. It can be stated in general as:

$$\mu A + \mu B = \mu(A \ \cent \ B) \qquad (10.3\text{-}1)$$

where μ is a measurement operation, A and B are objects to be measured, and $\cent$ is a specified means of combination. The additivity question is whether or not (10.3-1) is an equation. If the magnitudes are equal, the attribute measured by μ is said to be "additive."

For example, the attribute length is additive because when two rods are measured separately and the numerals obtained are added, the sum is equal to the numeral obtained from the measurement of the two rods joined end to end. In this case, the specified interpretation of $\cent$ is "joined end to end." Obviously, length is not additive if $\cent$ is interpreted as joined side to side. By contrast, the attribute temperature is not additive. If $\cent$ is interpreted as pouring liquids A and B together, the temperature of $\mu(A \ \cent \ B)$ is not equal to $\mu A + \mu B$. More generally, there is no known interpretation of $\cent$ which results in (10.3-1) being an equation when temperature is the attribute measured.

It is clear that additivity is nothing more than an elementary example of the empirical testing of predictions. The sum of μA and μB is a prediction—the anticipation of unobserved phenomena. The empirical test of that prediction is to measure $\mu(A \ \cent \ B)$ and then to compare the numeral obtained to the numeral obtained from summing μA and μB. If they are equal, the prediction is verified. After a sufficient number of verifications of this kind, we gain enough confidence to deem the attribute to be additive, that is, to accept the prediction as true without verifying it each time.

The empirical nature of the test cannot be overemphasized. The literature contains a number of discussions that list necessary but not sufficient conditions for additivity—for example, sameness of attribute. The insufficiency of such characteristics can be demonstrated by considering the addition of temperature. It is, of course, possible to add 7° and 5° and to obtain a logically true sum of 12°. The same attribute has been added. However, that is not sufficient to satisfy the additivity criterion. The symbol "12°" has no known empirical referent; and, therefore, it suffers from all of those deficiencies discussed throughout this essay. First, we cannot adjudicate disputes. For example, I could argue that temperature is multiplicative instead of additive. It is logically true that the product of 7° and 5° is 35°, just as it is logically true that the sum is 12°. So, 12° and 35° are both logically true; and in the absence of an empirical test, there is no way to determine which, if either, is right. Second, the numerals also illustrate the close connection of empirical testability and relevance—both 35° and 12° are irrelevant. They have no known use since they are not specified by any extant law or theory.

10.3.1 Additivity of Exit Values. We noted above that exit values are not additive when ¢ is interpreted as selling together. That is, $\mu A + \mu B \neq \mu(A \text{ ¢ } B)$ where μ is exit value and ¢ is the act of selling together. However, there is another interpretation of ¢ that does result in an equation. We can define ¢ as combining the *output* of A and B instead of interpreting it as combining the objects A and B.

Outputs are regularly combined in science. The by now familiar example of potential energy illustrates the case. There is no known way of combining objects which embody potential energy. An elevated ball embodies potential kinetic energy, and a battery embodies potential electrical energy. We can measure the potential energy of each, but we cannot combine the ball and the battery and measure their combined potential energy. However, we can combine the energy *output* of each and that output is additive. We can add the ergs. The sum of work performed by the energy output of each separately is equal to the work performed by the energy output combined. Thus, potential kinetic energy and potential electrical energy meet the additivity criterion where ¢ is interpreted as combining the outputs.

The same is true of objects which embody identical kinds of energy. Coal and oil are both sources of potential heat energy. Under ordinary industrial conditions their combination is not additive. Although it is possible to burn oil in a coal burner, it is not "efficient." That is, oil will not perform as much work as it will when it is burned in an oil burner. Thus, if ¢ is interpreted as *burning together,* potential heat energy is not additive. However, if ¢ is interpreted as burning separately in their respective burners, potential heat energy is additive. The Btu's are additive. The sum of the work performed by the separate outputs is equal to the work performed by the combined output.

The empirical test (experiment) for this can be outlined as follows:

Object $A\rightarrow$Energy received from $A\rightarrow$Work performed by A

Object $B\rightarrow$Energy received from $B\rightarrow$Work performed by B

At the object stage, there are serious questions about the additivity of potential energy. To continue with the coal and oil example, we could say that A has 100 Btu's and B has 200 Btu's, but if we interpret ¢ as burn together, the total Btu's will be different from 300. At the output stage of energy received, however, we do have additivity. The experiment is trivial: (1) Burn A and B separately and measure the separate Btu's. (2) Sum the numerals obtained in (1). (3) Combine the heat output (in a combustion chamber) obtained in (1) and measure the Btu's of that combination. (4) Compare the sum obtained in (2) to the measure obtained in (3).

Since we will find an equality in (4), we can say that potential heat energy is additive under the interpretation that ¢ means to burn separately and combine the energy received. Once we have performed a sufficient number of such experiments to satisfy ourselves that the result is general, we can accept the prediction as being true without verifying it in every case. That is, we can move from having combined energy received to the anticipation of combining energy receivable. This permits us to sum the energy receivable and use it in decisions, for example, to decide whether to keep the objects or to burn them and receive the heat energy. For objects A and B it permits

Object A	100 Btu's
Object B	200 Btu's
Total	300 Btu's

and that sum is empirically testable as well as relevant. In general, the sum specifies the available alternatives. For example, if the work to be performed in project i requires anything greater than 300 Btu's, project i is not an available alternative in the absence of obtaining additional objects. To put it another way, the sum specifies the total ability to perform work.

The same kind of empirical test (experiment) can be done for exit values.

Asset $A\rightarrow$Dollars received from $A\rightarrow$Goods obtainable by A

Asset $B\rightarrow$Dollars received from $B\rightarrow$Goods obtainable by B

At the asset stage, there are serious questions about the additivity of exit values. If we interpret ¢ as sell together, we are likely to find that exit values are not additive. At the output stage of dollars received, however, we do have additivity. The experiment is exactly the same as the one outlined for potential heat energy. (1) Sell *A* and *B* separately and measure (count) the separate dollars received. (2) Sum the numerals obtained in (1). (3) Combine the dollars received (in one stack) in (1) and measure (count) the number of dollars in that combination. (4) Compare the sum obtained in (2) to the measure obtained in (3).

Since we will find an equality in (4), we can say that exit values are additive under the interpretation that ¢ means sell separately and combine the dollars received. Once we have performed a sufficient number of experiments to satisfy ourselves that the result is general, we can accept the prediction as being true without verifying it each time. That is, we can move from having combined dollars received to the anticipation of combining dollars receivable. This permits us to sum the dollars receivable and use the sum in decisions, for example, to decide whether to keep the assets or to sell them and receive the dollars. For assets *A* and *B*, it permits

Asset *A*	$100
Asset *B*	200
Total	$300

and that sum is empirically testable as well as relevant. In general, the sum specifies the available alternatives. For example, if the entry value of project *i* is greater than $300, project *i* is not an available alternative in the absence of additional financing. To put it another way, the sum specifies the total ability to command goods.

In the specific case at hand, we can add the exit value of the depreciable asset to the cash on hand under this interpretation of ¢. In the same way that we can add some extant heat energy (in a combustion chamber) to some potential energy (in a ton of coal), we can add some extant dollars (in the till) to some potential dollars (in depreciable assets). For example,

Cash (amount at time *t*)	$ 100
Automobile (exit value at time *t*)	3,000
Total (COG at time *t*)	$3,100

yields an empirically testable sum. In the scientific literature such sums are often called "explanations." For potential energy: If the potential energy of object *A* is added to the potential energy of object *B*, the sum is a measure of the work that can be performed. For exit values: If the exit value of asset *A* is added to the exit value of asset *B*, the sum is a measure of the goods that can be commanded.

I expect that many colleagues will not be satisfied with the above explication of the additivity of exit values. I must confess that I too am not entirely happy with it. It would be much simpler if we could just add prices without regard to the way the assets were combined. It was this desire for simplicity that caused me to attempt to bypass the additivity question in *Enterprise Income*. In the firm model examined therein—trading in the wheat market—the market is perfect; therefore, the prices are additive. The exit value of the inventory is equal to the sum of the exit values of the units. When we consider imperfect markets, this happy situation does not exist and the problem must be dealt with. In dealing with the problem we must take the world as it exists: we must combine dollars receivable rather than combining assets, just as we must combine energy receivable rather than combining objects containing energy.

10.3.2 Additivity of Other Values. We must also apply the additivity criterion to the other valuation methods. If we apply a criterion to one method, we must apply it with equal force to its competitors. Then we must compare how each method fares under the application of the criterion. Most of the extant literature is concerned with the additivity of exit values. There is little literature concerned with the additivity of other valuation methods. I will not attempt a definitive analysis of the additivity of other valuation methods. Instead, I will raise some questions and invite the proponents to supply the definitive analysis of the additivity of their endorsed method.

Little has been written about the additivity of historic costs. Ijiri is one of the few who discusses the issue. He has, evidently, also attempted to bypass the additivity problem by defining historic costs to be additive.

> The second factor which makes current cost income more disputable than historical cost income is the non-additivity of current costs. The historical cost of Resource *A* and Resource *B* is *by definition* the sum of the historical cost of Resource *A* and Resource *B*. (IJIRI, "A Defense," p. 6)

The first thing to note about this approach is that if we allow an attribute to be additive by definition, then I can, with equal justification, define exit values to be additive.

The more important point is to distinguish measure theory from measure*ment* theory. Measure theory is a branch of mathematics concerned with proving theorems assuming certain conditions, one of which is additivity. Thus, measure theory postulates or assumes additivity and then works out the logical consequences of that assumption. (See, e.g., Halmos, *Measure Theory,* p. 30.) On the other hand, measurement theory is a branch of empirical science, and additivity is an open empirical question. That is, whether or not, for example, electrical resistance is empirically additive can be determined only by comparing the measurement of resistors separately and jointly. If the comparison reveals an equality, it is additive; otherwise it is not additive.

The same empirical test must be applied to accounting. It is, of course, appropriate and helpful for Ijiri and others to work out the logical consequences of an assumed or defined additivity. We will then know the general characteristics of additivity. Eventually, however, we must also ask about the empirical additivity of historic costs.

In order to ask the empirical question intelligently, we must first distinguish purchase prices from historic costs. I believe that when Ijiri speaks of the additivity of historic costs, he has purchase prices in mind. He is not thinking of adding allocated purchase prices. Therefore, we will begin by considering the additivity of purchase prices and then turn to the additivity of historic costs.

We find little disagreement about the additivity of purchase prices. If we are contemplating the purchase of asset i for $10 and asset j for $15, the $25 sum is accepted without raising the additivity question. I believe the reason the question is not raised is due to our familiarity with accounting for purchase prices. Compare the reverse situation. If we are contemplating the sale of asset i for $10 and asset j for $15, we do worry about whether i and j together would fetch $25. We raise the additivity question in regard to sales, but we do not raise it in regard to purchases. The question must apply equally to purchases and sales because there cannot be a seller without a purchaser. If i and j were purchased together, they might require the expenditure of something other than $25. Thus, purchase prices (entry values) are no more and no less additive than sales prices (exit values). For both of them, the thing that is additive is the number of dollars that would be received or spent under the specified conditions that the two resources are to be sold or purchased separately. If we consider their purchase or sale jointly, any question about the additivity of one applies with equal force to the other. Thus, entry values are additive under the interpretation of purchasing separately.

Historic-cost proponents object to the additivity of purchase prices

Exhibit 10.3-1

Cash at t		$60
Uses of Cash:		
Purchases of Asset i	10	
Purchases of Asset j	15	
Total Uses		25
Cash at $t + 2$		$35

unless the exchange occurs. They view the process of valuing assets at either entry or exit values as a "hypothetical exchange," and they contrast it to the purchase prices in an "actual exchange." Let us consider these actual exchanges. Suppose we start with $60 cash at time t and purchase assets i and j for $10 and $15 at time $t + 1$. The figures are additive. The empirical test is simple. One can predict

$$60_t - (10_{t+1} + 15_{t+1}) = 35_{t+2}$$

and one can test that prediction by counting the cash on hand at $t + 2$. Since they are additive and since the explanation is likely to be relevant, I agree that they should be reported. I would put them in the form given in Exhibit 10.3-1 and title the report a "Cash Flow Statement" or "Funds Statement." Thus, I have no argument with the additivity of such purchase prices. What we are adding is dollars. In the same way that we can add dollars received or receivable to dollars on hand, we can add (subtract) dollars spent to dollars on hand.[2]

The difficulty that I have with such purchase prices is in reporting them on the balance sheet. If the purchase prices are not allocated (reported like land is reported), the historic-cost balance sheet at time $t + 2$ will be:

---

2. I also have no argument with those who want to report cash flows. Indeed, I think that cash flow reporting is a relevant explanation. Unfortunately, I have not made this view explicit in some of my previous work. I would like to make it quite explicit here and apologize for not having done so previously. My only excuse is that I thought it was obvious because cash flows are the same regardless of what valuation method is employed. That is, a dollar spent or received is the same regardless of what value one assigns to the object received or given in exchange. As I view it, the cash flow report would be the same for all valuation methods; therefore, there was no dispute. For this reason, I was most puzzled when cash flow advocates began to criticize my previous work. It finally occurred to me that my critics view exit values as competitive with cash flows, while I view them as complementary.

Cash	$35
Asset *i*	10
Asset *j*	15
Total Assets	$60

The $60 is reported as total assets at time $t + 2$. There is no empirical phenomenon extant at $t + 2$ represented by that figure. The $60 cash existed at time t, but it does not exist at $t + 2$. If we begin to consider the $60 of total assets at $t + 2$, we can run through a long list of things that it does *not* represent but I cannot find anything that it *does* represent. The best interpretation that I can come up with is a statement in the subjunctive mood: $60 is the amount of cash that would be in the till if $25 had not been spent. But that is a hypothetical statement since the dollars were actually spent, and the historic-cost proponents have strong objections to reporting hypothetical statements.

When we consider allocated figures the difficulty is compounded. The historic-cost balance sheet is given in Exhibit 10.3-2, and the total asset figure is completely inexplicable. There is no empirical test that would either confirm or disconfirm the $4,100. Of course, we can recalculate the figures as auditors do. We can also define depreciation as a rational allocation that is not a measure of anything; we can define assets as accounts that have a debit balance after the books are closed; and we can define total assets as the sum of the debit balances.[3] Such a string of definitions is what Peirce ("Pragma-

Exhibit 10.3-2

Cash		$ 100
Automobile	5,000	
Accumulated Depreciation	1,000	
Unexpired Cost		4,000
Total Assets		$4,100

3. For those that are not familiar with this literature, I should point out that these statements are taken from the literature. The definition of depreciation was quoted in Section 6.1. The definition of assets as debit balances after the books are closed and the definition of a balance sheet as a tabular statement of balances are found in American Institute of Certified Public Accountants, "Accounting Terminology," pp. 12–13.

Some colleagues think that I invent such definitions in order to try to be humorous. If you find them ridiculous or humorous, I cannot take the credit—they are, in fact, definitions taken from the literature.

tism") meant by "gibberish"—words being defined by other words, and they by still other words without any of the referents being capable of investigation by the observational methods of science.

Of course, the culprit is the conventionally allocated figure of $4,000. We should not expect a sum to have an empirical referent if one or more of the addends does not also have an empirical referent. For that reason, replacement costs and discounted values suffer the same fate. Since replacement-cost depreciation is a conventionally allocated current purchase price, adding it to cash will not yield an empirically testable sum. Since a discounted value is an arithmetically adjusted forecast, adding it to cash will not yield an empirically testable sum. I cannot prove the nonadditivity of these values for the same reason that I cannot prove the nonexistence of a green swan (as discussed in Section 9.4). Instead, I must challenge the proponents of such valuation methods to provide proof of the additivity of their endorsed value.

In summary, I find entry values to be additive on the same grounds as the additivity of exit values. I find that historic costs, replacement costs, and discounted values fail the additivity criterion.

10.3.3 Categories of Assets.

Choosing account categories is an important problem that remains intractable, albeit usually unrecognized. The nature of the problem can be most easily understood by casting it in familiar terms of historic-cost depreciation. Prior to calculating depreciation we must decide what constitutes the account category.

In broad terms we have the choice of component depreciation, unit depreciation, or group depreciation. Textbooks provide us with examples of depreciating the components of assets as opposed to depreciating the asset as a whole. Tax considerations often lead us to component depreciation. Textbooks also provide examples of depreciating groups of assets as opposed to depreciating the individual assets. Convenience considerations often lead us to group depreciation. Obviously, the three different methods result in different depreciation expenses and in different historic costs being reported on the balance sheet.

The problem is that there is no apparent way to decide which method to use. We are free to categorize the asset as a component, as a unit, or as a group. That is, we can establish accounts for components, units, or groups. In attempting to describe what practicing accountants do (as opposed to prescribing a preferable rule), I have previously suggested that the usual method of purchasing dictates the categories. For example, if a firm purchases chassis and engines, it will usually establish account categories of "chassis" and "engines" and will employ component depreciation. If it normally purchases individual automobiles, it will establish account categories of "automobile #1" and "automobile #2" and will employ unit depreciation. If it purchases fleets of automobiles, the account category will be "fleet," and group depreciation will be employed. But this is a description, as opposed to a solution, and tax and convenience considerations may result in it being breached as often as it is observed. Moreover, it does not begin to describe the possibilities. We could break it down into finer categories of tires, wheels, carburetors, and the like or even into still finer categories of nuts, screws, bolts, and the like. Or we could utilize broader categories. Instead of establishing an account for fleets of automobiles we could establish one for automotive equipment which would include automobiles, trucks, semi-trailers, and the like. Or we could utilize a still broader category which would include fork lifts, front loaders, and the like. It is conceivable to have a very broad category entitled "plant and equipment" which would include everything except current assets. There are examples of such broad accounts found in practice albeit they are rare.

What is the appropriate category? If the same asset and expense figures were obtained from employing different categories, e.g., if the sum of unit depreciation were equal to the group depreciation of the same units, there would be no problem. But the figures are different and therefore the selection of categories is a type of additivity problem in historic-cost accounting.

The categorization problem plagues all of the valuation methods. The sum of replacement-cost unit depreciation is different from replacement-cost group depreciation. The discounted value of the group is different from the sum of discounted values of the units. The entry value of the group is different from the sum of the entry values of the units. The same is true of exit values. In regard to exit values this is known as the "aggregation problem" and has been examined by Ijiri (*Accounting Measurement*), McKeown ("Additivity"), Thomas (SAR #3), and Trowell ("Additivity").

I freely admit that exit values suffer from this problem. I also admit that I have no solution. In this essay I am assuming a category of one automobile; I am attempting to bypass the question because I do not have an answer.[4] If the categorization problem is sufficient

---

4. See Chambers ("Second Thoughts") and McKeown ("Additivity") for different approaches to a solution in regard to exit values. To the best of my knowledge, no one has suggested a solution for other valuation methods. Indeed, in so far as I am

reason to reject the exit valuation method, we must reject all other valuation methods on the same grounds. It is a problem common to all valuation methods proposed to date. My only defense is that when the categorization or aggregation problem is considered, exit values fare no worse than the other valuation methods.

10.3.4 Value of the Firm. At one time or another, all of the methods of valuing assets have been subjected to the criticism that they do not sum to the "value of the firm" or that they do not sum to the "going concern value." A major problem in attempting to analyze these criticisms is that "value of the firm" or "going concern value" is invariably undefined. In some of the literature, the authors appear to mean discounted value of the firm. They reject the particular valuation method under discussion because it does not sum to this "ideal" or "true value." In other literature the authors seem to mean the price of the firm. They reject the particular valuation method under discussion because it does not sum to this price.

Once we have discerned what the authors mean by "value of the firm" or "going concern value," we can see the error. They are switching attributes. There is no reason to expect the sum of the entry values of the assets to equal the discounted value of the firm, nor is there any reason to expect the sum of the discounted values of the assets to equal the entry value of the firm. Since entry values and discounted values are different attributes, we cannot reasonably expect one to sum to the other. Such criticism is similar to requiring, say, electrical resistance to sum to voltage.

Even if we do not switch attributes, the total value of the firm will be different from the sum of the values of the assets. The entry value of the firm is likely to be different from the sum of the entry values of the assets. I do not know what "historic cost of the firm" means, but the existence of "purchased goodwill" as well as of the purchase versus pooling controversy is direct evidence of an inequality. Likewise, the discounted value of the firm is likely to be different from the sum of the discounted values of the assets due to the interaction effects of combining assets—the economies or diseconomies of scale or the incremental discounted value of the incremental asset. The same is true of the replacement cost of the firm in relation to the replacement costs of the assets.

---

aware, no one had addressed the problem in the context of other valuation methods. Devine ("Essays") alludes to the problem, without providing a solution, in regard to historic costs.

If this inequality is evidence of an additivity problem, it is a problem which plagues all of the valuation methods. If we condemn any method of valuing assets for not summing to the value of the firm, we will be forced to condemn all methods of valuing assets.

10.3.5 Price of the Firm. The price of the firm as a whole is likely to be different from the sum of the prices of the assets of that firm. The sum of the exit value of the assets is likely to be different from the exit value of the firm, and the same is true of entry values.

Firms and assets are traded in different markets. The market for firms is separate from the market for assets. Thus, we should expect different prices. To put it negatively, if a collection of assets was a perfect substitute for a firm, there would be no reason for the different markets to exist. Since they are not perfect substitutes, since they are different goods, different markets exist and they trade for different prices.

There are many analogous situations. For example, the market for automobiles is different from the market for automobile parts. The sum of the prices of the parts of an automobile is different from the price of that automobile. There is a "going automobile price" just as there is a "going concern price," and both are different from the sum of the prices of the components. The difference is not evidence of an additivity problem. Rather, it is merely a difference that should be recognized and dealt with. I believe that the appropriate way to deal with it is to inquire into the way in which it will affect decisions, as will be done in the following Section.

10.4 Relevance to Single Owners and Creditors

> Those who study the financial statements of an enterprise want to know (for any one of a variety of reasons) what its financial strength is. This may be because they want to buy it or sell it, to lend it money or borrow from it. . . .
>
> ROSS, *Financial Statements*, p. 8

In previous applications of the relevance test we have been concerned with the kind of decisions normally made by managers. The keep versus replace decision, for example, is usually classified as a managerial decision. In general these kinds of decisions constitute the "composition problem" in the apt phraseology of Edwards and Bell (*Theory and Measurement,* p. 34). The manager needs to decide on the composition of assets to be held. The total exit value is also relevant to this type of decision, as was mentioned during the discussion of the additivity of exit values. Thus, we have demonstrated the relevance of exit values to managerial decisions.

We now turn to the kinds of decisions made by owners. If the owner allows the managers to make the decisions regarding composition of assets, the owner's major decision is to keep versus dispose of the firm. I say "dispose of" the firm because if the decision is to not keep it, the owner can either sell the firm or sell the assets since the price of the firm is different from the sum of the exit values of the assets. That is, the owner faces three alternatives:

—Keep the firm.

—Sell the firm.

—Sell the assets (liquidate).

The relevant decision variables are

D_{ft} = discounted value of firm f at time t

P_{ft} = price of firm f at time t

X_{ft} = sum of the exit values of the assets of firm f at time t

The way in which the variables are ordered indicates the relative profitability of the alternatives.[5] There are six cases:

(1) $D > P > X$ ⎫ owner keeps firm
(2) $D > X > P$ ⎭
(3) $P > D > X$ ⎫ sell firm
(4) $P > X > D$ ⎭
(5) $X > D > P$ ⎫ sell assets.
(6) $X > P > D$ ⎭

Only in cases (1) and (2) would the owner be inclined to keep the firm. His discounted value of keeping is greater than the value of selling the firm or the assets. However, he may have other alternatives with greater discounted values. For this reason, he must consider the relative values of the other alternatives. Adding a subscript o to indicate the owned firm and u to indicate an unowned firm, if $D_{ut} > D_{ot}$ and $P_{ut} = P_{ot}$ it is more profitable to purchase the unowned firm. In case (1) he would sell for P_{ot}, purchase for P_{ut} and expect to be better off by $D_{ut} - D_{ot}$. In case (2) he would sell the assets

---

5. For ease of exposition I refer to the price instead of the entry and exit values of the firm. In the ordinary case of negotiated exchanges—a monopolist facing a monopolist—there may be no difference. When there is a difference the relevant figure is exit for contemplated sales and entry for contemplated purchases.

for X_{ot}, purchase for P_{ut} and expect to be better off by $D_{ut} - D_{ot}$, as well as presently being better off by $X_{ot} - P_{ut}$. Thus, all three variables are relevant to the decision.

The greater of P_{ot} or X_{ot} is the sacrifice required to keep the firm. The owner must compare that required sacrifice to the discounted value in accord with the profitability principle. In addition, the greater of P_{ot} or X_{ot} is a determinant of the available alternatives. Neglecting additional financing, if $P_{ut} > P_{ot}$ and $P_{ut} > X_{ot}$, the purchase of the other firm is not an available alternative.

In cases (3) and (4) it is more profitable to sell the firm and invest the proceeds at the discount rate. In cases (5) and (6) it is more profitable to sell the assets and invest the proceeds at the discount rate. Again, all three variables are relevant to the decision. The cases are nothing more than an application of the profitability principle in which the required sacrifice is greater than the discounted value. The required sacrifice in these cases is the greater of either P_{ot} or X_{ot}.

The market forces are such that we can infer the normal relationships of the values. Let us consider the pairwise relationships. First, we can expect $D > P$ in the normal case. If $D < P$ for the present owner, it is more profitable to sell the firm than to continue operations. But the potential purchaser will purchase if and only if his D is greater than P. Thus, there may be a transitional stage in which $D < P$ for the present owner, but this status indicates that a sale is imminent. After the exchange, $D > P$ for the new owner; otherwise, he would not purchase.

Second, we can expect $D > X$ in the normal case. If $D < X$ it is more profitable to sell the assets than to continue operations. That is, it is more profitable to liquidate the firm and invest the proceeds at the discount rate. After the liquidation the firm does not exist, and therefore D and X do not exist. Thus, there may be a transitional stage in which $D < X$, but this status indicates that liquidation is imminent. For this reason we can infer that $D_{ft} > X_{ft}$ for all f except those in a transitional stage.

This result may be the basis for the going concern assumption. In this context the going concern assumption is tantamount to assuming $D_{ft} > X_{ft}$ for all f at all t. I have many reservations about the going concern notion, not the least of which is the insistence upon classifying it as an assumption. In my view, going concern is a *decision* to be made by *creditors* and/or *owners,* not an *assumption* to be made by *accountants.* At any given moment in time, it is possible for $D < X$; therefore, it is an error to assume $D > X$. For example, we have recently witnessed a rash of liquidations of small oil firms. The sudden increase in the price of crude resulted in a sudden increase in the exit value of oil leases. A number of owners decided to sell their leases at the increased price instead of continuing operations. It was a profit maximizing decision, because the sum of the exit values of the leases was greater than the discounted value of operating; that is, $X > D$. Such voluntary liquidations are not uncommon.

We must also consider involuntary liquidations. Adding presubscripts to indicate the owner's and creditor's discounted values, it is possible for $_oD > X$ and $_cD < X$. In that case the creditor may decide to force the firm into liquidation. The creditor's decision requires the comparison of his independently assigned discounted values to the liabilities, L_{ft}, and to the exit values. There are six cases:

(1) $_cD > X > L$
(2) $_cD > L > X$
(3) $X > _cD > L$
(4) $X > L > _cD$
(5) $L > _cD > X$
(6) $L > X > _oD$

In cases (1), (2), (3), and (5) the creditor's profit maximization decision is to permit the firm to continue operations. In cases (1), (2) and (3) the creditor expects to be paid in full. The only difference in these cases is the risk. Since $X > L$ in cases (1) and (3), the loans are low risk. The immediately available value is greater than the amount of the loan. Full payment of the debt in case (2) depends on the future expectations being realized. Therefore, it is a higher risk loan. Since $L > X$ the difference depends on the future, that is, on $_cD$. Case (5) is an attempt to minimize the loss on the loan. If the creditor forces liquidation the loss will be $L - X$ which is greater than the expected loss of $L - _cD$ from continued operations.

In cases (4) and (6) the profit maximizing decision is to force liquidation. The loan will be fully paid upon liquidation in case (4), while in case (6) the loss will be less from liquidation than the expected loss from continued operations.

To summarize, we can expect $_oD > X$ for all extant firms except those in transition. When $X > _oD$, the firm will be voluntarily liquidated and cease to exist leaving only those firms where $_oD > X$. Continuation versus liquidation is a decision to be made by the owner, not an assumption to be made by the accountant. The creditor also needs to compare $_cD$, L, and X in order to decide whether to force liquidation.

That is a decision to be made by the creditors, not an assumption to be made by the accountant. In both voluntary and involuntary liquidations, X is relevant. One cannot make a profit-maximizing decision without comparing X to other variables.

Third, we can expect $P > X$ in the normal case. If $P < X$ the owner would not be willing to sell the firm since it is more profitable to liquidate. Hence, X provides a floor for the owner's asking price.

In the same way, N_{ft}, the sum of the entry values of the assets of firm f at time t, provides a ceiling for the purchaser's bid price under certain conditions. If $P > N$, it is obviously cheaper to purchase the assets from a dealer than to purchase the firm from the owner. However, in many cases firms are in fact purchased when $P > N$. One reason is to obtain the share of the market that the firm has developed. Another reason is to purchase the absence of competition. There are other profit-maximizing reasons to purchase a firm instead of purchasing equivalent assets and establishing a firm. For purposes of analysis this fact is unfortunate, because it would be easier if we were confident that $N > P > X$ in all cases.

Note that this does not deny the relevance of N to the purchaser. In order to make a profit-maximizing decision, the purchaser needs to know both values. The difference $P - N$ is the premium he is paying for, say, the share of the market, and it is relevant to his decision. Of course the purchaser would prefer $P < X$ just as purchasers of assets would prefer $n_{it} < x_{it}$ as discussed in Section 8.2. If $P < X$ it would allow the purchaser to profit from the simple expedient of purchasing the firm and selling the assets. Given profit-maximizing owners and adequate information, we should expect that such situations could not occur. That is, if $P < X$ and the owner did in fact sell, we would be forced to conclude that he lacked adequate information.

We have now completed the three pairwise comparisons and found that in the normal case $D > P$, $D > X$, and $P > X$. Thus, in the normal case $D > P > X$. This is the equilibrium position. But we must remember that we are always driving toward equilibrium instead of being at equilibrium. The adjustments are being continuously made. Thus, at any given moment in time we can expect some firms to be in a transitional stage where $D < P$ and $D < X$. Only after the exchanges have been consummated will $D > P$ for the new owner, and only after liquidation has been accomplished will D and X cease to exist for liquidated firms. By contrast we should never observe an exchange of firms when $P < X$, even in a transition stage. The only time that an owner would sell the firm for P when $P < X$ is when he is ignorant of X. Therefore, observation of $P < X$ in an exchange of firms is evidence of inadequate information.

Finally, we need to consider relative riskiness. The gamma index presented in Section 8.2 is applicable. Recall that gamma was defined as

$$\gamma = (n_{it} - x_{it})/n_{it}$$

The basis of this risk indicator is that x_{it} is the immediately recoverable amount and therefore $n_{it} - x_{it}$ is the amount put at risk. To put it another way, x_{it} is the floor of the downside risk if expectations are not realized.

The same is true for X_{ft}. In the normal case $D > P > X$ and therefore X provides a floor for the downside risk if expectations are not realized. $P - X$ is the amount put at risk upon purchase. Of course, the new owner may be able to negotiate a new price greater than the exit value, in which case the new price would be the amount recovered if expectations were not realized. However, the slumbering market for firms prohibits the observation of the new price until the negotiations have been completed. Since X provides a floor, the total downside risk—the ultimate fallback position—is X.

For these reasons, in assessing riskiness of firms equation (8.2-1) should be restated as:

$$\gamma = (P - X)/P \qquad (10.4\text{-}1)$$

When $\gamma = 1$, all of the value depends upon the future, upon D. None of the value is immediately recoverable. Decision makers recognize this risk relationship by classifying firms that currently report large amounts of goodwill or other zero exit value intangibles as high-risk situations. When $\gamma = 0$, the entire amount is immediately recoverable. This is also recognized by decision makers. They classify firms that currently report large amounts of liquid assets as low-risk situations. They also classify firms that have large amounts of unreported exit values as low-risk situations.

In general, $P - X =$ sunk costs or the amount put at risk. If one can find a case where $P < X$, it is a negative risk situation, as indicated by $\gamma < 0$, since one can profit by the simple expedient of purchasing the firm and liquidating it. In short, X can be used in the same way x_{it} was used in the assessment of risk in Section 8.2. Thus, X is relevant to the determination of the relative riskiness of firms.

10.5 Relevance to Multiple Owners

The aim should be to satisfy (so far as is possible and prudent) the investor's need for knowledge, rather than the accountant's sense of form and respect for tradition.

AMERICAN INSTITUTE OF ACCOUNTANTS, "Audits," p. 9

Firms are often owned by groups of people. Such owners are known as partners or shareholders depending upon the legal arrangement of the firm. Denoting λ_{ft} as the total shares outstanding of the firm f at time t, we can define the average of the various values,

$$\bar{p}_{ft} = P_{ft}/\lambda_{ft}$$
$$\bar{x}_{ft} = X_{ft}/\lambda_{ft}$$
$$\bar{d}_{ft} = D_{ft}/\lambda_{ft}$$

and utilize these averages to determine the fraction of the values pertaining to a particular multiple owner. For example, if a firm is sold for P, a partner with a one-third share would receive $P/3$; and a shareholder who owned 100 of 1,000,000 shares would receive $(P/1,000,000)100$.

If the firm were liquidated, the amount received by the partner would be $X/3$; and the shareholder would receive $(X/1,000,000)100$. The discounted value per share is an individual determination. Each owner will assign a D to the firm that is likely to be different from the D assigned by any other owner or potential owner. Hence $\bar{d}$ represents the discounted value per share assigned by a particular individual.

Given these definitions we can simply substitute $\bar{p}$, $\bar{x}$, and $\bar{d}$ for P, X, and D in the previous analysis of decisions. The structure of the decision models is not altered by multiple ownership. The relevant variables are merely scaled down to the amount owned by each multiple owner. However, there are two complications: the need to obtain agreement and the existence of share prices.

10.5.1 Agreement. There is the need to obtain agreement among multiple owners before certain actions can be taken. The firm cannot be sold or liquidated without the consent of the partners or the ratification of the shareholders. In the terms of this essay, the need to obtain agreement affects the available alternatives. It is not an alteration of the decision process, but it is a limitation of the alternatives available to the decision maker. For example, if an owner assigns a $\bar{d}$ such that $\bar{d} < \bar{p}$, it is a profit-maximizing decision to sell the firm for P. However, without the consent of the partners or the ratification of the shareholders, it is not possible to sell the firm. Since it is not an available alternative, there is no point in considering its profitability. To put the agreement in the terms of a decision, the owners may receive an offer of P which each must compare to his D. If all assign a D such that $_jd > p$ for all j, or vice versa, there is agreement. Otherwise there is disagreement. Thus, obtaining the consent of the partners or the ratification of the shareholders depends upon the discounted values that each assigns. The same is true for the decision to liquidate the firm or to continue operations. If all agree that $X > D$, it is more profitable to liquidate than to continue operations. Agreement means that $\bar{x} > \bar{d}$ for each owner. However, if some owners assign a D such that $\bar{d} > \bar{x}$, there will be disagreement; and liquidation of the firm may not be an available alternative. Again, agreement depends upon the discounted values assigned by each owner. The only case in which we can expect agreement is in the decision to sell the firm or to liquidate it. This, of course, requires the prior condition that each fractional owner's discounted value is less than X and P. In that case all would agree to sell when $P > X$, and all would agree to liquidate when $X > P$.

It is possible to sell the share instead of selling the firm. This is always an available alternative for shareholders of corporations, and the decision will be considered below. Selling a share of a partnership is an available alternative only when agreement of the other partners is obtained.

Purchasing a share also requires that the partners agree since they have the right to refuse admission to the partnership. Assuming that they agree, p is the observed, negotiated price for the share. If there were an active market for firms, the participants could observe P and divide by λ to obtain $\bar{p}$. Since the market for firms slumbers, P is not observable.[6] The market for partnership shares is equally sleepy; so p must be negotiated, albeit both participants may estimate P and use their estimate as the basis for their negotiations of the value of p.

---

6. We can reverse the process and infer P from the observation of p. That is, since the market for firms slumbers we cannot regularly observe either p or P. When a fraction is sold, we can observe p, and that is our best available evidence for the value of P. This is current practice for partnerships. Textbooks provide illustrations of the calculations of the "value [price] of the firm" when a fraction of the ownership changes hands. The calculation is merely $P = p\lambda$ where p and λ are observed and P is the dependent variable. The texts also urge that assets be stated at "fair market value" when a fraction of the ownership changes hands. They show the dire inequities that occur if the assets are not revalued, if historic costs are carried forward. They use these inequities and the legal concept that a new partner results in a new firm to justify restating the asset at fair market value. They define the excess of the price of the firm over the fair market value of the assets as goodwill. If the fair market value is taken to mean the exit value, $P - X =$ goodwill.

As before, the value of p will be bounded by the discounted values assigned by the owner and purchaser. If they can negotiate a p such that it is greater than the discounted value of the owner and less than the discounted value of the purchaser, a bargain will be struck and the share will change hands.

We noted above that if $X > P$, it is a profit-maximizing decision to liquidate rather than sell. The same is true if $\bar{x} > p$. The partner would prefer to liquidate rather than sell his share. But liquidation of the partnership requires obtaining agreement of the other partners. If they do not agree, liquidation is not an available alternative to the selling partner. Therefore, $\bar{x}$ is irrelevant to his decision. The decision must be based solely on a comparison of $\bar{d}$ to p because the alternatives have been constrained to keep versus sell. Under these conditions we cannot specify the relationship of $\bar{x}$ to p or $\bar{x}$ to $\bar{d}$. Since $\bar{x}$ is not an available alternative, the partner may sell even if $\bar{x} > p$.

It must be stressed, however, that $\bar{x}$ is irrelevant to the selling partner because of another decision to which $\bar{x}$ was relevant. If all partners assigned $\bar{d}$ such that $\bar{x} > \bar{p} > \bar{d}$, agreement to liquidate would be obtained. Thus, $\bar{x}$ is irrelevant to the selling partner because the other partners found $\bar{d} > \bar{x}$.

The purchaser will find $\bar{x}$ to be relevant to his risk assessment in the same way that X was relevant in the single ownership case. In this case the purchaser may be in the happy position of $\bar{x} > p$. This indicates a negative risk. Even the worst case of unrealized expectations, even immediate liquidation, will result in a profit to the purchaser. The amount put at risk is negative. Thus, as before, the purchaser can calculate γ as his risk indicator. He prefers a larger $\bar{x}$ to a smaller $\bar{x}$, other things being equal. If he can find a situation in which $\bar{x} > p$, he can decrease his risk position.

Also as before the purchasers of a share will find $\bar{n}$ to be relevant where $\bar{n} = N/\lambda$. If $\bar{n} < p$ the purchaser would be inclined to purchase the assets instead of purchasing the share. This decision also requires obtaining agreement from others. He must find others who agree that $\bar{d} > \bar{n}$ in order to form a partnership. If he cannot do that, $\bar{n}$ is irrelevant to the purchaser because forming a partnership is not an available alternative. Thus, he may purchase even if $\bar{n} < p$. But $\bar{n}$ is irrelevant only because of the prior decision of others in which $\bar{n}$ was relevant.

To summarize, multiple ownership decisions are identical to single ownership decisions except for the need to obtain agreement. In single ownership, D, P, and X are relevant to the owner and D, P, X, and

N are relevant to the purchaser. In multiple ownership, $\bar{d}$, p, and $\bar{x}$ are relevant to the owner and $\bar{d}$, p, $\bar{x}$, and $\bar{n}$ are relevant to the purchaser. Where partners do not agree that $\bar{d} < \bar{x}$, liquidation is not available to a partner and therefore $\bar{x}$ is irrelevant to his keep versus sell decision. Where potential partners do not agree that $\bar{d} > \bar{n}$, forming a partnership is not available to a purchaser; and therefore, $\bar{n}$ is irrelevant to his decision to purchase or not to purchase. Therefore, the owner may sell when $\bar{x} > p$, and the purchaser may purchase when $\bar{n} < p$. Thus, we may observe $\bar{n} < p$ and $\bar{x} > p$ because of the failure to obtain agreement among the multiple owners.

10.5.2 Share Prices. For publicly traded corporations there is an active market for shares. The price, p, of such shares can be readily observed. That price is compared to the discounted value, d, of the dividends and the terminal price in order to decide whether to purchase or not to purchase, to sell or not to sell.

Note that this is the same decision model that has been used throughout this essay. We have continually compared the required sacrifice to the discounted value in order to determine the profitability of the project. The only difference is the terms used. Previously we have referred to "asset i," whereas here we refer to "share of the fth firm." We previously referred to "future cash flows" which included the "salvage value," whereas here we call them "dividends" and "terminal price." Thus, a share of stock is just another asset with a different name. For this reason, all of the previous decision analysis is applicable. For example, neglecting commission costs, that is, neglecting the distinction between entry and exit values, a maximizer would not purchase an unowned share or keep an owned share if $p > d$.

If we view the stock market as an isolated activity, the above is all we need to say. That is, if we take the view that there is no relationship between the share prices and the firm's asset prices and cash flows, then we need go no further. The investor needs only to focus on the present and future share prices and the future dividends. Reports on assets are irrelevant regardless of how they are valued. Thus, under this view, reporting assets at their historic cost is just as good as reporting them at their replacement cost since both are irrelevant and since both have no connection to share prices. Indeed, under this view all financial statements are irrelevant.

Some accountants apparently hold this view. They seem to believe that financial statements are now irrelevant to investors and that we should not try to make them relevant. Some take this position on the basis of the difficulty of empirically determining what information is relevant to investors. Some argue that it is inappropriate to "normatively" determine what information is relevant. Others cite the difficulty of the normative determination instead of or in addition to the inappropriateness of normative determination. Others argue that we ought to adopt the objective of "stewardship," as opposed to "decision relevance," on the basis of tradition and/or because it is impossible to know what is relevant.

Others take the position on the assumption that accounting is necessarily conventional. They argue that since we cannot report "scientific truths," we must report "conventions" and, therefore, the best we can do is to warn investors that our reports have little, if any, relevance to their decisions. We should "educate" investors on the limitations of our reports. Others take the position on the basis of the efficiency of the market. They argue that since the market can "see through" the accounting figures, it makes no difference what we report. Alternatively, since all stocks are priced "fairly," reflecting all available information, one cannot earn an abnormal return from studying financial statements. Since a random selection is an optimal investment strategy, financial statements are irrelevant to the investment decision.

I disagree. Obviously, I do not accept the view that we should not try to make our reports relevant to investors, else I would not be writing this essay. Moreover, I do not accept the view that the stock market is an isolated activity. Since a share is a representation of the ownership of a fraction of the assets of the firm, there must be a relationship. To illustrate the relationship, let us examine a simplified case.

Consider a firm whose only asset is a bond that is traded in the near-perfect bond market and it has no debt. To make the discounting process apparent, assume that the bond pays interest of $150 per year in perpetuity. The current market price of the bond is $1,000. Thus, the "yield rate" or "market rate" is 15 percent. By definition, then, the discounted value of the firm, D, is $1,000, the same as the market price.

In deciding whether to purchase or not to purchase an unowned share or to sell or not to sell an owned share, the investor needs to compare the price of the stock, p, to the discounted value, d, of dividends and terminal price. The best estimator of the dividends is the future cash flows of the firm scaled down by the number of shares outstanding. In this case the expected dividends are $150/5 = $30 per year. In more complicated cases different investors may forecast different cash flows of the firm and therefore forecast different dividends; but in this simplified case, cash flows of the firm are known, and therefore the investors should have homogeneous expectations.

Given homogeneous expectations, the only source of variation in d is the different discount rates. As noted in Section 9.3.5, different investors will have different discount rates and therefore the discounted value of the $30 per year dividends will differ among investors. Now the investor compares his individual d to p, as given by the last trade on the stock exchange. Obviously, each purchaser would prefer a smaller p, and each seller would prefer a larger p. But there are market forces which will set p at $200, one-fifth of the market value of the bond. If p were less than $200, one could purchase all the stock, sell the bond, and profit by the difference. Given the near perfection of both markets, it would be easy for anyone either to form a coalition or to obtain debt financing to buy all of the stock when it sells for less than $200. But the present owners would not be willing to sell for less than $200 for the same reasons. The present owners would like to sell for more than $200 because they could then buy an identical bond and profit by the difference. But the potential purchasers would not be willing to pay more than $200 for the same reasons. To put it another way, if the price deviated from $200 per share, it should attract arbitrageurs who would drive the price back to $200. Thus, the best estimate of the market price of the stock is the scaled-down market price of the bond.

We now have stock priced at $200 per share and expected dividends of $30 per share in perpetuity. Thus, the "yield rate" or "market rate" on the stock is 15 percent and the discounted value is $200. Investors whose individual discount rates are greater than 15 percent will not purchase or they will sell, and those with rates less than 15 percent will purchase or hold. The point is that in such near perfect markets, with the attendant near perfect information, the price of the shares is simply the price of the assets scaled down by the shares outstanding.

Assuming that the firm can reinvest at the same rate, it makes no difference whether the firm pays all of its earnings in dividends or retains them. If it were known that the firm was going to pay $50 in dividends and retain $100, the expected price one year hence would increase by the amount of the retained earnings divided by five shares. In this case the price one year hence—the "terminal price"—is expected to be $220. The increase in the price of $20 plus the $10 dividend received yields the same return and the same results. (For a lengthy discussion of this result see Miller and Modigliani, "Dividend Policy.") The same result is also obtained if the market price of the bond fluctuates. If the price of the bond increases to $1,500, this means that the "market rate" is now 10 percent. We can go through the same analysis as above to determine that the price per share should now be $300 instead of $200.

The benefit of examining such simplified cases is that they clearly show the logical relationship of asset prices to share prices. They show the relevance of (1) asset prices and (2) future cash flows to share price decisions. We cannot empirically test the relationship because asset prices are not now reported.[7] If asset prices were reported, we could perform systematic empirical tests.

Although systematic empirical tests are not possible, some empirical evidence exists. Consider the case where the shareholders have collectively decided to dispose of the firm. They can either sell the firm or sell the assets. Obviously the decision depends on the relation of P to X. Now suppose we observe cases in which $X > P$, but the shareholders collectively sell for P. They each received p which is less than $\bar{x}$.

If we observe such cases, they must be anomalies. Either the owners are philanthropists or they lack adequate information. We have in fact observed such cases, albeit we have not yet recognized them to be anomalies. Court cases provide ample documented evidence. Gerstle vs. Gamble-Skogmo, Inc., is a clear example. This was a class

---

7. Note that the relationship sought is share prices to reported asset *prices*, not share prices to reported asset book values based on *conventions*. A number of tests have been performed to determine the relationship of changes in share prices to changes in accounting conventions. These tests have, in the main, had negative results. The failure to observe changes in share prices associated with changes in accounting conventions is the basis of the notion that the market "sees through" the accounting reports.

We should not expect to observe an association. There is nothing in economic theory that specifies a relationship between changes in accounting conventions and the action of capital market agents. No one has tested the association between changes in share prices and changes in asset prices, and there *is* an economic reason to expect to observe that association.

The distinction is crucial. Those who have overlooked the distinction have drawn conclusions that exceed the results of their tests. They have argued that since the market does not react to a change in reported assets and income occasioned by a change in an accounting convention (e.g., accelerated to straight-line depreciation), it would also not react to a change in reported assets and income occasioned by a change in asset prices. The structure of the argument is that if a is not empirically related to b, then a is not empirically related to c. But one cannot *deduce* the empirical relationship of a to c; one must empirically *test* that relationship. That test has not been performed. It cannot be performed until the asset prices are reported.

action (i.e., collective action by shareholders) against Gamble-Skogmo arising from Gamble's purchase and liquidation of General Outdoor Advertising, Inc. The price that Gamble paid was less than the sum of the exit values of the assets of General. That is, $P < X$, and the owners sold for P. Shortly after the purchase, Gamble sold the assets of General and reaped a substantial profit of $X - P$. The court action was an attempt to recover the losses of the owners (i.e., $X - P$) based on the failure to disclose X in the proxy statement. That is, the plaintiffs alleged ignorance of X and claimed that they would not have sold for P had they known that $P < X$. The court found for the plaintiffs and awarded damages.

Cases such as these provide an incontrovertible demonstration of the relevance of X to shareholders as well as to purchasers. It is logically true that one cannot choose between X and P without knowing the magnitude of both. It is empirically true that shareholders have made erroneous decisions when they did not know the magnitude of X. The courts have corroborated both the logic and the empirics—the evidence presented allowed the court to decide that the shareholders did not know the value of X and that the value of X was necessary for their decision. Thus, these cases are falsifications of those allegations that exit values are irrelevant to shareholder decisions.

In general, X is relevant to owners because it provides a floor for P. Therefore, $\bar{x}$ provides a floor for p for each shareholder when they act collectively. Without knowledge of $\bar{x}$, the individual shareholder cannot decide whether he should accept a tender offer of p or to vote to liquidate the firm. If $\bar{x} > p$ it is more profitable to vote to liquidate, and if $\bar{x} < p$ it is more profitable to accept the tender offer. Of course, if $\bar{d} > \bar{x}$ and $\bar{d} > p$, the shareholder should keep the share.

From the purchaser's point of view X is relevant in one or both of two ways. If the purchaser's purpose is to operate the firm, he will purchase if $D > P$, and X is relevant to the indication of the risk. The purchaser would prefer $P < X$ because it results in a negative amount put at risk. If the purchaser's purpose is to liquidate the firm, X must be greater than P in order for him to profit from liquidation.

People who purchase firms for the purpose of liquidating them are known as "raiders" or "pirates" or worse names. They make an estimate of $\bar{x}$ and then tender an offer of p such that $P < X$. Other raiders purchase shares in the open market rather than making a tender offer. They are called "sneaky" since they do not announce their willingness to purchase and just quietly purchase shares when $p <$

$\bar{x}$.[8] If they can acquire control of the firm by either method, they profit from liquidation or from "milking" the firm or "dissipating" the assets. The amount of their profit is $X - P$ and therefore X provides a ceiling for P.

I have often wondered why raiders are held in such disdain, as indicated by the pejorative names given to them and pejorative terms used to describe their actions. The only thing they are doing is making a profit. Since others who make a profit are described merely as "businessmen" and are held in high esteem, the fact that raiders make a profit cannot be the reason. It may be that the people who sell to them feel cheated. But the reason that they are cheated is that they did not know the magnitude of X. It seems to me that the fault lies in the information system, rather than in the people who profit from inadequate information. Thus, the ire should be directed toward the information system instead of toward the people who profit from its inadequacies.

The only thing that raiders are doing is buying in one market and immediately selling in another. They buy in the capital market and immediately sell in the factor market. Others who buy in one market and immediately sell in another are known as "arbitrageurs" and are thought to be of benefit to the economic system since they keep prices in proper proportion. For example, arbitrageurs who buy in the Chicago Wheat Market and immediately sell in the Kansas City Wheat Market, or vice versa, keep the prices in proper proportion in that they are equal plus or minus transportation costs.

It seems that raiders could serve as arbitrageurs between the capital market and the factor market. If so, they would bid p up to $\bar{x}$ minus liquidation costs. The exit value per share would provide a ceiling for raider's bids on share prices. The exit value per share minus liquidation costs would also provide a floor for owners' asking prices per share.

We would still observe $p > \bar{x}$ for firms that are expected to be profitable. That is, if investors or operators, as opposed to raiders, assigned a $\bar{d}$ such that $\bar{d} > \bar{x}$, they would bid up p above $\bar{x}$. For

8. Some managers who own a fraction of the firm have attempted a similar feat. They have used the firm's assets to purchase shares in the open market, thereby decreasing the number of shares outstanding which increased the fraction of the firm that they owned. When $p < \bar{x}$, they can purchase all of the other shares outstanding, leaving themselves as sole owners of the remaining assets. For every share purchased they profit by $\bar{x} - p$. This was the motivation for some firms to "go private" during the recent depressed market.

an expected profitable purchase, we would observe the ordering $\bar{d}$ $> p > \bar{x}$. The investor would purchase if and only if his assigned discounted value per share was greater than the price per share. Thus,

$d - p$ = net discounted value assigned by the individual

as before. And since the market as a whole expects the firm to be profitable, then $p > x$ and

$p - x$ = net discounted value assigned by the market

because p is a weighted average of the value of d of all market participants.

Note that the ordering of $\bar{d} > p > \bar{x}$ for an expected profitable purchase of a share is the same as the ordering of $d_{it} > n_{it} > x_{it}$ for the expected profitable purchase of a depreciable asset as discussed in Section 8.2. A similar analysis is applicable. We can restate equation (8.2-1) or (10.4-1) as

$$\gamma = (p - \bar{x})/p \qquad (10.5\text{-}1)$$

since the total downside risk is given by $\bar{x}$.

The only difference, but it is a *significant* difference, between purchasing a share and purchasing a depreciable asset is the secondary market for the share. If one purchases a depreciable asset, the alternatives are to use the asset or sell it. If one purchases a piece of paper that represents a claim on a depreciable asset, the alternatives are to use the asset, sell the asset, or sell the piece of paper. Thus, the shareholder has one additional alternative. But the addition of that alternative should not obscure the basic fact that the piece of paper is a claim on the depreciable asset. It is a claim on either the cash flow from using the asset or the cash flow from selling it. No matter how wild the stock market gets, no matter how much it seems to have a separate life of its own, the assets of the firm underlie the piece of paper; therefore, there must be a relationship between the two. Under the present financial reporting system, we cannot empirically identify the relationship because asset prices are not reported. If we adopt a system of reporting asset prices, it will provide the empirical base for research on the relationship of asset prices to share prices.

In the meantime, we must admit ignorance. We cannot specify all of the variables relevant to the investor's decision. However, we can specify some of those variables. First, the investor's assigned discounted value of the share which in turn depends upon the investor's assigned discounted value of the firm is relevant. Second, the price of the share is relevant. Third, the exit value of the assets is relevant. We can point to the occurrence of anomalies and inequities due to failure to report exit values. Since the investor is the best source of his assigned discounted values and since the stock market is the best source of the prices of shares, I conclude that the accounting system ought to report exit values to shareholders.

11

Financial Statements: Income and Funds

> Financial reporting is not an end in itself but is intended
> to provide information that is useful in making business
> and economic decisions. The primary focus of financial
> reporting is information about earnings and its
> components.
>
> FINANCIAL ACCOUNTING STANDARDS BOARD, "Concepts
> No. 1," pp. vii, ix

We now turn to a consideration of the nature of income and the
income statement. I agree with the FASB that information about income
must be useful or, in my terms, relevant. I would only add that a
necessary but not sufficient condition for relevance is that it refer
to empirical phenomena.

11.1 Income—Changes in Wealth

> Personal income connotes, broadly, the exercise of
> control over the use of society's scarce resources. It
> has to do not with sensations, services, or goods, but
> rather with rights which command prices (or to which
> prices may be imputed). Its calculation implies estimate
> (a) of the amount by which the value of a person's
> store of property rights would have increased, as be-
> tween the beginning and end of the period, if he had
> consumed (destroyed) nothing, or (b) of the value of
> rights which he might have exercised in consumption
> without altering the value of his store of rights.
>
> SIMONS, *Personal Income Taxation*, p. 49

The undisputed definition of *income* is that it is the difference
between *wealth* at two points in time after adjusting for consumption
for individuals or investment for firms. Thus, if we have an appropriate

measure of wealth, we also have an appropriate measure of income. In general,

$$A_{ft+1} - A_{ft} - I_{fT} = Y_{fT} \qquad (11.1\text{-}1)$$

where

$$A_{ft} = \text{sum of the assets of firm } f \text{ at time } t$$
$$I_{fT} = \text{sum of investment and disinvestment exchanges of firm } f \text{ for time period } T$$
$$Y_{fT} = \text{net income of firm } f \text{ for time period } T$$

Since we often want to know the components, an equivalent expression is

$$\vec{A}_{ft+1} - \vec{A}_{ft} - \vec{I}_{fT} = \vec{Y}_{fT} \qquad (11.1\text{-}2)$$

where the arrow indicates a vector. $\vec{Y}_{fT}$ displays the income by components of assets, that is, the net change in each asset, and it sums to Y_{fT}. In the previous chapters, I have proposed that "wealth" be interpreted as Command Over Goods (COG) because this interpretation meets the interrelated criteria of empirical testability and relevance. Thus, Y is the increment of COG.

The income statement is an *explanation* of Y, the increment in COG. It is an analysis of Y in the sense that it breaks Y down into its components. Thus, $\vec{Y}_{fT}$ is one explanation since it shows the income asset by asset. Usually, we want a more detailed explanation in the sense that we want to separate the increases and decreases in each asset instead of the net change. For example, we display the cash inflows separately from the cash outflows instead of showing the net change in cash. When we do this, we assign special names to the increases and decreases.

In general, the components of income are exchanges and value changes. The exchanges with customers result in increments in COG called revenues and the exchanges with employees result in decrements in COG called wages. The value changes result in increments in COG called appreciation or decrements in COG called depreciation. Displaying these components and demonstrating that they sum to Y constitute the explanation.

In the simplified case under consideration, revenues (cash receipts from sales) and wages (cash expenditures to employees) present no new problems. The accounting for these items is essentially the same as in current practice. The definition of depreciation (decline in exit value of the depreciable asset) is the only proposed change. The exit-value income statement for this firm is in the following form:

Revenues	$\$\Delta^+ x_{1T}$
Wages	$\Delta^- x_{2T}$
Depreciation	$\Delta^- x_{3T}$
Net Income	$\$Y_{fT}$

This income statement is an explanation of changes in empirical phenomena that occurred during a time period T. Specifically, it explains the change in COG that resulted from exchanges with customers and employees *and* from the decrement in exit value of the depreciable asset. The net income figure is the algebraic sum of the increments and decrements in COG. Just as revenues are increments in COG and wages are decrements in COG, depreciation is a decrement in COG. Thus, the income statement is an accounting for or explanation of the increments and decrements in COG. It subtracts decrements in an attribute from increments in the same attribute, resulting in a net increment of that attribute. It is the same type of explanation as:

> The increment in the potential energy of i less the decrement in the potential energy of j yields the net increment in potential energy in this system, which is a measure of the net increment of work that can be performed.

In this case:

> The net increment in the exit value of cash minus the decrement in the exit values of automotive equipment yields the net increment in exit values, which is a measure of the net increment of the goods that can be commanded.

To put it another way, the income statement is a prediction, in the scientific sense, of the increment in goods that can be commanded in the market. If one has a measure of the increments in potential energy, one can predict the incremental work that can be performed. In the same way if one has a measure of the increments in exit values, one can predict the incremental goods that can be commanded. The relationship between explanations and predictions will be discussed further infra.

I have spent a good deal of space trying to demonstrate the empirical testability and relevance of exit values. It seems obvious to me that if the exit values of assets are empirically testable and additive, the increments and decrements are also empirically testable and additive.

It is equally obvious that if the exit values of assets and sums of assets are relevant, the increments and decrements are also relevant. Nonetheless, there are some aspects which require further elucidation.

11.2 Stocks and Flows

> The first quantity is a *stock* (or *fund*) of wealth; the second quantity is a *flow* (or *stream*) or wealth. . . . The distinction between a fund and a flow has many applications in economic science. The most important application is to differentiate between capital and income.
>
> FISHER, *Nature of Capital*, pp. 51, 52

Wealth is a stock; income is a flow. Stocks are a function of flows, and flows are a function of changes in stocks. We cannot measure one without also at least implicitly measuring the other. In general,

$$a_{it} = \sum_{j=0}^{t} \Delta a_{ij} \qquad (11.2-1)$$

where

$$a_{it} = \text{stocks of } i \text{ at time } t$$
$$\Delta a_{ij} = \text{flow (in or out) of } i \text{ at time } j$$

This is true of mass flowing in and out of a system or of water flowing in and out of a bathtub, as well as income flowing in and out of a firm. The present stock of any additive attribute is the sum of all past flows. Reversing the procedure we can write,

$$\sum_{j=t-1}^{t} \Delta a_{ij} = a_{it} - a_{it-1} \qquad (11.2-2)$$

that is, we can determine the net flows from the change in stocks just as we can determine the stocks by summing the flows. Therefore, if the stocks are correctly measured, the net flows are also correctly measured. If the flows are correctly measured, the stocks are also correctly measured.

I present this general relationship of stocks to flows in an attempt to lay to rest an ancient, pervasive myth in accounting. That myth is that one can have an accurate measure of flows while having an inaccurate measure of stocks. Specifically, that one can have an accurate income statement (flows) which yields an inaccurate balance sheet (stocks). One of the arguments advanced in favor of LIFO, for example, was that it gave an accurate representation of cost of goods sold.

Its proponents admitted that it gave an inaccurate representation of inventory. It was thought that FIFO did the opposite. Thus, one was given a choice of an accurate stock or an accurate flow but not both. From this idea of mutually exclusive accurateness came the notion that one must decide which statement—income or balance sheet—is more important so that one would be able to make it accurate and leave the less important statement inaccurate. This was considered a dilemma of major proportions.

One proposed solution was to abandon the requirement that the balance sheet and income statement articulate. An example of that proposal was to use LIFO values for both cost of goods sold and for inventory. Those who proposed this claimed that articulation was an outmoded constraint that should be abandoned. Others maintained articulation by writing the inventory up to LIFO values and crediting a new kind of nonincome, noninvested equity. They thought that one could have a wealth increment without a corresponding income increment—a violation of the definition of income and wealth. Such proposals were an attempt to avoid the dilemma, to avoid being forced to choose the most important statement.

The plain fact is that if one has an additive attribute, an inaccurate measure of stocks will yield an inaccurate measure of flows and vice versa.[1] For example, if a bathtub were empty at time 0, inflows of 10 gallons occurred at time 1, and outflows of 7 gallons occurred at time 2, the stocks at time 2 must be 3 gallons. That is, we would expect

$$3 = 10 + (-7)$$

and if we found the stocks to be different from 3 gallons, we would conclude that the flows were inaccurately measured. For example, if the stocks were found to be 2, we would have

$$2 = 10 + (-7)$$

which is a logical contradiction of the meaning of the numerals and an empirical contradiction of the additivity of volumes of water. In such a case we might look for errors in the form of unrecorded flows (such as a leak), check the accuracy of the gauges, or take into account outflows due to evaporation or the changes in volume due to temperature changes. I cannot be sure of all the things we might do, but

---

1. An alternative interpretation of the dilemma is that historic costs are not additive. Some of the LIFO-FIFO debates came close to saying that. In the context of the debate they would claim that adding (subtracting) LIFO costs from inventory left a balance that did not make sense. See Johnson ("Inventory Valuation") and Moonitz ("Case Against LIFO").

I can be sure that we would *not* conclude that it is possible for the sum of accurate measures of flows to yield an inaccurate measure of the stocks.

Despite these lessons from ordinary experience (as well as from the laws of physics), the notion persists. Many accountants still believe that one must choose which statement one wants to be accurate and, as a result, the other statement will be inaccurate. From this reasoning comes the notion that one may have a correct theory of income or a correct theory of wealth but not both. Accountants even get classified as "balance-sheet theorists" versus "income-statement theorists." My view is exactly the opposite. Since income and wealth are inextricably entwined, an incorrect measure of one yields an incorrect measure of the other and vice versa.

Although less pervasive than it was during the great LIFO–FIFO debate, more than remnants of this notion remain. One still finds claims that the income statement is more important than the balance sheet. From this comes the recurring proposal that we use one valuation method for the income statement and a different valuation method for the balance sheet. Several people have claimed, for example, that although exit values may be appropriate for the balance sheet, they are not appropriate for the income statement. They suggest presenting a replacement-cost income statement.

In my view, this is a fundamental error. I view the income statement as an explanation of the changes on the balance sheet. Just as one cannot explain changes in weight by presenting volume flows, one cannot explain changes in exit values by presenting replacement-cost flows. And vice versa. Therefore, I think that we ought to choose the best valuation method rather than choosing the most important statement. Once we choose a valuation method, we ought to use it for both statements.

There are some variations on this theme that do not commit the error and therefore are exempted from the above comments. In general, those variations are that we should add and subtract some entry value figures in the body of the income statement without disturbing the bottom line. Since the same magnitudes are added and subtracted, the effect on net income is zero. (See, e.g., Friedman, "Exit-Price Income.") This proposal is to report net exit-value income augmented by entry-value data. For example, one proposal is to subtract the entry value of units sold from revenues in order to display the Edwards and Bell concept of current operating profit. Then, the difference is added back so that it does not affect the net income reported. Since these variations do not violate the relation of income to wealth,

I have no objections on that score. Since entry values are empirically testable, I also have no objections on this score.[2,3] Obviously, these variations are based on the belief that current operating profit is relevant. Of that I am skeptical. Sometimes I seem to catch a glimmer of the relevance of current operating profit, but every time I try to demonstrate it to myself, I fail. Since the demonstration remains elusive, I will remain skeptical of the relevance. Perhaps a reader can provide a demonstration.

11.3 Explanations, Predictions, and Forecasts

> In explaining we look for true premises from which the already verified conclusion is deducible, and in predicting we verify the premises before verifying the conclusion.
>
> PAP, *Introduction*, p. 344

The income statement is an explanation of the changes in COG for a given period of time. By the very nature of the term "explanation," the time period lies in the past. If it referred to the future, it would be termed a "forecast." One oft-repeated objection to income statements in general and exit-value income statements in particular is that they are "obviously irrelevant" because they are concerned with the past, while decisions require forecasts. It is true that decisions require

2. I do have objections to those variations that propose replacement costs since they are not empirically testable. Thus, the comments refer to the variations that specify entry values.

3. Some historic-cost proponents do object because the exchanges are "hypothetical." In the scientific literature they are called "counterfactual conditionals." In English they are called "statements in the subjunctive mood" which was the basis for Rosenfield's ("Subjunctive Gains and Losses") terminology.

Scientists do not object to employing counterfactual conditionals. Quite the contrary, they are indispensable in science. "Flexible" means, "If I were to subject this object to force, it would flex." "Potential energy" means, "If I were to burn this object, it would yield so many Btu's." In the same way, these proposals say, "If I bought these units now, I would pay the entry value."

Of course, no scientist reports that he has flexed or burned something that he has not actually flexed or burned, but scientists do report what would happen *if* they flexed or burned it, and that is empirically testable. In the same way, reporting what one would pay if he purchased something now is empirically testable.

At first glance it appears that the proposal is to report that something was purchased that was not in fact purchased. That would be false in the same way that it would be false if a scientist reported burning something that he had not in fact burned. The truth value of the statement is saved when they add the difference back. In effect, the adding back says, "But I did not purchase those units now, so I must add their cost back to get the true command over goods." It is the same as the scientist saying, "If I had burned this object, I would have performed so much work; but I did not burn the object, so I must add it back to calculate the true work performed."

forecasts, but it does not follow from the truth of that proposition that explanations of the past are irrelevant. On the contrary, explanations are the logical obverse of predictions; and, as such, they may aid in developing a forecast even though they may not be forecasts. Again, the accounting error is to equate prediction to forecast and, worse, to disparage a measure because it is not a forecast.

With admirable scientific simplicity, Pap (*Introduction*, pp. 343ff) elucidates the similarity of and difference between prediction and explanation by employing the familiar example of milk turning sour. The explanatory form is: "This milk is sour because it was exposed to x temperature for y time." The explanation is informative in and of itself. Not incidentally, its logical obverse permits one to forecast what will happen to milk if it is subjected to x temperature for y time. If the explanation is true, the predictive form is: If milk is exposed to x temperature for y time, then it will turn sour. However, if one is not able to determine whether or not the milk will be subjected to x temperature for y time, one will not be able to forecast whether or not the milk will turn sour.

Many more examples come immediately to mind. Past weight gains or losses can be explained by differences between caloric intake by eating and caloric burning by exercise. Such explanations are informative despite the fact that you would be in a hazardous position if you tried to forecast my future weight gain or loss. The reason is not because of the irrelevancy of the explanation, but rather because you cannot forecast either my future eating or exercise habits. Hougen et al. (*Chemical Process*, pp. 248–49) explain a heat balance by means of a 20-term equation. One of the terms is the mass of CO_2 leaving the turbine. Since they cannot forecast this mass change, they cannot forecast the heat balance; but this does not invalidate the explanation or make it irrelevant.

The exit-value income statement is exactly the same form. It explains the increment in command over goods by taking the difference between the net increment in the exit value of cash (revenues and wages) and the decrement in the exit value of the depreciable asset (depreciation). If one can forecast future revenues, wages, and depreciation, one can also forecast future income. The fact that the inputs (being dependent upon fickle consumer tastes, technological changes, competitor's actions, and a raft of other things) are difficult, if not impossible, to forecast does not invalidate the explanation or make it irrelevant.

Sterling's law can be used to forecast the future exit value of automobiles. I am fairly confident that it will forecast next year's exit value, but I am less confident about the following year. After

10 years, I am quite uneasy about it. At 20 years out, we may all be riding monorails. I did not proffer the law because of its ability to forecast but rather because it refers to empirical phenomena. It is quite possible to measure the exit value of automobiles directly. A quick check of the latest, easily obtained Blue Book will reveal the exit value (wholesale price) of almost all models. The law happens to be more convenient (less costly) to apply than to measure directly. Thus, its ability to forecast is incidental. The important point is that it refers to empirical phenomena.

Even if the law is a perfect forecaster of depreciation, we still must forecast revenues and wages before we can forecast income. Of course, it is possible that exit-value income may be a good forecaster of itself. If so, we could just fit a trend line and project it into the future. I do not have much hope for this approach because like many economic measures, exit-value income will probably go up and down in no discernable pattern. Some economic measures have been shown to be a random walk, notably the prices of shares on the New York Stock Exchange. However, the fact that present and past prices do not yield a trend line does not invalidate their use as present measures and explanations of the past.

We also need to compare *what* is to be forecasted. If forecastability is the sole criterion, then historic-cost straight-line depreciation is the best depreciation method since this year's depreciation is a perfect forecaster of next year's depreciation. However, in the apposite terminology of Revsine ("Predictive Ability"), such depreciation is an "artifact," and there is no known relevance of either the calculation or forecast of such artifacts. By contrast, the change in command over goods is an empirical phenomenon, and the relevance of the attribute to some, but not all, decision models has been demonstrated supra. The first criterion should be relevance; after that we could consider the forecastability of the attribute. Artifacts may be easy to forecast; but since they are irrelevant, there is no point in forecasting them. Empirical phenomena may be difficult, even impossible, to forecast; but since they are relevant, there is a need to measure them, to explain them and to try to forecast them.[4]

---

4. This discussion should not be taken as an indication that exit values or command over goods are the only empirical phenomena that can be or need be measured and/or forecasted. To cite just one example, consider Beaver's ("Financial Ratios") work on the ability of ratios to forecast failure. Firm failure is obviously relevant and obviously an empirical phenomenon. On the other hand, it seems to be equally obvious that it is an error (and a misinterpretation of Beaver, Kennelly, and Voss ("Predictive Ability")) to say that an artifact which can be forecasted is somehow superior to an empirical phenomenon which cannot be forecasted.

11.4 Averaging, Forecasting, and Measuring

> But never do we say that we are measuring the value
> of a quantity at a future time, even though it may
> be possible to *predict* [forecast] that value on the basis
> of a measurement made at present.
>
> MARGENAU, *Physical Reality*, p. 374

A basic characteristic of present accounting practice is the calculation
of *average* costs. We divide the cost of an inventory lot by the quantity
of units to obtain the average cost per unit. We divide the cost of
an automobile by the years of service life to obtain the average cost
per year. The result is that an equal amount of cost is assigned to
each unit or year. This has a tendency to *smooth* the expenses and
income. By contrast, exit-value accounting often results in unequal
amounts being assigned to units or years. This has a tendency to
"rough" the expenses and income—to report differing amounts instead
of equal amounts.

This inequality of exit-value expenses and income is the basis for
objections to reporting it. Some use the derisive term "yo-yo profits"
to express this objection. They feel that reporting unequal amounts
would be inequitable or misleading. I am convinced that part of this
objection is due to the fact that we accountants are unfamiliar with
exit-value statements. We feel more comfortable with the historic-cost
income statements simply because they are familiar. There is no reply
except to say that every new method is, by definition, less familiar
than old methods. Since stability of method is desired, we cannot
accept every new method without first subjecting it to scientific tests
and criticism. However, we also cannot reject every new method solely
because it is unfamiliar if we are to ever accept new methods.

The accountant's general tendency is to prefer a constant or equal
expense per period or per product to a variable or unequal expense.
Gellein ("Decreasing Charge Concept," p. 57) noted this tendency
long ago:

> This convention, which for convenience will be called the "constant
> charge" concept of allocating costs, assumes that the same cost factor
> should be assigned to every like unit (whether a unit of time, product,
> or some other factor) in the series with which benefits from the use
> of an asset or service can be identified.
>
> The constant-charge notion probably appeals to the sense of logic
> of most people. An asset costing $240 benefits 120 like units; therefore,
> the cost per unit must be $2—that is popular reasoning. This sense
> of logic, however, may be nothing more than a manifestation of the
> typical American's sense of equality or maybe his taste for symmetry.
> It is possible, too, that dislike for a pattern of spreading benefits on
> some other basis is a result of conflict with long-established tradition.

It seems that we accountants think in terms of averages, of equality of expenses per period, and this is deeply ingrained. Our texts justify *not* expensing the cost of a depreciable asset at time of acquisition by simply pointing out that expensing at acquisition would result in irregular expenses and, therefore, irregular income. Thus, irregular income is to be avoided by regularizing expenses. An alternative "reason" is that since an asset is expected to benefit periods or products equally, ipso facto it should be expensed equally. Even accelerated depreciation is justified by arguing that if maintenance is added to depreciation, it results in a more nearly equal total expense per period over the life of the asset. Since equality of people is part of the democratic ideal, since the word comes from the same root as equity, and since the accountants' views about democracy and equity seem to have been transferred to expenses, there may be no argument that would persuade accountants to accept inequality of expenses.

The only response is to present the choice of measuring versus averaging. We often face such choices. For example, we can average the distance travelled by a free-falling body. It is quite simple to divide the total distance by the time interval to obtain the average distance per unit of time. The alternative is to measure the distance travelled per unit of time. If we measure the body's rate of fall we find that it accelerates—the body travels unequal distances per unit of time. If we want to know where it is at a given point in time, we must measure. Applying the average will give us a false position. No physicist confuses his desire for equality with the need to measure. When he *measures*, he discovers inequalities; measurement is a fundamentally different concept from the *calculation* of equal averages.

We face the same choice. We can discover the inequalities by measuring, or we can calculate equal averages. If we apply the average decline per unit of time, we will have a false position in the sense that it does not describe empirical phenomena. Then we can fall back to defining what we do as not being a measure of anything, of accounting being necessarily conventional, an art instead of a science. Alternatively, we can measure.

But the situation is worse in accounting because the average is a forecast. We cannot calculate the average distance travelled by a falling body until the time interval has elapsed. If we make the calculation before the body comes to rest, we must forecast the time interval and this yields a forecasted average. The same is true when we forecast the service life of a depreciable asset. The depreciation is a forecasted average cost per year. I fail to understand how one can reject measuring the *present* exit value on the basis that it is a forecast. I fail to understand how one can accept a forecasted average on the basis that since the cost is historic, it is not a forecast.

In my view we should measure rather than forecast; we should measure rather than average. We should suppress our desire for equality and set out to discover the inequalities of the empirical world.

11.5 Funds Statements

> The purpose of the funds statement needs to be resolved. The funds statement should either report on flows into and out of some corpus of funds or serve to classify the different kinds of changes that occur in designated balance sheet categories or accounts.
>
> SPILLER and VIRGIL, "Effectiveness," p. 132

The income statement does not provide a complete explanation of the changes in successive balance sheets. Notably, it omits investments and disinvestments as well as changes in the composition of assets and equities. The purpose of the funds statement is to provide the explanation of those items that are not explained by the income statement. Taken together, the income statement and the funds statement are intended to provide a complete explanation—an explanation of *all* flows that occurred during a period.

The usual approach in preparing a funds statement is to take the difference between two balance sheets (a vector) and then to add back value changes such as depreciation. This results in an implicit definition: the funds statement is an explanation of *all* exchanges occurring during a period of time. To put it negatively, it does not explain value changes. Since it explains all exchanges, it overlaps the income statement by repeating the income-type exchanges. Thus, the funds statement displays income-type exchanges and nonincome-type exchanges. The income statement displays income-type exchanges and value changes. In historic-cost accounting, these value changes are allocations such as depreciation and bond discount amortization. In exit-value accounting, the value changes would be changes in the exit value.

Although these definitions appear simple, there are some confusing aspects that result in inconsistencies in present practices.[5] It may be that some of the confusion can be clarified by a systematic classification of exchanges and the consideration of them one by one.

---

5. These confusing aspects have little to do with the valuation system in use, and therefore what follows does not depend upon the adoption of exit values. It is general—not specific to a particular valuation system.

11.5.1 Investment Exchanges. Recall that equation (11.1-1) contained Y_{fT} and I_{fT} where I_{fT} was defined as the sum of investments and disinvestments by owners and creditors of firm f during period T. These investment exchanges are currently displayed on the funds statements. Specifically, I_{fT} is analyzed and assigned names such as "issuance of capital stock," "dividends," and "retirement of bonds."

It would be possible, of course, to display the investment exchanges on a separate statement. For purposes of analysis of different types of exchanges, let us assume that we prepare a separate report entitled "investment statement."

Most investment exchanges are quite clear. It is easy to identify investments and disinvestments by owners and creditors. It is also apparent that all investments are sources of assets and all disinvestments are uses of assets. Therefore, preparation of the investment statement should not present any major difficulties.

It will avoid some difficulties. One is the barter problem. If plant is acquired and bonds are sacrificed, the funds statement must either omit the exchange or report it as *funds* provided by bonds and *funds* used for plant. Some people are troubled by this "fiction." I am not troubled, but it is clear that reporting *assets* provided by bonds on an investment statement is not a fiction. Therefore, reporting the "fiction" can be avoided by preparing a separate statement which utilizes a more precise terminology.

The netting problem would not be avoided. We would still need to decide whether to report both the investments and disinvestments of a particular type or to report the net amount. In present practice, we sometimes report the net change in an active equity account as a source or use of funds. For example, if notes payable is an active account, we sometimes report the net change instead of segregating the borrowings from the repayments and reporting them separately. Some are troubled by this method of reporting and recommend that we report the sources of funds from borrowings and the uses of funds from repayments since that is "actually" what happened. If the purpose is to display cash flows or funds flows, I must agree. However, if the purpose is to explain the change in the amount of assets, that is given by the net change in the notes payable account. Perhaps this problem could be solved by clarifying the purpose of the statement.

11.5.2 Equities—Sources of Assets. If we are interested only in explaining the change in the amount of assets, we need go no further. Taken together the income statement and the investment statement provide a complete explanation of the changes in the amount of assets.

Changes in the amount of assets come from three sources:

(1) Creditors
(2) Owners
(3) Customers

The investment statement provides an explanation of the changes due to exchanges with creditors and owners; the income statement provides an explanation of exchanges of the changes due to exchanges with customers and exchanges for customer service such as wages, as well as value changes such as depreciation. Thus, the two statements are all that we need to provide a complete explanation of changes in amount of assets.

We are usually not satisfied with this explanation. We also want to provide an explanation of changes in composition. Prior to discussing composition exchanges, let us return to the relation of stock to flows in order to explicate the relation of the three statements. As noted in Section 11.2:

$$a_{it} - a_{it-1} = \sum_{j=t-1}^{t} \Delta a_{ij}$$

where

$$a_{it} = \text{stock of } i \text{ at time } t$$
$$\Delta a_{ij} = \text{flow (in or out) of } i \text{ at time } j$$

The income and investment statements display the values of Δa_{ij}, the flows, for time period $t - 1$ to t. The only thing that we are doing is classifying these flows: some are classified as investments and others as income. Then we subclassify them. We use the general categories of creditors and owners to subclassify investments. We use the general categories of revenues and expenses to subclassify income. If we sum these classes, we get total flows for the time period. The total flows for a time period explain the change in total assets for that time period. Thus, $Y_{fT} + I_{fT}$ are the total flows. We also noted in Section 11.2 that

$$a_{it} = \sum_{j=0}^{t} \Delta a_{ij}$$

That is, the present stock is the sum of all past flows from the beginning to now. The same is true of total assets.

$$A_{ft} = \sum_{T=0}^{t} (Y_{fT} + I_{fT})$$

That is, the total assets at the present time are the sum of all past flows from the beginning to now. Prior to the existence of the firm it had no assets, all accounts had a zero balance. From the beginning to now, all assets have flowed in from three sources: creditors, owners and customers. The accounts now have nonzero balances due to the debits and credits entered to record these flows as they occurred.

Thus, if we combine the income and investment statement, we obtain an explanation of the change in total assets from the beginning (when they were zero) to now. Summing that combination by account class would be adding both sources and uses which would yield the *net* source of that account class.

Vector notation may help in visualizing this:

$$\vec{A}_{ft} = \sum_{T=0}^{t} (\vec{Y}_{fT} + \vec{I}_{fT})$$

For example, when we sum the sources of assets from bond issues in one statement with the uses of assets from bond retirement in another statement, we obtain the *net* sources of assets from bonds. Another name for net sources from bonds is "bonds payable," a subclass of liabilities which is a subclass of equities.

The same is true for all other equity account classes. The net source is the balance of the account. Thus, "equities" is another name for "net source of assets." In general, we have three classes of equities:

(1) Creditors—liabilities
(2) Owners—contributed capital
(3) Customers—retained earnings

All equities are similar in that they are sources of assets. They are also different, and these differences are the bases for the classification.

The broad differences are contractual or legal. In general, creditors are to be repaid at a specific time, while owners are to be repaid at a specific event. Liquidation is the event at which owners are to be repaid, while liabilities are to be repaid at the due date. Although rare, there are some exceptions (e.g., perpetual bonds) but the common assertion that owners are never to be repaid is a misstatement since the contractual agreement between owners and firms invariably specifies the distribution of assets at the event of liquidation. Another difference is that the amount to be repaid is fixed for creditors, while the amount to be repaid to owners is residual. But it also has exceptions since there are different levels of preference for creditors and owners, resulting in several levels of residuals upon liquidation, as well as several levels of residuals prior to liquidation for the distribution of income, for example, preferred versus common shareholders.

Note that the basis for distinguishing owners and creditors is the difference in the *claims* on the assets of the firm. Although both are classified as sources, they are subclassfied on the basis of claims. The same type of distinction is used to classify customers. Upon completion of the exchange, the customers have no further claim on the firm. To put it in economic terms, an investment is an unrequited exchange. Owners and creditors make unrequited exchanges with the firm which means that a future requital is contracted. Customers' exchanges are requited. They have received their product or service from the firm for which they act as a source of assets to the firm; but once that product or service is received, the customers have no further claim on the assets of the firm. Instead, the owners have the claim on assets in the amount of that net source. Retained earnings represent a net source from customers and a claim by owners.

There has been a long-standing dispute among accountants regarding the nature of equities. Some argue that they are sources but not claims, while others argue that they are claims but not sources. One focal point of the dispute is the nature of owners' equity. Some argue that since there is no due date for owners' equity, it cannot be considered a claim. Retained earnings are similar, so the argument goes, in that they are not a claim by customers despite the fact that they are a source. From this some people conclude that the only description of equities is that they are sources, not claims. The opposition focuses on accounts such as taxes payable and points out that the government does not supply assets specific to the firm (although it supplies public goods such as police protection); therefore, these accounts cannot be considered a source. The opposition thus concludes that the only proper description of equities is that they are claims, not sources. Indeed, it is true that the government does not supply assets to the firm, but it is also true that the taxes have been deducted from income and from retained earnings. The net source of assets from customers has therefore been reduced by the amount of the taxes payable. This is a part of the netting problem. The balance of the retained earnings is the net amount after deducting taxes. If desired, we could display the gross source from the customers and omit the taxes payable as a source. To put it another way, it is similar to retained earnings. The taxes payable figure is a source from customers and a claim by the government, just as the retained earnings figure is a source from customers and a claim by owners. To put it a third way, the taxes payable figure is a composition exchange of the kind to be discussed below, not an investment exchange.

I am here trying to ameliorate this long-standing dispute. I think that it is a false issue. To my mind, equities are sources *and* claims. They are all sources which are subclassified by their claim status. More importantly, assets are stocks which are sums of flows. Y_{fT} + I_{fT} is an expression of the total flows for time period T. When T is an interim time period, Y_{fT} and I_{fT} are called revenues and expenses, sources and uses; and the statements are called income and investment. When T runs from the inception of the firm, Y_{fT} and I_{fT} are called equities; and the statement is called a balance sheet.

11.5.3 Composition Exchanges. In addition to income and investment exchanges, the funds statement explains exchanges of assets for assets and equities for equities. The problem is that Y_{fT} and I_{fT} provide an explanation of changes in total assets, but they do not provide an explanation of the changes in the composition of assets and equities. Thus, Y_{fT} and I_{fT} do not provide a complete explanation of the changes in successive balance sheets. For this reason it is thought advisable to include composition exchanges on the funds statement.

An example of a composition exchange is the purchase of a plant for cash. Giving a note payable for an account payable is another example. Since such exchanges would not be included in either the income or investment statement, we need a third flow statement to account for them. The net composition exchanges are given by the difference in vectors. In order to visualize the statement, we must define a vector, $\vec{B}_{ft}$, which includes all accounts on the balance sheet. I will adopt the convention that all equity accounts (or credit balances) have a negative sign so that the sum of assets and equities is zero. Then

$$\vec{B}_{ft+1} - \vec{B}_{ft} - \vec{Y}_{fT} - \vec{I}_{fT} = \vec{C}_{fT}$$

An alternative way to visualize the statement is as a worksheet which includes all the balance sheet accounts at two dates as well as columns for eliminating investment exchanges, income exchanges, and value changes. After elimination the crossfoot yields the net effect of all composition exchanges.

Obviously, $\vec{C}_{fT}$ sums to zero—the worksheet balances. Displaying the components of $\vec{C}_{fT}$ on a composition statement would then constitute an explanation of the net composition exchanges. If desired, we could show both the inflows and outflows of each account instead of the net changes.

We are usually not satisfied with simply displaying the composition exchanges. Instead we want to highlight the cash flows or funds flows. In order to accomplish this, we set one account (cash) or a group of accounts (funds) apart and explain the composition exchanges in terms of the inflows and outflows of that account or accounts. In effect, since

$$B_{ft} = \{b_{1t}, b_{2t}, ..., b_{mt}\}$$

and

$$0 = b_{1t} + b_{2t} + ... + b_{mt}$$

then

$$- b_{1t} = b_{2t} + ... + b_{mt}$$

and account 1 is to be explained by the changes in all the other accounts. The vector subtraction results in

$$-b_{1t+1} - (-b_{1t}) - (-y_{1T}) - (-i_{1T})$$
$$= (b_{2t+1} - b_{2T} - y_{2T} - i_{2T}) + ... + (b_{mt+1} - b_{mt} - y_{mT} - i_{mT})$$

and the change in account 1 is explained by showing that it is equal to the sum of the changes in all the other accounts. If account 1 is cash, we have explained the change in cash due to composition exchanges.

We would still face the problem of barters and netting. If plant were exchanged for equipment, for example, we would need to decide whether or not the barter should be reported as if the exchange had been a sale of plant for cash and a purchase of equipment for the same amount of cash. I am not troubled by reporting such "as if" or counterfactual conditional exchanges. It seems to me that a barter which bypasses cash has exactly the same effect as if there had been two exchanges which went through cash; and, therefore, I do not consider the method of reporting to be a problem. The same is true for netting. Showing the exchange broad or net is merely a question of how much detail one wants to show.

11.5.4 Purpose. I think that the lingering confusion about the funds statement is due to a failure to be clear about the purpose of the statement. Is its purpose to explain *all* of the changes in successive balance sheets? If so, *all* exchanges *plus all* value changes must be included. The income statement would then be a proper subset of the funds statement. Is the purpose to explain changes in successive balance sheets due to exchanges? If so, *all* exchanges, income, investment, and composition must be included. The income statement would then intersect with the funds statement since both would include income exchanges. But the funds statement would exclude value changes. Is the purpose to explain exchanges that resulted in a change in total assets? If so, the funds statement is a proper subset of exchanges since composition exchanges would be excluded; and, as before, the funds statement would intersect with the income statement since both report income exchanges.

Is the purpose to explain cash flows? If so, we must include all composition exchanges, such as collection of accounts receivable, as well as investment and income exchanges. Is the purpose to explain funds flows, with funds defined as net quick assets or as net working capital? If so, we must exclude composition exchanges within the defined fund category. (For example, collection of accounts receivable would be excluded.)

I cannot provide an answer to the question of the purpose of the funds statement. I suspect that all cash flows (including "as if" cash flows for barters) would provide the most relevant information. However, this opinion is based on a suspicion rather than a demonstration. Since I have not demonstrated the conclusion, I will leave it as a suggestion rather than argue that it is superior to the adoption of other purposes. Perhaps a reader can provide a demonstration.

If we were to adopt this purpose, it would result in the funds statement reporting *all* exchanges. It would intersect with the income statement to the extent of income exchanges; thus the same information would be reported twice. The additional information on the income statement would be value changes. The additional information on the funds statement would be investment and composition exchanges.

11.5.5 Cash Flow Income. Sometime ago financial analysts began talking about "cash flow income." They adjusted the income statement by adding back allocations such as depreciation. The resulting figure was termed cash flow income or cash flows from operations, and it was considered to be more useful than the net income figure. Most accountants reacted with alarm. They pointed out that cash-basis accounting had long ago been abandoned and replaced by accrual-basis accounting because the accrual basis provided the more accurate, more useful figures.

The battle lines were drawn with financial analysts opting for cash-flow income and most accountants opting for accrual income. This was prior to the exposure of the allocation problem by Thomas, and so the terminology used in the debate was a good deal less precise than that used in the current literature. The arguments in favor of cash-flow income were based on two rather vaguely stated reasons: (1) cash flows were important; (2) allocations such as depreciation were not cash flows—they were not "real." The reply by accountants was equally vague. They said that depreciation was a "real" expense and that the net income figure must reflect the "cost expiration" of plant just as it reflected the "cost expiration" of cash paid in wages.

Some accountants sympathized with the financial analysts. One (Drebin, "'Cash Flowitis'") phrased the question as to whether cash-flow income was a malady or syndrome. These accountants suspected that there was something wrong with allocations such as depreciation and, therefore, suspected that the fault lay with accounting, not with financial analysts. The financial analysts were exhibiting a syndrome rather than a malady. However, such accountants were a small minority. The conventional wisdom was that accrual net income was obviously superior to cash-flow income. The subject was not open to question.

Ironically, at the present time many accountants have adopted the view that cash-flow income is the superior concept. Although not yet a majority, their numbers are growing rapidly. In the current terminology, the reasons are three: (1) cash flows are relevant; (2) the concept avoids the allocation problem; (3) it avoids the valuation problem.

I agree with reason (1). Cash flows are relevant. My only disagreement is that I think that all cash flows are relevant. We should not restrict the reporting of cash flows to those from operations. When we discount future cash flows we must include the future entry value of plant to be purchased and the future exit value of plant to be sold. In the same way, when we report past cash flows we should include plant purchased and sold. That is, we should include composition and investment exchanges as well as income exchanges on the funds statement.

I also agree with reason (2). Reporting cash flows avoids the allocation problem. Cash flows are exchanges, not allocations. If we adopt the goal of reporting exchanges, the allocation problem does not arise.

Reason (3) is more complex. In one sense it does avoid the valuation problem in the same way that it avoids the allocation problem. If we adopt the goal of reporting nothing but exchanges, the valuation problem does not arise. But we must ask ourselves whether we want to report exchanges *and* values or exchanges *or* values.

Many cash-flow proponents apparently hold the view that reporting values and value changes is an alternate to reporting exchanges. They are seen to be mutually exclusive alternatives. On the basis of this view, cash-flow proponents have criticized the various valuation methods in general and exit values in particular. Those who have criticized me have evidently done so because in my past work I have not explicitly affirmed the relevance of cash flows. I hereby correct that ommission: cash flows are relevant and should be reported. I failed to mention it previously because it seemed to me that the relevance of cash flows was too obvious to require mention.

In my view, the two are complementary, not competing. We should prepare both an income statement and a funds statement, as well as a balance sheet. In this sense, reporting cash flows does not avoid the valuation problem. In the same way if we decide to continue to allocate instead of measure, we do not avoid the allocation problem.

On this basis we can subdivide the cash-flow proponents. I have no quarrel with those who want to report cash flows in addition to values and value changes or with those who want to provide funds statements in addition to income statements and balance sheets. We are focusing on different problems, not disagreeing. However, I disagree with those who want to report cash flows instead of values and value changes.

It is difficult to know the exact basis of the disagreement. Obviously, I applaud those who are attempting to avoid the allocation problem by not allocating. However, I disagree with those who are attempting to avoid the valuation problem by not valuing. Since they focus exclusively on the flows, I do not know what kind of stocks they would report, if any. Do they mean to report flows alone, to refuse to report stocks, or do they mean to report flows as well as some nonallocated, nonvalued stocks? If the latter, I am puzzled. I cannot conceive of a stock that is nonallocated and nonvalued. I would merely ask the proponents to make their proposed stocks explicit so we can examine them.

Although it seems difficult to believe, some proponents are apparently suggesting that we do not report any stocks, that we report flows alone. They explicitly argue that flows are relevant, and they come perilously close to implicitly deducing that stocks are irrelevant. Those who make such deductions must be overlooking the relation of stocks to flows. Surely they would not deduce that *cash stocks* are irrelevant from the premise that *cash flows* are relevant. If not, we must report cash stocks as well as cash flows. If we report cash stocks, we are faced with the problem of measuring or valuing or allocating them.

It seems obvious to me that cash stocks are equally as relevant as cash flows. If cash stocks are relevant, we have to ask if near-cash stocks (for example, short term, liquid receivables) are relevant, and then if other noncash stocks are relevant. I think the answer will be affirmative for each class of stocks. If so, we must report stocks as well as flows. And we must face the problem of valuing those stocks.

12

Conclusions

> Like as to make that the computations agree with the
> Sugars, the Silks, the Wools, it is necessary that the
> accomptant reckon his tares of chests, bags, and such
> other things: So when the *Geometricall* philosopher
> would observe in concrete the effects demonstrated
> in the abstract, he must defalke the impediments of
> the matter, and if he know how to do that, I do assure
> you, the things shall jump no less exactly than *Arith-*
> *metical* computations. The errours therefore lyeth
> neither in abstract, nor in concrete, nor in Geometry,
> nor in Physicks, but in the Calculator, that knoweth
> not know how to adjust his accompts.
> GALILEUS, *The Systeme of the World,* p. 185

The primary problem of accounting is that our figures do not have empirical referents. The fault lies neither in the abstract nor in the concrete but in ourselves—we do not know how to adjust our accounts. If figures do not represent empirical phenomena, then it is the preparers and purveyors of the figures who are at fault, not the phenomena.

The solution to the problem is to adopt the objective of reporting figures that represent empirical phenomena. The first, and most important, generally accepted accounting principle should be that we account for empirical phenomena. The *kind* of phenomena that we decide to account for is important, but secondary. We must first decide to account for *some* kind of phenomena. A corollary of this principle is the establishment of the generally accepted auditing standard that reported figures be empirically tested. The first, and most important, objective of auditing should be the assurance that the figures accurately represent the empirical phenomena that they are intended to represent.

A prerequisite to adopting this principle and standard is the recognition that it is a matter of choice. We must rid ourselves of the belief that accounting cannot be an empirical science. If it is possible for

213

us to decide that depreciation is a rational allocation that is *not* a measure of *anything,* then it is also possible for us to decide that it *is* a measure of *something.* If we can define our subject matter to be nonempirical, we can also define it to be empirical. Once we have defined it to be empirical, we can subject it to empirical testing.

To illustrate that empirical testing is possible, that it is a matter of choice, consider a bit of history. Most accountants remember the McKesson-Robbins case as a scandal, a blot on our record. Although I agree that it was a scandal, I remember it as resulting in the most important improvement in accounting in this century. It was a significant, albeit unrecognized, theoretical advance because it *partially transformed* accounting into an empirical science. Prior to the trial, empirical testing of asset quantities was not a generally accepted auditing standard. Instead of looking at the assets, auditors looked at the accounts and records. We did not recognize that to look at the accounts and records was a decision that we had made. Instead, we told ourselves that it was impossible to verify asset quantities because auditors lacked the expertise, because it was not a proper part of the auditing function, because it would be too costly, and so forth. At the trial, we attempted to defend ourselves by citing the fact that verifying quantities was not GAAS. We lost. The court recognized that this was a matter of choice, and it decided that auditors should get out of their ivory towers of accounts and records and get into the real world of asset quantities. Since then auditors have become quite proficient at verifying quantities.

At the present time the arguments for our inability to account for and verify asset values are almost identical to those used in regard to asset quantities. Instead of looking at present prices occasioned by the exchanges of other entities, we look at the records that show the past prices occasioned by the exchange of the entity we are accounting for. Instead of verifying that the figures accurately represent some extant value, we "examine" the accounts and recalculate the allocations of those past prices. We do not recognize that looking at those accounts and records is a decision that we have made. We tell ourselves that it is impossible to account for and verify asset values because we lack the expertise, because it is not a proper function of accounting, because it would be too costly, and so forth. In recent trials we have tried to defend ourselves by citing GAAP. We have lost. The courts, particularly in the Continental Vending case, have told us that GAAP is not a defense; instead we must assure ourselves that the financial statements are true, correct, and understandable by nonaccountants. They have not yet told us to account for and verify asset values, but they have come close. Before the courts decide this for us, before we are rocked by another scandal to which we must react, I hope we preact. I hope that we recognize that there is a decision to be made and that we set about explicitly making that decision. I hope that we decide to get out of our ivory tower of unexpired costs and get into the real world of market prices. The goal, then, is to extend the advance made by the McKesson-Robbins case to asset values, to *fully* transform accounting into an empirical science.

There have been a growing number of accountants who have more or less clearly recognized the need to transform accounting into an empirical science. Several proposals satisfy the requirement of empirical testability. These include unallocated entry values, undiscounted cash flows, and physical capacity, as well as exit values. Since all of these meet the criterion of empirical testability, the decision as to which one or which collection of these attributes that we should account for requires an additional criterion. Thus, the second problem facing accountants is the selection of which empirically testable attribute(s) we should measure and report.

The solution to this problem is the rigorous application of the relevance criterion. Instead of making vague assertions that this or that figure is "useful," we must get deeply involved in the decision process; we must carefully examine the various decision models that are designed to allow decision makers to achieve their individual objectives. This is a difficult task. It requires the accountant to examine the myriad decision situations that decision makers face and then examine the decision models to see what information is specified by (relevant to) those models.

In general, it requires that accountants become involved in decision science. Decision theorists build models with little regard for information constraints; accounting theorists design systems with little regard for model specifications. Close coordination is essential to the efficient operation of both the decision and the information system. As a subset of the total information system, accounting information must be controlled by decision-model specification, subject to measurement constraints and cost-benefit considerations. Thus, accountants must become cognizant of and responsive to decision-model specifications.

The adoption of the related criteria of empirical testability and relevance is the most important message of this essay. A less important message is that exit values satisfy both criteria. One reason that this is less important is that exit valuation is a conclusion drawn from the application of the criteria. Another reason is that it would be a vast improvement of accounting if any of the empirically testable attributes were adopted. Reporting unallocated entry values, for example, would be much superior to current practice. I do not understand the relevance of entry values, but they are empirically testable and therefore we could adjudicate our disputes. Ability to adjudicate disputes by empirical test would have the benefit of impeding the drift toward legalistic accounting. Entry values are not conventions to be decided by a legislature but rather either direct measurement or hypotheses which are true or false. Thus, reporting entry values would make accounting an empirical science and thereby stem the never-ending flow of regulations.

Although empirical testability is of great importance and would result in vast improvements, relevance is also important if we are to meet the needs of users. The decision models examined in this essay clearly indicate that for owned assets, the exit value is the relevant attribute. This conclusion was drawn in the specific case of accounting for automobiles. The reason for selecting automobiles, in addition to making the recommendations concrete, was the ready availability of prices in the second-hand market. Since the prices are available and since the empirical testability and relevance have been demonstrated, the conclusion is that we should begin to report exit values of automobiles on balance sheets and the difference in exit values on income statements, as well as purchases and sales of automobiles on funds statements.

Previous conclusions to report exit values of marketable securities have been resisted on the grounds of the lack of availability of exit values of other assets. A number of people have already raised the same objection to reporting exit values of automobiles. They point out the lack of availability of prices in the second-hand market of other depreciable assets. The studies that have been done indicate that exit values are much more readily available than is generally thought and that the incremental cost of obtaining them is relatively small. However, the total evidence is sparse and it is likely that obtaining second-hand prices for all assets will be a serious problem. But note that it is a *measurement* problem. If we can be clear on the *objective* in cases where measurement is not a problem, then we can address the issue of measurement where it is a problem. Thus, my recommendation is to begin with automobiles (and other easily measured assets such as marketable securities) and then extend it to other assets as we gain experience and as we solve the measurement problems. I cannot be sure that we will solve all the measurement problems, but I can be sure that we will not solve them if we do not try. I am also sure that it is a logical error to refuse to report measurements of one asset on the grounds that is difficult or impossible to measure other assets. Thus, the first problem to be solved is the conceptual one of establishing the criteria, the objective. After that we can extend exit-value accounting to other assets as the measurement circumstances permit.

This is an incremental approach. My recommendation is that we convert to exit values on an asset by asset basis. Many people prefer the revolutionary approach. They want to wait until all problems are solved before any changes are made. One objection to incremental-ization is made on the grounds of internal inconsistency of the statements. It is considered to be an error to report the exit value of some assets unless the exit values of all asset are reported. Those who take this position must be overlooking the vast inconsistencies that now plague our financial statements. We now report accelerated depreciation for automobiles and straight-line depreciation for build-ings. On the basis of consistency it would be no worse if we reported exit values of automobiles and book values of buildings. On other bases it would be much better to report exit values of automobiles. Other objections stem from broader issues such as social welfare considerations. It is alleged that we cannot report exit values of automobiles until we assess all of the distributional effects that would be caused by such a change. But then it is pointed out that we cannot determine those effects; and if we could, we could not compare interpersonal utilities to see whether or not the change would be desirable. Imposing such criteria paralyzes accounting. It prohibits any change and thereby freezes accounting at its position at the time the criteria are imposed. This reveals a fundamental problem. Had we imposed the criteria in, say, 1930, we would still be using 1930 practices. Had we imposed them in 1940, we would still be using 1940 practices. Since it would be absurd to allow practices to be determined by the accident of the time at which the criteria were imposed, we must compare the social welfare effects of the 1930 to the 1940 practices to see which we prefer. For the same reason, we must compare the social welfare effects of present practices to proposed practices to see which we prefer. Until we can do that, we cannot refuse to make changes on the basis of a social welfare criterion. Social welfare considerations do not necessarily favor the status quo. I have no objection to social welfare considerations, but I do object to the idea that such considerations prohibit change. Thus, my recommendation is that we begin to report exit values while continuing research on the broader issues.

There are many other objections to exit-value accounting. Some of those objections were considered and rejected in the preceding chapters. One further objection is discussed in the appendix. Undoubtedly there are many more objections which I have overlooked. I invite the readers to raise their objections in general but especially in the context of the firm model discussed in this essay. I think that exit values will be able to withstand objections if the same type of objections are applied with equal vigor to the competing valuation methods, but I cannot be sure of that until the objections are raised and considered. However, exit values are secondary. The primary message is that we abandon the specific criteria of accounting and adopt the general scientific criteria of empirical testability and relevance. That is the first step and the most important step toward a science of accounting.

Appendix
An Extreme Case

> . . . at times theory can be tested only by an extreme
> example. If theory does not stand up under such a
> test, suspicion is aroused that the theory does not
> furnish a sound foundation for any superstructure of
> accounting principles.
>
> GILMAN, "Accounting Principles," p. 116

In the previous chapters we have considered an asset whose exit value declines gradually over time. Many accountants concede the possibility of exit-value accounting in such cases. However, I often encounter an intense negative reaction to exit-value accounting when those values change abruptly. The most extreme case is when the exit value of a costly asset goes to zero immediately after acquisition. Colleagues often present me with such a case and ask what I would do. My reply is that if the exit value is in fact zero after acquisition, I would write it down to zero on the first reporting date following acquisition. This reply is considered to be a *reductio ad absurdum* proof of the error of adopting exit-value accounting. I have been presented with this case and observed the negative reaction so often that, at the suggestion of Professor Donald Corbin, I have named it "the case of the $1,000,000 oil drilling rig in the middle of the Sahara Desert." Since many accountants think that this case provides prima facie evidence of the absurdity of exit-value accounting, since it is supposed to be the most telling case against exit-value depreciation, I will now discuss it. If an effective defense for exit values can be presented in response to the most difficult case, then it should provide some indication that exit values could also be defended against less difficult cases.

The case is that an oil explorer expends $1,000,000 for a drilling rig and begins exploration in the Sahara Desert. Immediately after the rig is put into operation, the exit value goes to zero; that is, the cost of dismantling and transporting the rig to a market where it could be sold equals or exceeds the proceeds that would be derived from its sale. Under exit-value accounting $1,000,000 would be reported as an expense in the first year. The cash used to purchase the rig had an exit value or command over goods of $1,000,000. This has disappeared since the rig has been purchased, and the rig has an exit value of zero. Other costs such as wages would also be reported as expenses as the cash is paid or the liability is incurred. They would not be capitalized or amortized.

The prospective deposit would be valued at the amount for which it could be sold. That would be zero initially. The amount may go up if the geological reports are encouraging or remain at zero if they are discouraging. If encouraging geological reports resulted in increments in the exit value of the prospective deposits, they would be reported as value increments in the years in which they occur. If subsequent geological reports are discouraging resulting in a decrease in the exit value, then the prospective deposit would be written down in the year in which the decrease occurred. If a deposit is discovered, the value increment of the deposit would be reported at the time of the discovery. That deposit would be valued at the amount it would fetch in an immediate sale, that is, the amount for which the entire deposit in the ground could be sold.[1] When a deposit is discovered, the explorer has the option either to sell the deposit as a whole or to pump the oil from the ground and sell it by the barrel. If the explorer takes the former route, there is no problem. The proceeds from the sale of the deposit would be approximately equal to the exit value. The gain would not be recognized at the time of the sale since it would have been reported as a value increment at the time of the discovery. An adjustment may be required for any difference between the sales proceeds and the previously assigned exit value of the deposit, but no conceptual problems arise in this option. If the explorer decides to pump the oil and sell it by the barrel, the accounting is straightforward. The cash proceeds from the sale of the oil and the cash disbursements for lifting costs would be reported as revenues and expenses in the period in which the cash was received or disbursed or the receivable or payable was incurred. Since the

1. "Exit value" differs from "net realizable value" in that in the latter we are required to deduct lifting costs, transportation expenses, and the normal profit margin from the refinery price of the crude. What is sought in exit-value accounting is the immediate sale price of the oil *as is*. Thus, the exit value of the deposit will be different from the net realizable value of the oil.

exit value of the deposit is dependent upon the price and the quantity of the crude, we can note that if the price remains constant, the exit value of the deposit will decline as the oil is lifted. However, given the volatility of the price of crude, it is quite possible for the exit value of the deposit to increase even though the quantity has decreased. Therefore, the best we can say about the pattern of the exit value of the deposit is that it will have to be determined at the date of statement preparation.[2] The change in the exit value of the deposit would be reported as either a value increment (appreciation) or a value decrement (depreciation) on the income statement for the period in which the change occurred.

There are many alternative methods of accounting for this case. Within the historic-cost method there are several thousand submethods which would result in different values and different incomes. The cost of the rig could be depreciated while drilling is going on or it could be deferred until drilling is completed. If the hole is dry, the deferred cost of the rig could be expensed immediately or it could be amortized over time or over other discoveries. If a deposit is discovered, the deferred cost of the rig could be depleted over the quantity in the well, or it could be added to other costs and depleted over the quantity in a field. The deposit would not be reported, which is equivalent to valuing it a zero. Those who consider it absurd to value the rig at zero under exit-value accounting have no qualms about valuing the deposit at zero under historic-cost accounting.

I am less certain about how to generalize replacement-cost accounting for this case. The question is: Should it be the replacement cost of the rig or the deposit or both? Many replacement-cost proponents accept all historic-cost procedures except for the substitution of current purchase prices for past purchase prices. For this group, the depletion per barrel would be current cost of the rig divided by the estimated barrels. This is updated historic-cost accounting with the deposit reported at zero. If the replacement cost of the deposit is accounted for, I assume that the deposit would be written up to its current purchase price, and this would be the basis for the depletion per barrel. But what happens to the replacement cost of the rig under this option? If both the replacement cost of the deposit and the replacement cost of the rig were deducted from the sales proceeds,

---

2. It turns out that exit values of deposits are relatively easy to determine. Oil companies regularly buy and sell deposits or fractions of deposits (called participating units); therefore, the market, albeit far from perfect, is well established and the prices are known within relatively narrow limits.

the current operating profit could easily be negative even though the incremental revenues from lifting were greater than the incremental costs of lifting. Since this would violate the purpose of reporting current operating profits and since this would yield an erroneous signal, perhaps the proponents would value the rig at zero and the deposit at its current purchase price. If so, the net result would be similar to exit-value accounting. The main difference might be the timing of the write-off of the rig. I would prefer to write off the rig at acquisition. Under replacement costing, the write-off may be deferred until discovery. But I do not understand the rationale for deferring the write-off, nor do I understand the rationale for valuing the rig at its exit value of zero when the avowed purpose is to report replacement costs.

I have similar problems with the other valuation methods. The rig and the deposit are incommensurable units which render physical capacity an enigma. The range of the future cash flow runs from zero for a dry hole to perhaps $100,000,000 for a major discovery. Assigning subjective probabilities to those cash flows is only one of the seemingly insurmountable empirical problems of reporting discounted values.

I will not go into detail in describing the competing methods. Instead, I will ask readers who are proponents of competing methods to supply the details for themselves. There are many objections to exit-value accounting. There are even more objections when the case is as extreme as the one just described. I will consider some, but only some, of those objections.

A.1 Averaging Versus Measuring

Exit-value accounting for this case would result in irregular expenses and, therefore, irregular income. I am convinced that one of the main reasons for the intense negative reaction to exit-value accounting in such cases is simply that it does result in a high variation in expenses and income. This is a rather curious reaction because on the one hand we accountants argue against the smoothing of income and expenses. On the other hand it seems that we experience uneasy feelings when income and expenses are not smooth. This is the only basis I can find for our inclination to average (amortize or allocate) the expenses—it results in a smoother income. I agree that averaging will result in a smoother income but the choice, as I see it, is to measure or to smooth. If we choose to measure, we will find that exit values are in fact highly variable. The question then is whether we report the variations as we find them or conceal those variations by averaging.

It is fairly easy to demonstrate the relevance of the exit value of the rig at each point in time. For example, if the explorer is drilling, he needs to compare his updated forecast of the possibility of discovering oil to the zero exit value of the rig in order to determine whether to continue drilling (and to incur the incremental costs of drilling) or to abandon the project. Thus, each time the explorer receives a new geological report, the exit value of the rig is relevant to the decision of whether or not he ought to continue drilling. By contrast, I cannot conceive of the relevance of an averaged or allocated conventional value of the rig whether it be by replacement or historic costing.

A.2 Time and Measurements

The income statement specifies a particular time interval and the balance sheet specifies a particular point in time. All measurements are made at a point in time. The purpose of the measurement is to discover the magnitude at that point in time without regard to what has gone before or what will come after that point in time. What will come after the measurement is a separate process known as forecasting. What has gone before is a separate process known as history. It is an error to confuse measurement with history or with forecasts.

Those accountants who argue that we ought not to report a zero value for this oil rig "because that expenditure will benefit the future" are confusing measurements with forecasts. It may very well be that this oil rig will result in a discovery that will have a value in the future, but that does not mean that it has a value in the present. It is undeniable that the oil rig required the sacrifice of a past value, but that does not mean that it has a present value.

I think that the main problem is one of language. We have not carefully distinguished forecasts from measurements and our manner of speaking often permits us to confuse the two. Margenau (*Physical Reality*, p. 374) draws the distinction clearly: "But never do we say that we are measuring the value of a quantity at a future time, even though it may be possible to *predict* [forecast] that value on the basis of a measurement made at present."

We may eventually decide to report forecasts. I am not so much concerned at the moment about whether or not we should report forecasts but rather with the need for clearly distinguishing measurements from forecasts. To continue to use the same term for both processes is almost certain to be productive of errors.

Even if we agreed to forecast, we would still find it necessary to measure. As I have tried to demonstrate in Section 11.3, one needs to compare the present measured exit values to the forecasted discounted values. Therefore, we need measurements of exit values; and if those exit values are zero, we should show them at zero regardless of their forecasted future magnitudes or their past magnitudes. By extension, since the income statement is an explanation of value changes, the income statement should show the decline in exit values for a given interval of time regardless of past events or forecasted future events.

A.3 The Rig Versus the Deposit

It is a non sequitur to argue that the oil *rig* should be reported as having a $1,000,000 value because the oil *deposit* has or is expected to have a greater than $1,000,000 value. If a deposit has been discovered, we ought to try to measure the value of that deposit separately from measuring the value of the rig. They are two different assets.

This is also a problem with language. We often encounter arguments in the accounting literature which, when examined carefully, turn out to be an argument that says that we ought to assign x value to asset A because asset B has or had or is expected to have a value greater than or equal to x. For example, in the historic-cost method of valuation, we would value the oil rig at $1,000,000 because the cash expended for that rig had a value of $1,000,000 and because an oil deposit of greater than $1,000,000 was or is expected to be discovered. The oil deposit is not shown on the balance sheet, but the rig is shown on the balance sheet because the deposit exists or is expected to be discovered. The fact that the *deposit* has or is expected to have a value does not allow one to conclude that the *rig* has a value.

The same is true of discounted values. The forecasted cash flows from selling the oil do not inure to the drilling rig. If we want to report the discounted values of the deposit, we should label those values as being from the deposit, not the rig.

Again, we may eventually decide to report forecasted values. Even if we do, we should be clear as to what it is that we are valuing. For the reasons previously presented, I think that we ought to also measure the exit value of the assets. If the deposit has an exit value, we should report it. If the rig has a zero exit value, we should also report that. By extension, since the exit-value income statement is an explanation of the changes in exit values, we should report the increment in value from the deposit as a positive item and the decrement in value (depreciation) of the rig as a negative item.

A.4 The Various Statements

Many accountants argue that we need to provide a record of past expenditures even if they represent sunk costs or zero exit values. I agree. Exit-value accounting does not destroy the permanent record of past expenditures. The original purchase price of the rig would be recorded in the journal and the ledger. It would be reported as a use of funds on the funds statement, and it would also be reported as an expense on the income statement. The annual report contains statements for the past five or ten years so that the expenditure continues to be reported.

Thus, the argument is not truly concerned with providing a record of past expenditures; instead, it is concerned with *what* statement the purchase price should be reported on. Specifically, historic-cost proponents argue that it should be reported as an asset on the balance sheet. This is a non sequitur. To argue that the expenditure ought to be reported does not imply that it ought to be reported as an asset. In addition, to report the expenditure on the balance sheet is redundant. Since the other statements report the expenditure, to continue to show that expenditure on the balance sheet is unnecessarily repetitious.

In short, the funds statement would show the expenditure for the oil rig. The income statement would show the decline in the value of the rig. Between the two, they provide a complete history of the rig. Therefore, there is no need to continue to show a book value of the rig on the balance sheet for the purpose of providing a history of the project or the firm.

A.5 Comparability Over Time

We often state that consistency over time is desirable, forgetting that the purpose of consistency is to permit comparability. It is thought to be inconsistent to write down an asset to zero at acquisition and then to have no further expenses to charge to subsequent periods. Thus, consistency is used to defend the practice of allocating the cost over time.

This is an error. It is not inconsistent to charge one time period with the entire expenditure and subsequent time periods with a zero amount of the expenditure; instead, it is a recognition of the change in exit values. The difference is between reporting a change in some empirical phenomena and reporting an allocation. It is not an inconsistency in reporting.

There are many analogies. The weather service reports a *measurement* of rainfall regardless of whether or not the measured amount is consistent with past measured amounts. We would all recognize it as an error if the weather service "deferred" a flood and allocated it evenly over a future expected drought. The very purpose of measurement is to discover variations in empirical phenomena. By contrast, it seems that the purpose of allocation is to make the empirical phenomena appear to be smooth regardless of the actual variations.

Of course, there is nothing wrong with averaging past measurements over time periods. The weather service reports average rainfall per year. There are many uses for such averages. One use is to compare a current year's measurement to an average in order to get an idea of how unusual the current year is. Another use is to forecast next year's measurement. In the absence of other information, we often extrapolate past averages into the future. When the future becomes the present we can make another measurement and compare it to the forecast. Note, however, that if we allocate we no longer have a measurement to compare to the average. If the weather service reports this year's rainfall as an allocation of last year's flood, we cannot determine the variation from the average. We do not know what in fact (empirically) happened this year, so we cannot compare it to a forecast or to an average of the past years' measurements.

Exit-value accounting is an attempt to measure the change in COG of a given firm. If it is discovered empirically that such changes are equal, the equality of changes will be reported. If it is discovered that they vary, such variations will be reported. In the extreme case under consideration, the changes are highly variable by assumption. That high variation would be reported. In some contexts we clearly recognize the inappropriateness of allowing management to smooth income. In other contexts we seem to implicitly justify a smoothing on the basis of some ill-defined notions of "properly matching." Those who want to argue that we ought to continue to smooth should be required to make their justifications explicit so that they can be examined. In addition, note that if we do permit such allocations, we are back to the point of having defined an unresolvable issue. As Lutz and Lutz (*Theory of Investment*, p. 7) have said, the depreciation problem has been unresolved for over 100 years. If we define it as a cost allocation, I expect that it will remain unresolved for the next 100 years.

The notion of comparability means that we ought to be able to compare one period to another period by measuring the same attribute. It does not mean that the measure of that attribute shows an equal change in each time period. Thus, if we decide on other grounds that exit values are the appropriate attributes to measure, it is proper for us to report the unequal changes in exit values even if that means writing a large expenditure down to zero at acquisition.

A.6 Comparability Among Firms

For purposes of illustration, suppose that one driller has expended $1,000,000 for an oil rig to drill in the proven reserves of the Permian Basin. The other driller has expended the same amount to drill in the highly speculative unproven reserves of the Sahara Desert.

In order to be able to compare these firms or projects, we must measure the same attribute: we cannot allocate. If we were to allocate, it would be possible to report equal book values for these two disparate projects. It would also be possible to report different book values, but the difference would not necessarily have any relation to empirical phenomena. Thus, any attempt to compare firms from conventional accounting statements alone (excluding competitive sources of information) is productive of errors.[3]

Exit-value financial statements allow one to make a specific kind of comparison. They allow one to discriminate between empirical phenomena. In this case the exit value of the rig in the Sahara is zero by assumption. Let us assume that the rig in the Permian Basin has an exit value of $900,000. This means that the Permian Basin project or firm has the ability to command goods of $900,000 more than the one in the Sahara. That is a significant difference, a relevant bit of information.

Some colleagues will argue that it is the future cash flows from the deposit that are relevant, not the exit values of the rig. It cannot be denied that the future cash flows are relevant, but it does not

3. Evidence for this comes from an oft-repeated behavioral experiment in my theory seminar. When we begin to discuss problems of comparability, some students invariably argue that historic-cost statements permit comparisons. This argument is tested by giving the entire class five sets of financial statements, two of which refer to the same firm with different allocation procedures, different forecasts of life, etc. The task is to identify the two sets of statements that refer to the same underlying empirical phenomena. Over the years the students, despite their expertise in accounting, have not been able to do better than chance.

follow that exit values are not relevant. The drillers must forecast the future cash flows in order to decide whether or not to continue drilling. However, the decision requires that the discounted values be compared to the exit values. In the Sahara case, it is a profit-maximizing decision to continue drilling if the discounted values are greater than zero. In the Permian Basin case, the discounted values must be greater than $900,000. That is, in the Sahara case a $1,000,000 expense has in fact been incurred (sunk), and there is nothing that can be done in the future to change that. In the other case, only a $100,000 expense has been incurred; the $900,000 can be recovered by selling the rig.

This comparison is also relevant to present and potential investors and creditors. It tells them how their investment is split between present and future. In the Sahara case their return depends entirely on future events; in the Permian case some of the value exists in the present. In the same way that recoverable costs are relevant to the management decision, they are relevant to the investors' decisions. Suppose that a majority shareholder forecasted the net cash flows to be less than $900,000 from the Permian project or to be less than zero (forecasted incremental costs greater than incremental revenues) from the Sahara project. Given these forecasts, the majority shareholder could instruct management to cease drilling and liquidate the rig. Alternatively, he could sell his stock on the market if the price per share is greater than the exit value per share. In both cases, the exit value in addition to (not instead of) the forecasted cash flows is relevant to the decision. Although a small shareholder does not have the same options, he needs to make similar comparisons. In addition, small shareholders may band together to form a controlling interest, but they can do so only if they can make the comparisons.

The exit values also supply a risk indicator. In the Sahara case the risk must be exceptionally high. The asset is so specialized it cannot be used for anything except drilling that one well. If any other oil explorers held positive expectations about the Sahara project, they would be willing to purchase it for some positive amount. Thus, the fact that it has a zero exit value is an indication of its high risk. By comparison the Permian project is much less risky. Both levels of risk and risk comparisons are relevant to investors.

In short, exit-value statements permit comparison among firms or projects in regard to the one attribute of COG. They do not permit comparisons in regard to other relevant attributes, such as discounted values. By contrast, book values do not permit comparisons of any empirical attribute that I know.

A.7 Conclusions

Careful examination of the objections advanced to extreme cases reveals vast confusion. We confuse the rig with the deposit, past expenditures with present measurements, forecasted magnitudes with present measurements, averaging with measuring, the need to provide a permanent record with the reporting of assets, and so forth. My hypothesis is that such confusion springs from ingrained habits of thought. We have become so accustomed to reporting large expenditures as assets that we cannot objectively examine proposals to report them as expenses. The language "costs that benefit the future" has trapped us into a mode of thinking that prevents us from considering the case on its merits. If exit values are found to be the preferred valuation method on grounds of empirical testability and relevance, then we should seek to measure and report the exit value, regardless of its magnitude. If we find the magnitude to be zero, we should report it.[4]

---

4. One minor confusion stems from such locutions as, "What happens if there is *no* exit value?" This sometimes means an undetermined (or difficult to determine) exit value, and other times it means a zero exit value. The former expresses a measurement problem. The latter expresses a psychological problem of reporting a zero asset when a large expenditure was made.

Works Cited

American Institute of Accountants. "Audits of Corporate Accounts." New York: American Institute of Accountants, 1934.

American Institute of Certified Public Accountants. "Accounting Terminology Bulletins, Number 1, Review and Resume." *Accounting Research and Terminology Bulletins*. New York: AICPA, 1961.

Baxter, W. T. *Depreciation*. London: Sweet & Maxwell, 1971.

Beaver, William H. "Financial Ratios as Predictors of Failure." *Journal of Accounting Research* 4 (1966), Supplement *(Empirical Research in Accounting, Selected Studies 1966)*, pp. 71–111.

———; Kennelly, John W.; and Voss, William M. "Predictive Ability as a Criterion for the Evaluation of Accouting Data." *The Accounting Review* 43 (1968):675–83.

Beidleman, Carl R. *Valuation of Used Capital Assets*. Studies in Accounting Research No. 7. Sarasota, Fla.: American Accounting Association, 1973.

Benston, George J., and Krasney, Melvin A. "DAAM: the Demand for Alternative Accounting Measurements." *Journal of Accounting Research* 16 (Supplement 1978):1–45.

Berkeley, Bishop George. *A Treatise Concerning the Principles of Human Knowledge*. Garden City, N.J.: Doubleday, Doran & Co., Inc., 1935.

Bierman, Harold, Jr. "Measurement and Accounting." *The Accounting Review* 38 (1963):501–8.

Blough, Carman G. "Development of Accounting Principles in the United States." In *Berkeley Symposium on the Foundations of Financial Accounting*, pp. 1–14. University of California, Berkeley: Schools of Business Administration, 1967.

Boulding, Kenneth E. *Economics as a Science*. New York: McGraw-Hill Book Co., 1970.

Bowman, Robert G., and Lookabill, Larry L. "Accounting Research, Education and Practice Revisited." Mimeographed. Eugene, Ore.: University of Oregon, 1978.

Braithwaite, Richard Bevan. *Scientific Explanation: A Study of the Function of Theory, Probability and Law in Science.* Cambridge: The Cambridge University Press, 1953.

Bridgman, P. W. *The Logic of Modern Physics.* New York: The Macmillan Co., 1927.

Brodbeck, May, ed. *Readings in the Philosophy of the Social Sciences.* New York: The Macmillan Co., 1968.

Bronowski, J. *The Ascent of Man.* Boston: Little, Brown and Co., 1973.

Butterfield, Herbert. *The Origins of Modern Science.* New York: The Free Press, 1966.

Cadenhead, Gary M. " 'Differences in Circumstances': Fact or Fantasy?" *Abacus* 6 (1970):71–80.

Catlett, George R. "Achieving Progress." In *In Pursuit of Professional Goals: Selected Addresses and Articles by George R. Catlett and Norman O. Olson, 1960–1972*, pp. 67–70. Chicago: Arthur Andersen & Co., 1973.

Caws, Peter. "Accounting Research—Science or Methodology?" In *Research Methodology in Accounting*, edited by Robert R. Sterling, pp. 71–73. Lawrence, Kan.: Scholars Book Co., 1972.

————. *The Philosophy of Science.* Princeton, N.J.: D. Van Nostrand Co., Inc., 1966.

Chambers, Raymond J. *Accounting, Evaluation and Economic Behavior.* 1966. Reprint. Houston: Scholars Book Co., 1974.

————. "Continuously Contemporary Accounting—Addivity and Action." *The Accounting Review* 42 (1967):751–57.

————. "Financial Information and the Securities Market." *Abacus* 1 (1965):3–30.

————. "NOD, COG and PuPU: See How Inflation Teases!" *Journal of Accountancy* 140 (Sept. 1975):56–62.

————. "Second Thoughts on Continuously Contemporary Accounting." *Abacus* 6 (1970):39–55.

Chasteen, Lanny G. "An Empirical Study of Differences in Economic Circumstances as a Justification for Alternative Inventory Pricing Methods." *The Accounting Review* 46 (1971):504–8.

Cohen, Morris R., and Nagel, Ernest. *An Introduction to Logic and Scientific Method.* New York: Harcourt, Brace & World, Inc., 1934.

Cournot, Augustin. *Research into the Mathematical Principles of the Theory of Wealth.* Homewood, Ill.: Richard D. Irwin, Inc., 1963.

Darwin, Charles. *The Origin of Species by Means of Natural Selection.* London: John Murry, 1873.

Daughen, Joseph R., and Binzen, Peter. *The Wreck of the Penn Central.*

Boston: Little, Brown & Co., 1971.

Davidson, Sidney. "Depreciation, Income Taxes and Growth." *Accounting Research* 8 (1957):191–205.

Devine, Carl. "Discussion." In *Berkeley Symposium on the Foundations of Financial Accounting*, pp. 15–19. University of California, Berkeley: Schools of Business Administration, 1967.

————. "Essays in Accounting Theory." Vol. 2, essay 13. Mimeographed. Tallahassee, Fla.: Florida State University, 1962, pp. 201–16.

Dopuch, Nicholas. "Discussion: 'Toward a Science of Accounting' by Robert R. Sterling." In *Stanford Lectures in Accounting 1975*. Presented by the Graduate School of Business, Stanford University, under the sponsorship of the Price Waterhouse Foundation, April 11, 1975.

————, and Sunder, Shyam. "FASB's Statements on Objectives and Elements of Financial Accounting: A Review." *The Accounting Review* 55 (1980):1–21.

Drebin, Allan R. " 'Cash-Flowitis': Malady or Syndrome?" *Journal of Accounting Research* 2 (1964):25–34.

Dyckman, Thomas R. "On the Investment Decision." *The Accounting Review* 39 (1964):285–95.

Edwards, Edgar O., and Bell, Philip W. *The Theory and Measurement of Business Income*. Berkeley and Los Angeles: University of California Press, 1961.

Einstein, Albert. Foreword to *Dialogue Concerning the Two Chief World Systems—Ptolemaic and Copernican*, by Galileo Galilei. Berkeley and Los Angeles: University of California Press, 1967.

————. *Out of My Later Years*. New York: Philosophical Library, 1950.

Eliot, T. S. "The Love Song of J. Alfred Prufrock." *The Complete Poems and Plays—1909–1950*. New York: Harcourt, Brace & World, Inc., 1971.

Epstein, Paul S. *Textbook of Thermodynamics*. New York: John Wiley & Sons, Inc., 1937.

Escholier, Raymond. *Matisse: From the Life*. Translated by Geraldine and H. M. Colvile. London: Faber and Faber, 1960.

Financial Accounting Standards Board. "Statement of Financial Accounting Concepts No. 1." Stamford, Conn.: Financial Accounting Standards Board, 1978.

Finney, H. A., and Miller, Herbert E. *Principles of Accounting Intermediate*. 5th ed., Englewood Cliffs, N.J.: Prentice-Hall, Inc., 1964.

Firth, C. H. *Oliver Cromwell and the Rule of Puritans in England*.

Black and White Library Edition. London: Putnam, 1938.

Fisher, Irving. *The Nature of Capital and Income.* New York: The Macmillan Co., 1906.

Foster, George J. "Mining Inventories in a Current Price Accounting System." *Abacus* 5 (1969):99–118.

Friedman, Laurence A. "An Exit-Price Income Statement." *The Accounting Review* 53 (1978):18–30.

Galileus, Galileus. *The Systeme of the World: In Four Dialogues Wherein the Two Grand Systemes of Ptolomy and Copernicus are Largely Discoursed of.* In *Mathematical Collections and Translations,* Vol. 1 by Thomas Salusbury. London: William Leybourne, 1661.

Gellein, Oscar S. "The Decreasing-Charge Concept." *Journal of Accountancy* 100 (Aug. 1955):56–61.

Gerstle vs. Gamble-Skogmo, Inc. 478 F.2d 1281 (1973).

Geymonat, Ludovico. *Galileo Galilei.* Translated by Stillman Drake. New York: McGraw-Hill Book Co., 1965.

Gilman, Stephen. "Accounting Principles and the Current Classification." *The Accounting Review* 19 (1944):109–16.

Goldberg, Louis. "Concepts of Depreciation." *The Accounting Review* 30 (1955):468–84.

Goodman, Nelson. *Fact, Fiction, and Forecast.* Indianapolis: The Bobbs-Merrill Co., Inc., 1965.

Grady, Paul. *Inventory of Generally Accepted Accounting Principles for Business Enterprises.* Accounting Research Study No. 7. New York: AICPA, 1965.

Halmos, Paul R. *Measure Theory.* Princeton, N.J.: D. Van Nostrand Co., Inc., 1950.

Hardin, Garrett. *Nature and Man's Fate.* London: Jonathan Cape, 1960.

Hatfield, Henry Rand. *Modern Accounting: Its Principles and Some of its Problems.* New York: D. Appleton and Co., 1919.

Hausman, Jerry A. "Individual Discount Rates and the Purchase and Utilization of Energy-Using Durables." *The Bell Journal of Economics* 10 (1979):33–54.

Hempel, Carl G. *Fundamentals of Concept Formation in Empirical Science.* International Encyclopedia of Unified Science, edited by Otto Neurath, Rudolf Carnap, and Charles W. Morris, vol. II, no. 7, Chicago: University of Chicago Press, 1952.

——— . *Philosophy of Natural Science.* Englewood Cliffs, N.J.: Prentice-Hall, Inc., 1966.

Hougen, Olaf A.; Watson, Kenneth M.; and Ragatz, Ronald A. *Chemical*

Process Principles. Part I—Material and Energy Balances. 2nd ed., New York: John Wiley & Sons, Inc., 1959.

Huxley, Aldous. *Words and Their Meanings.* Los Angeles: The Ward Ritchie Press, 1940.

Ijiri, Yuji. "A Defense of Historical Cost Accounting." In *Asset Valuation and Income Determination: A Consideration of the Alternatives,* edited by Robert R. Sterling, pp. 1–14. Lawrence, Kan.: Scholars Book Co., 1971.

————. *Theory of Accounting Measurement.* Studies in Accounting Research #10. Sarasota, Fla.: American Accounting Association, 1969.

————, and Jaedicke, Robert K. "Reliability and Objectivity of Accounting Measurements." *The Accounting Review* 41 (1966):474–83.

Johnson, Charles E. "Inventory Valuation—The Accountant's Achilles Heel." *The Accounting Review* 29 (1954):15–26.

Johnson, Kenneth P. "Discussion: 'Toward a Science of Accounting' by Robert R. Sterling." In *Stanford Lectures in Accounting 1975.* Presented by the Graduate School of Business, Stanford University, under the sponsorship of the Price Waterhouse Foundation, April 11, 1975.

Johnson, L. Todd, and Bell, Philip W. "Current Replacement Costs: A Qualified Opinion." *Journal of Accountancy* 142 (Nov. 1976):63–70.

Kuhn, Thomas S. *The Structure of Scientific Revolutions.* Chicago: University of Chicago Press, 1965.

Langford, Jerome J. *Galileo, Science and the Church.* Ann Arbor: University of Michigan Press, 1971.

Larson, Kermit D. "Descriptive Validity of Accounting Calculations." *The Accounting Review* 42 (1967):480–96.

————, and Schattke, R. W. "Current Cash Equivalent, Additivity, and Financial Action." *The Accounting Review* 41 (1966):634–41.

Lawler, John. "The Quest for Accounting Philosophers." In *Empirical Research in Accounting: Selected Studies 1967,* pp. 86–92. Chicago: The Institute of Professional Accounting, 1968.

Lazarsfeld, Paul F. "Evidence and Inference in Social Research." *Daedalus* 87 (Fall 1958):99–130.

Lewis, C. S. *Rehabilitations and Other Essays.* London: Oxford University Press, 1939.

Lintner, John. "The Aggregation of Investor's Diverse Judgments and Preferences in Purely Competitive Securities Markets." *Journal of Financial and Quantitative Analysis* 4 (1969):347–400.

Lutz, Friedrich, and Lutz, Vera. *The Theory of Investment of the*

Firm. Princeton: Princeton University Press, 1951.

McDonald, Daniel L. "A Test Application of the Feasibility of Market Based Measures in Accounting." *Journal of Accounting Research* 6 (1968):38–49.

McKeown, James C. "Additivity of Net Realizable Values." *The Accounting Review* 47 (1972):527–32.

————. "An Empirical Test of a Model Proposed by Chambers." *The Accounting Review* 46 (1971):12–29.

Margenau, Henry. *The Nature of Physical Reality: A Philosophy of Modern Physics.* New York: McGraw-Hill Book Co., 1950.

Menninger, Karl. *Whatever Became of Sin?* New York: Hawthorn Books, Inc., 1973.

Mill, John Stuart. *Principles of Political Economy.* Edited by W. J. Ashley. London: Longmans, Green & Co., 1909.

Miller, Herbert E. "Audited Statements—Are They Really Management's?" *Journal of Accountancy* 118 (Oct. 1964):43–46.

Miller, Merton H., and Modigliani, Franco. "Dividend Policy, Growth, and the Valuation of Shares." *Journal of Business* 34 (1961):411–33.

Minard, Lawrence. "Cheerful Days in the Dismal Science." *Forbes,* Jan. 8, 1979, pp. 34–39.

Moody, Ernest A. "William of Ockham." In *The Encyclopedia of Philosophy,* edited by Paul Edwards, vol. 8, pp. 306–17. New York: Macmillan Co. and The Free Press, 1967.

Moonitz, Maurice. "The Case Against LIFO as an Inventory-Pricing Formula." *Journal of Accountancy* 95 (June 1953):682–90.

Morris, Charles. *Signs, Language, and Behavior.* New York: Prentice-Hall, Inc., 1946.

Morris, Richard B., and Irwin, Graham W., eds. *Harper Encyclopedia of the Modern World.* New York: Harper & Row, 1970.

Pap, Arthur. *An Introduction to the Philosophy of Science.* New York: The Free Press of Glencoe, 1962.

Parker, James E. "Testing Comparability and Objectivity of Exit Value Accounting." *The Accounting Review* 50 (1975):512–24.

Paton, W. A., and Littleton, A. C. *An Introduction to Corporate Accounting Standards.* American Accounting Association Monograph No. 3. Chicago: American Accounting Association, 1940.

Peirce, Charles Sanders. "What Pragmatism Is." *The Monist* 15 (1905):161–81.

Polanyi, Michael. *Personal Knowledge: Towards a Post-Critical Philosophy.* New York: Harper & Row, 1964.

Pope, Alexander. *An Essay on Man.* Menston, England: The Scholar Press, Ltd., 1969.

Popper, Karl R. *Conjectures and Refutations: The Growth of Scientific*

Knowledge. London: Routledge and Kegan Paul, 1963.

———. *The Logic of Scientific Discovery.* New York: Basic Books, 1959.

———. "Philosophy of Science: A Personal Report." In *British Philosophy in the Mid-Century,* edited by C. A. Mace, pp. 155–91. Oxford: Alden Press, 1957.

"Progress on Inflation Accounting." *The Accountant* 165 (1971):115.

Radford, K. J. *Complex Decision Problems: An Integrated Strategy for Resolution.* Reston, Va.: Reston Publishing Co., 1977.

Reichenbach, Hans. *Experience and Prediction: An Analysis of the Foundations and the Structure of Knowledge.* Chicago: University of Chicago Press, 1938.

———. *The Rise of Scientific Philosophy.* Berkeley: University of California Press, 1968.

Revsine, Lawrence. "Data Expansion and Conceptual Structure." *The Accounting Review* 45 (1970):704–11.

———. "Predictive Ability, Market Prices, and Operating Flows." *The Accounting Review* 46 (1971):481–89.

———. *Replacement Cost Accounting.* Englewood Cliffs, N.J.: Prentice-Hall, Inc., 1973.

Rogers, Eric M. *Physics for the Inquiring Mind.* Princeton, N.J.: Princeton University Press, 1960.

Rosenfield, Paul. "Reporting Subjunctive Gains and Losses." *The Accounting Reivew* 44 (1969):788–97.

Ross, Howard. *The Elusive Art of Accounting.* New York: The Ronald Press Co., 1966.

———. *Financial Statements: A Crusade for Current Values.* New York: Pitman Publishing Corporation, 1969.

Russell, Bertrand. *Philosophical Essays.* New York: Simon & Schuster, 1966.

Shackle, George Lennox Sharman. *Decision, Order and Time in Human Affairs.* Cambridge: Cambridge University Press, 1961.

Simons, Henry C. *Personal Income Taxation.* Chicago: University of Chicago Press, 1938.

Slaughter, Frank G. *Immortal Magyar: Semmelweis, Conqueror of Childbed Fever.* New York: Henry Schuman, 1950.

Spacek, Leonard. "The Need for an Accounting Court." In *A Search for Fairness in Financial Reporting to the Public,* vol. 1, pp. 27–38. Chicago: Arthur Andersen & Co., 1969.

Spiller, Earl A., and Virgil, Robert L. "Effectiveness of APB Opinion No. 19 in Improving Funds Reporting." *Journal of Accounting Research* 12 (1974):112–42.

Sprouse, Robert T., and Moonitz, Maurice. *A Tentative Set of Broad*

Accounting Principles for Business Enterprises. Accounting Research Study No. 3. New York: AICPA, 1962.

Stamp, Edward, and Marley, Christopher. *Accounting Principles and the City Code: The Case for Reform.* London: Butterworths, 1970.

Staubus, George J. *Making Accounting Decisions.* Houston: Scholars Book Co., 1978.

——— . "The Responsibility of Accounting Teachers." *The Accounting Review* 50 (1975):160–70.

Sterling, Robert R. "Accounting at the Crossroads." *Journal of Accountancy* 142 (Aug. 1976):82–87.

——— . "Accounting in the 1980s." In *Accountancy in the 1980s— Some Issues,* edited by Norton M. Bedford, pp. 225–68. Proceedings of the Arthur Young Professors Round-Table, March 30–31, 1976, University of Illinois, Urbana.

——— . "Accounting Power." *Journal of Accountancy* 135 (Jan. 1973):61–67.

——— . "Accounting Research, Education and Practice—Conflicts, Compromises or Complements." *Journal of Business Administration* 4 (1973):15–30.

——— . "Board to Adjudicate Accounting Disputes." Paper read at the Ernst & Ernst Symposium for Educators, July 12, 1973.

——— . "An Explication and Analysis of the Structure of Accounting, Part Two." *Abacus* 8 (1972):145–62.

——— . "A Glimpse of the Forest." *The Accountant's Magazine* 72 (1968):589–94.

——— . "The Going Concern: An Examination." *The Accounting Reivew* 43 (1968):481–502.

——— . "Introduction." In *Research Methodology in Accounting,* edited by Robert R. Sterling, pp. 1–7. Lawrence, Kan.: Scholars Book Co., 1972.

——— . "An Operational Analysis of Traditional Accounting." *Abacus* 2 (1966):119–36.

——— . "Relevant Financial Reporting in an Age of Price Changes." *Journal of Accountancy* 139 (Feb. 1975):42–51.

——— . "A Statement of Basic Accounting Theory: A Review Article." *Journal of Accounting Research* 5 (1967):95–112.

——— . "A Test of the Uniformity Hypothesis." *Abacus* 5 (1969):37–47.

——— . "On Theory Construction and Verification." *The Accounting Reivew* 45 (1970):444–57.

——— . *Theory of the Measurement of Enterprise Income.* 1970. Reprint. Houston: Scholars Book Co., 1979.

——— , ed. *Institutional Issues in Public Accounting.* Lawrence, Kan.: Scholars Book Co., 1974.

————, and Radosevich, Raymond. "A Valuation Experiment." *Journal of Accounting Research* 7 (1969):90–95.

Stone, Marvin L. "Public Confidence in Private Enterprise—Let's Keep It." *Journal of Accountancy* 125 (Apr. 1968):52–56.

Sunder, Shyam. "Accounting Changes in Inventory Valuation." *The Accounting Review* 50 (1975):305–15.

Szasz, Thomas S. *The Myth of Mental Illness: Foundations of a Theory of Personal Conduct.* New York: Dell Publishing Co., Inc., 1974.

Thomas, Arthur L. *The Allocation Problem in Financial Accounting Theory.* Studies in Accounting Research No. 3. Menashaw, Wisc.: American Accounting Association, 1969.

————. *The Allocation Problem in Financial Accounting Theory, Part Two.* Studies in Accounting Research No. 9. Sarasota, Fla.: American Accounting Association, 1974.

Torgerson, Warren, S. *Theory and Methods of Scaling.* New York: John Wiley & Sons, Inc., 1967.

Torrey, Bradford, and Allen, Francis H., eds. *The Journal of Henry D. Thoreau.* New York: Dover Publications, Inc., 1962.

Trowell, John. "A Study of the Additivity of CCE With Respect to Assets." Master's Thesis, University of New England, Armidale, NSW, 1978.

Trueblood Committee. *Objectives of Financial Statements.* Report of the Study Group on the Objectives of Financial Statements. New York: AICPA, 1973.

Tweedie, D. P. "Cash Flows and Realisable Values: The Intuitive Accounting Concepts? An Empirical Test." *Accounting and Business Research* 8 (1977):2–13.

Vickrey, Don W. "A Comment on the Larson-Schattke and Chambers Debate Over the Additivity of CCE." *The Accounting Review* 50 (1975):140–46.

————. "Is Accounting a Measurement Discipline?" *The Accounting Review* 45 (1970):731–42.

————. "Realizable Market Value: Additivity, Multiple Measures, and a Plausible Measurement System for Accounting." Mimeographed. Tucson, Ariz.: University of Arizona, 1973.

————. "Two Views of Current-Exit Values: Addition and Additivity." *International Journal of Education and Research* 11 (1976):51–57.

Webster's Third New International Dictionary of the English Language Unabridged. Chicago: Encyclopedia Britannica, Inc., 1971.

"What *Are* Earnings? The Growing Credibility Gap." *Forbes,* May 15, 1967, pp. 28–44.

Whitehead, Alfred North. *Science and the Modern World.* New York: The Free Press, 1967.

Whorf, Benjamin L. *Language, Thought and Reality*. New York: John Wiley & Sons, 1956.

Wolnizer, P. W. "Current Prices and the Indexation Problems in the Steel Industry." Mimeographed. Sydney, NSW: University of Sydney, undated.

————. "Primary Production Inventories Under Current Value Accounting." *Accounting and Business Research* 7 (1977):303–10.

Zeff, Stephen A. "Comments on Accounting Principles—How They Are Developed." In *Institutional Issues in Public Accounting*, edited by Robert R. Sterling, pp. 172–78. Lawrence, Kan.: Scholars Book Co., 1974.

Index

Persons

Aristotle, 42, 43

Baxter, W. T., 67
Beaver, William H., 199n
Beidleman, Carl R., 76n
Bell, Philip W., xi, 69n, 124, 144,
    174, 196
Benston, George J., 88n
Berkeley, George, 5
Bierman, Harold, Jr., 10n
Binzen, Peter, 14
Blough, Carman G., 10n
Boulding, Kenneth E., xii, 46, 83
Bowman, Robert G., xi
Boyle, Robert, 72
Braithwaite, Richard Bevan, 159
Bridgman, P. W., 37, 64
Brodbeck, May, 66, 84, 145
Bronowski, J., 144n
Butterfield, Herbert, 9, 54

Cadenhead, Gary M., 23n
Catlett, George R., 4n
Caws, Peter, 10n, 11n, 12, 20, 119n,
    141
Chambers, Raymond J., 93, 107,
    121, 160, 162, 172n
Chasteen, Lanny G., 10n
Cicero, 124
Cohen, Morris R., 3, 35, 81
Confucius, 144
Copernicus, 42
Corbin, Donald, 219
Cournot, Augustin, 161
Cromwell, Oliver, 15–16

Darwin, Charles, x
Daughen, Joseph R., 14
Davidson, Sidney, 67
Devine, Carl, 10, 173n
Dopuch, Nicholas, 10n, 71n
Drebin, Allan R., 210
Dyckman, Thomas R., 50–52

Edwards, Edgar O., 144, 174, 196
Einstein, Albert, 10, 12, 24n, 75
Eliot, T. S., 100
Epstein, Paul S., 39
Escholier, Raymond, 10n

Finney, H. A., 10n
Firth, C. H., 16
Fisher, Irving, 194
Foster, George J., 76n
Friedman, Laurence A., 196

Galileo Galilei, 42–45, 49n, 54–55,
    58–60, 213
Gellein, Oscar S., 200
Geymonat, Ludovico, 49n
Gilman, Stephen, 219
Goldberg, Louis, 70
Goodman, Nelson, 45
Grady, Paul, 28, 93

Halmos, Paul R., 168
Hardin, Garrett, 15
Hatfield, Henry Rand, 117
Hausman, Jerry A., 138–39
Hempel, Carl G., 14, 39, 54n, 92, 93
Hougen, Olaf A., 78, 79, 198
Huxley, Aldous, 9, 19

241

Subjects